Oded Halahmy: Noble Exile (2008), aluminum sculpture, 26"H x 21"W x 6.75"D

Sheikh Hamad Award for Translation and International Understanding (SHATIU) is accepting nominations for the year 2021 in the following categories:

1. Translation from Arabic into English   (200,000 USD)
2. Translation from English into Arabic   (200,000 USD)
3. Translation from Arabic into Chinese   (200,000 USD)
4. Translation from Chinese into Arabic   (200,000 USD)
5. Achievement Award   (200,000 USD)

SHATIU is also accepting nominations for achievement awards in translation from and into the following languages:

- Translation from Arabic into Amharic
- Translation from Amharic into Arabic
- Translation from Arabic into Dutch
- Translation from Dutch into Arabic
- Translation from Arabic into Modern Greek
- Translation from Modern Greek into Arabic
- Translation from Arabic into Urdu
- Translation from Urdu into Arabic

The results will be announced on 22/12/2021

Please visit our website

www.hta.qa/en

for information about the Award, rules of submission and nomination forms.

  HamadTAward   Phone: (+974) 66570349   Email: info@hta.qa

Literature in translation from Banipal Books

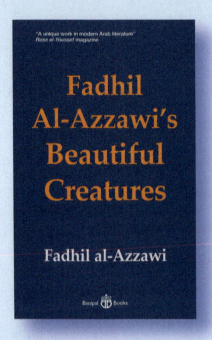

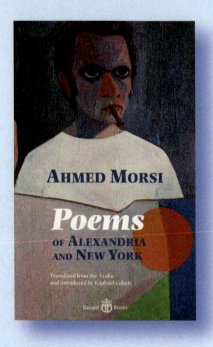

"Fadhil Al-Azzawi's Beautiful Creatures is a unique work in modern Arab literature"
Ahmed Abdel Muti Hijazi, Rose el-Youssef magazine (Cairo, 1969)

"Fadhil al-Azzawi has amassed an evolving set of lyrical and conceptual tools, accompanied by a canny capacity to reach far into the imagination" –
Khaled Mattawa, poet and translator

Introduced by Farouk Youssef
ISBN 978-1-913043-10-0 Paperback
ISBN 978-1-913043-22-3 Hardback
ISBN 978-1-913043-11-7 Ebook

"When I read the poems of Ahmed Morsi I begin to travel" –
Alfonso Armada, journalist, playwright, poet

"These two collections weave multiple relations, threaded with the themes of exile and alienation, between New York and Alexandria" – Hala Halim, New York University

"An impressive translation revealing the intense gaze of a magnificent narrator"
May Telmissany, author and film critic

Introduced and translated
by Raphael Cohen
ISBN 978-1-913043-15-5 Paperback
ISBN 978-1-913043-16-2 Ebook

Available online

www.banipal.co.uk

Literature in translation from Banipal Books

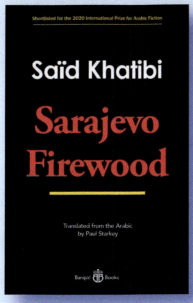

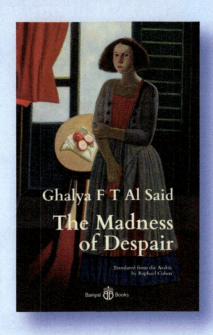

"A labyrinthine journey, with Algeria at one pole, Bosnia at the other . . . Along the way, we are forced to reconsider what we think we know about liberation, nationalism, decolonization, and war, as Khatibi masterfully shifts our focus from the state to the family and the continual trauma of self-understanding" – Ammiel Alcalay

"*Sarajevo Firewood* is an astonishing novel and Khatibi is one of the most original voices in Arabic literature today" – Amara Lakhous

ISBN 978-1-913043-23-0 Paperback
ISBN 978-1-913043-24-7 Ebook

"A talented and inventive storyteller, with a well developed sense of tragedy and comedy" – Susannah Tarbush

"*The Madness of Despair* depicts the tragedy of the Middle East, which will remain without solution until Arabs can live in freedom and dignity in their own lands rather than turning to life in exile" – Al-Jarida, Kuwait

"A love story where love becomes the mirror of longing for home'" – Katia al-Tawil

ISBN 978-1-913043-12-4 Paperback
ISBN 978-1-913043-21-6 Hardback
ISBN 978-1-913043-13-1 Ebook

In all good bookshops

Complete archive of issues for institutions and individuals
DIGITAL BANIPAL

- In this archive the digital subscriber can leap into translations of works from any Arab country – just type in which one – perhaps Morocco, or Iraq, or Palestine, Sudan, Syria, or Algeria.

- There are many major interviews with influential Arab authors – just search the name, such as Adonis, Tayeb Salih, Abdelrahman Munif, Etel Adnan, Gamal Al-Ghitani, Rashid al-Daif or Alaa Khaled, to name but a few.

- Though the scene for literature translated from Arabic has changed beyond recognition since 1998, there are still many authors well-known and hightly regarded in the Arab world, yet hardly, or not yet, translated except in Banipal. Check out, for instance, Ghalib Halasa (Jordan), Gha'eb Tu'ma Farman (Iraq), Alaa al-Deeb (Egypt) or Ihsan Abdel Kouddous.

- Banipal's digital edition offers readers all over the world the chance to flip open the magazine on their computers, iPads, iPhones or Android smartphones, wherever they are, check out the current issue, search through the back issues and sync as desired.

- Download the free iTunes App or get it on an Android smartphone.

- A year's digital subscription comes with full access to the full digital archive, back to Banipal No 1, February 1998 – for individuals and for institutions (based on FTE). Print and digital subscriptions are still separate for the moment.

For more information, go to:
www.banipal.co.uk/subscribe/digital/

Subscribe Directly to Digital Banipal with Exact Editions
Individual: exacteditions.com/banipal   Libraries: institutions.exacteditions.com/banipal

BANIPAL
Magazine of Modern Arab Literature

Banipal magazine, founded in 1998, takes its name from Ashurbanipal (668–627 BC), the last great king of Assyria and patron of the arts, whose outstanding achievement was to assemble in his capital Nineveh, Mesopotamia, from all over his empire, the first systematically organised library in the ancient Middle East. The thousands of clay tablets of Sumerian, Babylonian and Assyrian writings included the famous Mesopotamian epics of the Creation, the Flood, and Gilgamesh, many folk tales, fables, proverbs, prayers and omen texts.

Source: Encyclopaedia Britannica

PUBLISHER: Margaret Obank
EDITOR: Samuel Shimon

CONTRIBUTING EDITORS
Fadhil al-Azzawi, Peter Clark, Raphael Cohen, Bassam Frangieh, Camilo Gómez-Rivas, William M Hutchins, Adil Babikir, Imad Khachan, Khaled Mattawa, Clare Roberts, Mariam al-Saedi, Anton Shammas, Paul Starkey

CONSULTING EDITORS
Etel Adnan, Roger Allen, Isabella Camera d'Afflitto, Humphrey Davies, Hartmut Fähndrich, Ibrahim Farghali, Naomi Shihab Nye, Nancy Roberts, Susannah Tarbush

EDITORIAL ASSISTANTS: Rosie Maxton, Becki Maddock, Joselyn Michelle Almeida, Annamaria Basile

COVER: Photograph of Maryam al-Mulla, courtesy of her daughter Niran Bassoon

LAYOUT: Banipal Publishing
WEBSITE: www.banipal.co.uk
EDITOR: editor@banipal.co.uk
PUBLISHER: margaret@banipal.co.uk
ENQUIRIES: info@banipal.co.uk
SUBSCRIPTIONS: subscribe@banipal.co.uk
ADDRESS: 1 Gough Square, London EC4A 3DE
PRINTED BY Printforce, Biggleswade SG18 8TQ, UK
Photographs not accredited have been donated, photographers unknown.
This issue: *BANIPAL 72 – Iraqi Jewish Writers*
This selection © Banipal Publishing. All rights reserved.
This issue is ISBN 978-1-913043-28-5.
RRP £10, €12, US$15

No reproduction or copy, in whole or in part, in the print or the digital edition, may be made without the written permission of the publisher.

BANIPAL, ISSN 1461-5363. Published three times a year by Banipal Publishing, 1 Gough Square, London EC4A 3DE

www.banipal.co.uk

Shimon Ballas

Amira Hess

Samir Naqqash

Mona Yahia

Ronny Someck

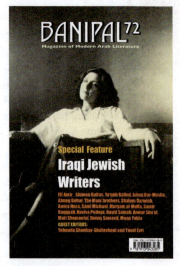

11   Editor's Foreword

IRAQI JEWISH WRITERS

12   Guest editors Yehouda Shenhav-Shahrabani and Yuval Evri: *Introduction*

16   Haviva Pedaya: *The Iraqi Jewish Literary Networks*

21   Ammiel Alcalay: *In & Out of Place – Memories of Nissim Rejwan, Shimon Ballas, and Samir Naqqash*

26   Yuval Evri: *Shimon Ballas, Exile by Choice*

32   Shimon Ballas: *The Imagined Childhood,* translated from the Hebrew by Eran Edry

40   Shimon Ballas: *He Loved Life* (Ahabba al-Hayat), a short story translated from the Arabic by Hana Morgenstern

48   Uri Horesh and Orit Bashkin: *Communism, Commitment and Humanity: David Semah*

50   David Semah: *He shall return*, a poem translated from the Arabic by Uri Horesh

56   Ryan Zohar: *Reading Sami Michael*

61   Sami Michael: *Blessed Is the Lord* (*Tabarak al-Rabb*), translated from the Arabic by Ryan Zohar

65   Sami Michael: *Two Women* (Imra'ataan), translated from the Arabic by Hana Morgenstern

68   Tami Israeli: *The Round Dove of Baghdad: The Poetry of Amira Hess in Context*

74   Amira Hess: *How Long Must We Be Remade,* poems translated from the Hebrew by Eran Edry

77   Reuven Snir: *Maryam al-Mulla, as an Iraqi-Jewish Feminist Activist*

82   Maryam al-Mulla: *His Tragedy, a Proverb,* translated from the Arabic by Aviva Butt and Reuven Snir

84	Almog Behar: *Exploring Ronny Someck*	
87	Ronny Someck: *Eight Poems*, translated from the Hebrew by Eran Edry	
92	Mona Yahia: *Matches*, a short story	
105	Lital Levy: *Reading Samir Naqqash*	
110	Samir Naqqash: *Shlomo the Kurd, Myself, and Time*, an excerpt, translated from the Arabic by Zeena Faulk	
124	Hadas Shabat Nadir: *The Quest for Home, the Quest for Identity: The Jewish-Muslim Prospect in Eli Amir*	

Haviva Pedaya

130	Eli Amir: *The Bicycle Boy*, an excerpt from the novel, translated from the Hebrew by Eran Edry
133	Nael el-Toukhy: *Complete but unfinished – on translating Chahla and Hezquel from Hebrew to Arabic*, translated from the Arabic by Jonathan Wright
138	Almog Behar: *Chahla and Hezquel*, an excerpt, translated from the Hebrew by Dan Cern and Eran Edry
150	Orit Bashkin: *Shalom Darwish (1913-1997) Gender and Intersectionality*

Sami Michael

152	Shalom Darwish: *In the Year 2532*, a story translated from the Arabic by Uri Horesh
155	Mati Shemoelof: *Can't Prostrate myself at my Grandmother's Grave*, a poem translated from the Hebrew by Eran Edry
158	Reuven Snir: *"Religion is for God, the Fatherland is for Everyone" – Anwar Sha'ul and the Rise and Demise of Arabic Literature by Jews*
165	Anwar Sha'ul: *Me and the Unknown Other Half: Which of Us Sought the Other?* translated from the Arabic by Zeena Faulk

David Semah

172	Ishaq Bar-Moshe: *Iraqi Days*, an excerpt from his novel *Ayyam al-Iraq*, translated by Jonathan Wright
176	Orit Bashkin: *Secularism, Spirituality and Reform – Ya'qub Balbul*
182	Haviva Pedaya: *"Baghdad"*, a poem, translated from the Hebrew by Howard Cohen
189	Almog Behar: *On the Poetry of Haviva Pedaya*

BOOK REVIEWS

192	Trino Cruz reviews *Poems of Alexandria and New York*
202	Susannah Tarbush reviews *The Madness of Despair*
206	Hannah Somerville reviews *Sarajevo Firewood*
210	Fayez Ghazi reviews *Foolishness as No One Told It* by Samir Kacimi

Anwar Sha'ul

214	**BOOKS IN BRIEF**
220	**EVENT** Berlin International Literature Festival
222	**CONTRIBUTORS**

Almog Behar

The Saif Ghobash Banipal Prize for Arabic Literary Translation

The 2021 Shortlist

Translated by **Marilyn Booth**	Translated by **Sarah Enany**	Translated by **Sawad Hussain**	Translated by **Elisabeth Jaquette**	Translated by **Jonathan Wright**
A novel of voices and letters, full of the uncertainties, ambiguities, and rootlessness of exile	A complex work of historical fiction in which the young Zeinab attracts the attention of Napoleon himself	A highly experimental collection of short stories, with a surrealist tinge	A novel within a novel that is a searing indictment of the Syrian regime	A novel of and in exile, whose narrator discusses his life with Emil Cioran, the Romanian nihilist philosopher
Voices of the Lost by Hoda Barakat (Lebanon) (Oneworld)	**The Girl with Braided Hair** by Rasha Adly (Egypt) (Hoopoe Fiction)	**A Bed for the King's Daughter** by Shahla Ujayli (Syria) (CMES, Texas University Press)	**The Frightened Ones** by Dima Wannous (Syria) (Harvill Secker)	**God 99** by Hassan Blasim (Iraq) (Comma Press)

THE JUDGES

Roger Allen (Chair)
Professor Emeritus of Arabic & Comparative Literature, University of Pennsylvania

Rosemarie Hudson
Founder publisher, HopeRoad Publishing

Ronak Hosni
Professor of Arabic and Translation Studies at the American University of Sharjah

Caroline McCormick
Director, Achates Philanthropy

The Prize is administered by the Society of Authors. The 2021 Winner will be announced on 12 January 2022, and the Award Ceremony, hosted on Zoom by the Society of Authors, will take place on 10 February 2022, with a Banipal celebration the following week (date tbc).

The Saif Ghobash Banipal Prize aims to raise the profile of contemporary Arabic literature as well as honouring the important work of individual translators in bringing the work of established and emerging Arab writers to the attention of the wider world. It was established in 2006 by Banipal magazine of modern Arab literature and the Banipal Trust for Arab Literature.

Full information available from: admin@banipaltrust.org.uk or
www.banipaltrust.org.uk/prize/

 facebook.com/SaifGhobashBanipalPrize    twitter.com/BanipalPrize

EDITOR'S FOREWORD

IRAQI JEWISH WRITERS

In this issue of Banipal we are delighted to present to the reader a very important and special feature on Iraqi Jewish writers. It must be said that this feature would not have been possible without the cooperation and assistance of our guest editors Professor Yehouda Shenhav-Shahrabani and Yuval Evri. It must also be stated that the idea for the feature came to us after the publication of Dr Khalida Hatim Alwan's book *al-Riwa'iyun al-'Iraqiyun al-Yahud* (Iraqi Jewish Novelists), which was published in Baghdad in 2014. We began the process of translating many of the texts that appeared in her study, by authors such as Ishaq Bar-Moshe, Samir Naqqash, Sami Michael and Anwar Sha'ul.

A long review of Khalida Hatim Alwan's book by Jonathan Wright appeared in *Banipal 57* (Autumn 2016), but we did not publish any of the translated texts, for we realised that if we were to properly produce an edition of the magazine devoted to Iraqi Jewish writers, we would need to cooperate with someone fully *au fait* with the subject. Someone also well versed in three languages, Arabic, English, and Hebrew, so as to be able to easily deal with texts, authors and translators. Finally, and after much searching, we found the right person, our great friend Dr Yehouda Shenhav-Shahrabani, professor emeritus at Tel Aviv University, a research fellow at the Van Leer Institute and chief editor of the Maktoob project for the translation of Arabic literature into Hebrew.

We are proud of this special feature that includes creative work from 17 Jewish writers, men and women, of Iraqi heritage. We have devoted the entire edition to the feature – something we have never done before – and even so we have had to put much of the creative material online. On the Banipal website can be found "Poems for the Incarcerated" an article by Almog Behar on the Mani Brothers with poems, and stories by Samir Naqqash, Shalom Darwish, Anwar Sha'ul and Ya'qub Balbul. We have also shortened the longer introductory pieces on authors due to limits on space, but have reproduced them in full online.

Finally, I have to express my disappointment that for technical reasons we have been unable to include in the feature the work of poet and author Mikha'il Murad (b. Baghdad, 1906, d. Tel Aviv, 13 Feb. 1986), one of the first Arab poets to write prose poetry. We hope to bring his work to the reader in appropriate form in a subsequent issue of *Banipal*.

Samuel Shimon

Iraqi Jewish Writers

Introduction

When Samuel Shimon and Margaret Obank came to us with the task of editing this volume on Iraqi Jewish Writers, we felt honoured and obliged in equal measure. At last, here was an opportunity to place this formidable mass of writing within the greater sphere of Modern Arabic English-language literature.

To date, English translations of Iraqi Jewish literature have been few and far between. As such, this literature remains by-and-large unknown to the wider English readership. Few attempts have previously been made to compile such literary materials in English. Ammiel Alcalay's *Keys to the Garden* (1996) was the first anthology to feature works by writers of Arab origins, amongst whom were seven Iraqi authors (Nissim Rejwan, Shimon Ballas, Samir Naqqash, Amira Hess, Ronny Someck, Tikva Levi, and Lev Hakak. See also: Berg 1996; Snir 2019). It is therefore of great practical and symbolic importance that this volume is now published as a special *Banipal* issue.

***

For several centuries, Iraqi Jews cast a major shadow as key players and contributors to Iraq's rich social and cultural tapestry. They were active in all areas of life as novelists, poets, essayists, journalists, mu-

Yehouda Shenhav-Shahrabani   *Yuval Evri*

sicians, composers, singers, and artists. However, in the aftermath of the 1948 War, all Iraqi communities across the Middle East found themselves facing far-reaching consequences. In the second half of the 20th century, the vast majority ended up emigrating; mostly to Israel, but also to other Asian destinations (chiefly Iran and India), or Europe and North America, with only a handful remaining in Iraq until the late 1970s. This exodus left Iraq stripped of its Arab-Jewish artistic and intellectual backbone.

And whilst there is diversity between (and within) their identities, distinct Arab-Jewish overtones recur, if not altogether dominate, in these authors' oeuvres, taking on many forms and harnessing a myriad of possibilities. Known as 'the Jews of the Arabs' in the Arab world and respectively, as 'the Arabs of the Jews' in the Jewish world[1], this admittedly convoluted, double-edged positioning does however capture poignantly the many contradictions and paradoxes experienced by Iraqi Jews throughout their long history. It is worth recalling Jewish Iraqi author Shimon Ballas's choice of words when describing his move from Baghdad to Tel Aviv in 1950: "I never changed my native soil or homeland. I only moved from one place to another within the region. I am not in conflict with the Arab surrounding. I came from an Arab region and remained in constant dialogue with it." (Alcalay, 1994).

The displacement of Arab-Jewish communities radically changed the social and cultural landscape. The writers who had left the Arab world now had to brave new, uncharted political territories and social realities, dominated by cultural fragmentation and negation.

Questions of language and poetic writing now echoed greater political and ideological issues more than ever before. Until 1948, whilst still in in the Arab world, these authors wrote predominantly in Modern Standard (aka literary) Arabic (mostly in Iraq and Syria), Judeo-Arabic (chiefly in rabbinical circles), or imperial languages (French or English). However, after 1948 and their emigration to Israel, this linguistic topography shifted dramatically. Although few did carry on writing in Modern Standard Arabic, the majority gave it up altogether, seeing as how Arabic was branded by the Israeli cultural and political elite as the sign of an exilic and inferior culture, and the language of the enemy. Instead, several authors (now-Israel-based) gradually transitioned to writing in Hebrew, whilst others ceased writing or publishing altogether, feeling severed from their cultural milieu and readership.[2]

In this volume, we provide an original literary ontology, which cuts across existing classifications of place, time, and language. It includes short stories, excerpts from novels, and poems – written by 17 individuals – all of whom are of Iraqi descent. We hope that the collection transcends the national and colonial cartography that dominates the split between the Arabic and the Hebrew, and that it provides a more integrative approach, anchored and guided by a deep-seated affinity for Middle Eastern history and culture. It features authors and poets of different generations, traversing a wide range of languages – from the poetry of the Mani brothers at the turn of the 20th century to the works of Almog Behar and Mati Shemoelof in the early noughties. All texts were either translated directly from Arabic (approximately two-thirds) or from Hebrew, with the exception of Mona Yahia's, whose contribution was originally in English.

We included introductory essays for each author, and added several essays on the Iraqi-Jewish literary world. It is therefore our hope that this volume paves the road for further readings and reimagined analyses of Iraqi Jewish literature; no longer confining it to the context of local national literatures but rather, discussing and analysing it also in relation to the literary world's greater Arab diaspora. The texts featured in this special issue attest to the sheer wealth of an Iraqi Jewish literary body of work, whilst also taking on universal questions of belongingness, exile, diaspora, cross-national affinities, and cross-linguistic possibilities. Granted, the danger that accompanies any collection of this magnitude is the false impression of canonisation. To be precise, what it represents is a coincidental gathering and a series of opportunities that presented themselves to us at the time of compiling and curating the works.

We thank Samuel Shimon and Margaret Obank for their invitation, and for the fruitful dialogue and collaboration. We thank Eran Edry for his wonderful translations from Hebrew to English, and Reuven Snir, Orit Bashkin, Ori Horesh, Zeena Faulk, Hana Morgenstern, Aviva Butt, Ryan Zohar and Jonathan Wright for their translations from the Arabic. We are also very grateful to Almog Behar for his ideas and help in gathering the materials.

In September 2019 the great Iraqi Jewish author Shimon Ballas passed away. In his death, we lost not only a dear friend but also a teacher and an intellectual giant who, above all else, was a model and inspiration for generations of Arab-Jewish authors and activists. We dedicate this volume to him, in ever-loving memory.

Yehouda Shenhav-Shahrabani
Yuval Evri

Notes

[1] On the transformation of the Arab-Jewish world post 1948, see Shohat (2003) and Shenhav (2006).

[2] On the linguistic movement between Arabic and Hebrew in the Iraqi-Jewish literature, see Snir (2019), Berg (1996); Shohat (2015) and Levy (2014).

Bibliography

Ammiel Alcalay. *Keys to the Garden: New Israeli Writing* (City Lights, 1996)

Ammiel Alcalay, 'At home in exile: An interview with Shimon Ballas', *Literary Review*, 37, 2 (1994), pp. 180-189.

Orit Bashkin. *Impossible Exodus: Iraqi Jews in Israel* (Stanford University Press, 2017)

Nancy Berg. *Exile from Exile: Israeli Writers from Iraq* (SUNY Press, 1996).

Lital Levy. *Poetic Trespass: Writing between Hebrew and Arabic in Israel/Palestine* (Princeton UP, 2014)

Yehouda Shenhav. *The Arab Jews: A Postcolonial Reading of Ethnicity, Nationalism and Religion* (Stanford: Stanford University Press, 2006).

Ella Shohat (2003) 'Rupture and Return: Zionist Discourse and the Study of Arab Jews', *Social Text*, 21.2: 49-74

Ella Shohat (2015). 'The Question of Judeo-Arabic', *The Arab Studies Journal*, 23.1: 14-76

Snir, Reuven 2019. *Arab-Jewish Literature: The Birth and Demise of the Arabic Short Story*. Brill.

HAVIVA PEDAYA:
The Iraqi-Jewish Literary Networks

Just as high-quality historical writing depends on literary documents, literature is never written without its history. The massive immigration of Iraqi Jews from Iraq into Israel in the 1950s represented a tectonic shift, from the history of Jewish Hebrew and Arabic literature in Iraq to the histories of individuals, destined to infiltrate from then on under the rubric of "Mizrahi authors" into the emerging canon of the new state, forced to migrate in language after having migrated in space. This gave birth to two types of creative writers from Islamic countries: Hebrew and Arabic language writers. About twenty years ago, they began being described as a group in their own right, rather than individuals classified (or excluded) by the establishment. This is not enough, however. We strive for the description of a literature that accounts for the fracture between fifty years, without a history of its own, and hundreds or even thousands of years of continuous creation. Diaspora is a key concept in this regard as it forms a joint cross-section of problems shared by all Mizrahi authors, who have experienced exile in Israel not as outsiders per se, but as immigrants from Islamic (read non-Western) countries.

The chronicle of this literature will include in its last chapters the historical stage of the gathering of all Jews from Arab countries into a single collective with its labelling as "Mizrahi" or "Sephardic". The postcolonial criticism of this stage and this labelling cannot ignore the generalizing nature of the literary practices of the generations experiencing this gathering, this labelling, and its very definition as a stage in its own right.

The suppression of Arabic and the nationalization of Hebrew proceeded in tandem with the construction of the Hebrew canon. This was another way of emasculating bilingualism and bi-nationalism, together with the demand for an emasculated Hebrew style in the spirit of late modernism and universalism imposed in Israel since the 1960s. The joint construction of the canon of Hebrew literature and criticism must be deconstructed. What could have been understandable in the early years after Israeli independence is now an overgrown infant that has never been weaned from the urge to produce a canon. And although some of the proponents of the critical discourse have already moved on to a post-colonialist discourse, the criticism of Hebrew literature still perceived its role as having to constantly produce a canon while at the same time excluding the unworthy using passwords and emasculation codes.

***

In order to discuss Iraqi-Jewish literary works in Hebrew or Arabic, we must acknowledge five literary networks: (1) That of the millennia-old Babylonian Jewry; (2) Modern Arabic literature and the modern Arab fiction as written in 20th-century Iraq; (3) The rabbinical and secular *Haskalah* literature of the turn of the 20th century; (4) Mizrahi literature in Israel; and (5) The diasporic literature of both Jewish and Muslim Iraqi émigrés. This categorization will enable a series of comparisons to be made to canonical Hebrew literature in Israel and to the finest Arabic literature worldwide.

(1) The *longue durée* of Babylonian Jewry's literature stretches back to the deep roots of Mesopotamian civilization, making the history of the Jewish-Iraqi diaspora incomparably longer than any other Jewish diasporas. This literature includes some of the best known biblical works, such as the Book of Ezekiel (Jerusalem-Babylon, began prophesying in 593 BC).

(2) Arabic beginnings. This network comprises Jewish authors and poets who can only be fully understood in the context of modern

Arabic fiction. The first among these generations includes Jewish writers who immigrated to the new state of Israel. Born in the first two decades of the 20th century, they became immediately uprooted from their prominent social status in Iraq and relegated to a marginal place in Israel. Most of them wrote in Arabic, and some managed to publish their books in Iraq and to be read in that language by Jewish and Muslim intellectuals. This generation included Shalom Darwish (1913-1997); Ya'qub Balbul (1920-2003), who stopped writing after arriving in Israel; and Maryam al-Mulla (al-Bassoon, 1927-2013), who immigrated to Israel only in 1973 and never stopped writing in Arabic. Her best known work is the story "Ma'satuhu Mathal" (His Tragedy, a Proverb).

The most prominent among the authors of this generation, and the cornerstone of the entire Iraqi–Jewish literary corpus is Samir Naqqash. Despite being young relative to this network (1938-2004), he is more similar to the characteristics of Iraqi-born authors and poets who wrote mainly in Arabic and who formed a literary circle of Arabic-writing Jews. However, upon immigrating to Israel, Hebrew publishers showed no interest in their work. In the young state of Israel, there was hardly any concept of translation, and only one "source" was almighty, choking the bloodstream of this network. In fact, these authors are simultaneously included in the fifth network, the diasporic one, because even when living in Israel, they remained émigrés to a certain extent, members of the Iraqi linguistic diaspora.

(3) Beginnings from Hebrew and Jewish-Arabic. Despite its long history and continuity, this literature has been relegated to the canonical margins by the European originators of Israeli literature. Note, however, that despite the conventional wisdom that modern Hebrew literature has grown out of the European *Haskalah* literature, an analogous autonomous category has never been assigned by literary critics to Hebrew works in Islamic countries. Rather, these have been judged through the lens of the emerging Hebrew literature in Israel or in Europe.

This third network started with the birth of secularized literature in the *Haskalah* period from its rabbinical womb. When discussing the Iraqi-Jewish literary world, we need to address both several literary networks and the movement along the intergenerational axis. Note that since the literary activity in Israel and the discovery of the Mizrahi identity unfold along a journey of identity, the location on the intergenerational axis will not be related to the authors' age in any way, but to the timing of their first publication. This timing is usually related to a kind of maturation or intersection of the individual and collective axes within the identity journey, often involving doubts and torments of the members of the minor culture.

This network marks the edge of more than a thousand years of a tradition of rabbinical writing in Hebrew, Arabic and Judeo-Arabic. It is the stepping-stone to a Jewish modernism in a Hebrew literature that is undergoing self-renewal in Arab countries. Its founding fathers included rabbis and kabbalists, who emigrated to Palestine or other countries, and who wrote poetry or literature in Hebrew or Judeo-Arabic; some of them began acting as collectors and anthologists – another indicator of a *Haskalah* process.

The Manni brothers, for example, immigrated to Israel as children. Rabbi Saliman Manni (1850-1924) and Rabbi Abraham Baruch Manni (1854-1882) wrote, next to their rabbinical works, Hebrew poetry inspired by the Golden Age in Spain (*Andalus*), and developing into modern Hebrew poetry on "mundane" subjects.

Due to the limited scope of this short review, note that – although it seeks to shed light on the entire history of Iraqi-Jewish literature, whether written in Iraq, in Israel or in the Iraqi diaspora, it only offers examples for the fourth and fifth networks, and only those included in this feature.

(4) Migration across geographic and linguistic spaces. The fourth network is where the main drama of Mizrahi literature unfolds, with movement along a three-generational axis that involves a journey of identity, creativity, migration and in some cases trauma as well. A somewhat different fate met the authors who, in addition to emigrating from Iraq to Israel, also managed to immigrate to the Hebrew language. They include a wide range of authors, the best known of which are Sami Michael (b. 1926) and Shimon Ballas (1930-2019).

As opposed to these authors of the first "Iraqi-Israeli" generation, where the writers' age is more or less aligned with the age of their first publications following their arrival in Israel, the gap between the birth year and publication year increasingly yawns. I believe this gap is the result of the complexity of coping with identity issues in Israel. The generational element here is determined by the year of first publication, rather than according to age, since by then the authors were already part of the "Zeitgeist" of the generation in which they published. Social struggles and transformations in collective consciousness were part of what enabled the literary breakthrough that had been denied some of their predecessors.

The second Iraqi-Israeli generation cannot be properly understood without the Mizrahi revolutions that occurred in the late 1960s and throughout the 70s – the Black Panthers, and the popularization of what came to be known as "Mizrahi music". Prominent members include author Eli Amir (b. 1937, first published 1983) and poets Amira Hess (b. 1943, first published 1984) and Ronny Someck (b. 1951, first published 1976).

The third generation in Israel includes writers born in the sixth and seventh decades after statehood. I am a member of this generation as my first book was only published in 1996 (Haviva Pedaya, b. 1957). Two prominent representatives of this generation are authors and poets Mati Shemoelof (b. 1972; 2001) and Almog Behar (b. 1978; 2008).

(5) Diasporic literature in various languages. Some of the authors belonging to this network have spent long periods in Israel and other countries. To a varying extent, they experienced a sense of exile in the Israeli national space, but even if exile was not the dominant experience in their world, they always remained attached to their mother tongue, Arabic. Their diasporic quality refers primarily to the incompatibility of their geographic location and creative language.

Naqqash was active in both Israel and Britain, thus remaining within the bilingual space of the native and colonialist. He is the most prominent author who interfaces with each of the networks mentioned, given his profound familiarity with the biblical, *Haskalah*, Jewish-Arabic and Iraqi diasporic literature. He never found his home, however, in the "Mizrahi" category, as he never moved to Hebrew.

Mona Yahia (b. 1954) arrived in Israel in 1971 and then emigrated to Germany – all the while writing extensively in English. Finally, Arabic literature scholar David Semah (1932-1997), among the pioneers of its academic study in Israel, kept writing Arabic poetry.

Others whose Arabic writing was stifled, such as Shimon Ballas and Shmuel Moreh, became scholars of Arabic literature, the former of Palestinian literature, and the latter of Iraqi Arabic literature.

IRAQI JEWISH WRITERS

AMMIEL ALCALAY

In & Out of Place

Memories of Nissim Rejwan, Shimon Ballas, and Samir Naqqash

I.

While the circumstances are so very different, I almost feel like Harun Soussan, the narrator of *Outcast*, Shimon Ballas's masterpiece that I co-translated with Oz Shelach, still the only one of Ballas' novels to have been translated into English. Like Harun fumbling around for his glasses in the opening scene, I am fumbling around, looking for documentation, letters, and even tapes from my dear old, now departed friends Shimon, Samir, and Nissim. But those things, along with books they gave me, and various clippings I saved, are mostly in my office, now inaccessible because of the pandemic. So the only option is to speak, as Kazem, another character in *Outcast* remarks, "straight from the heart."

AMMIEL ALCALAY

II.

In 1987, I happened to be in London, just after the great Palestinian cartoonist and champion of freedom Naji al-Ali died, some five weeks after he had been shot in the street on his way to work, victim of an assassination. I went to the memorial at the Kufa Gallery and there, among the speakers, I saw the renowned Iraqi poet Buland al-Haydari. I knew that Buland and Nissim had been friends in Baghdad in the late 1940s, when Nissim managed the al-Rabita Bookshop, a gathering place for local poets and writers, so I approached him. When I mentioned Nissim's name I saw Buland's eyes light up: he told me to wait until the memorial was over and not to leave, under any circumstances, until we had had a chance to talk. As I approached him after the event, he asked after Nissim with great curiosity and told me to wait until he got a piece of paper so he could write a short letter that he wanted me to deliver to his old friend directly, by hand. I knew from Nissim that they had attempted to communicate with each other at various times but to no avail, so I had a sense of the momentous nature of the occasion. Nissim and I always met in Jerusalem, sometimes at a café in town, sometimes at the Jerusalem Post where he'd gotten me on the list of reviewers, sometimes at the university to hear a speaker or attend part of a conference, sometimes at a press conference or political meeting on the East side of the divided and occupied city but, most often, we met at his place. Once I got back from London, I called and told him I had a surprise for him and, as usual, he said I should just come over, if that would be convenient. Once there, I handed him the letter, saying it was from an old friend. As he quizzically took the letter and opened it, I could see an expression on his face I'd only seen once before, some months earlier, when the Iraqi writer Khalid Kishtainy had managed to come to Jerusalem and we'd all gone out together to see a performance by the al-Hakawati Theater. Khalid had recently published his book *Arab Political Humor* and the whole time they were together, neither could stop laughing. Having already known Nissim for a number of years, I found this highly unusual. Of course, he had a wry sense of humor and one could, every now and then, glean a sparkle in his eye and see the edge of a grin develop, but almost as if he were grinning to himself, nothing like these full outward displays of joy. Seeing him like that, I knew that he hadn't always been the way I thought he was, that there were other parts of him left behind in another world. Like so many of his contemporaries, whether they admitted it to themselves or not, all they had been through because of the "Zionist entity," had surely taken its toll, and it was no different with Nissim.

III.

I met and did not meet Shimon in many places: we never, for example, met in Paris, even though it was his second home and the setting for one of his most important novels, *Last Winter*. In 1998, along with some other friends, we were absent together in Beirut. After having been invited by Elias Khoury for events centered on Arab Jews as part of the 50th commemoration of the Nakba, we were advised not to go as our safety couldn't be ensured. But in our absence, others spoke for us, and the attempt to shut our appearances down had the opposite effect: people came from all over, as we heard later, particularly Palestinians from the camps ringing Beirut, to listen, to find out what all the commotion was about. They came to hear firsthand (or, in this case, because of the circumstances, secondhand), about the uprooting of Jewish communities from Arab countries, to hear about Zionism, paraphrasing Ella Shohat, a scholar with roots in Iraq, 'from the standpoint of some of its other victims.' In 2002 we met in New York, when I invited Shimon to participate in a momentous meeting with Elias Khoury and Juan Goytisolo, in that strange interlude between 9/11 and the war against Iraq, with the idea of making a statement of some kind, at least for the record. We once bumped into each other in the middle of Cairo, unaware that we would both be there at the same time. He was with David Semah, a colleague and poet, one of the first to write in response to the 1956 massacre of Palestinians in Kufur Qasim, with his Arabic poem "He Shall Return." We walked for a while, as Shimon and I often did in Tel Aviv but here, again, as when I gave Nissim the letter from Buland al-Haydari or when I saw him with Khalid Kishtainy in Jerusalem, I could see that in Cairo Shimon and David were attentive to and immersed in every sound and sensation, their ears bending and their mouths moving to different wavelengths. We were together in Toledo and Geneva, or maybe only one or the other, in meetings with the PLO at a time when such meetings were illegal. We often ended up together at political events, sometimes as speakers. On occasion we drove from Tel Aviv to Haifa, when Shimon had something to do at the university and he asked me to tag along. But, as with Nissim, we also often just met at his place, on Tchernikovski Street in Tel Aviv, the walls lined with books—in Arabic, Hebrew, French, and English—along with his wife Gila's over-sized art books, rows and rows and rows of them, enclosing a living world of beauty and imagination within.

IV.

I only met Samir Naqqash at his home in Petah Tikva. I vividly remember the light coming through from the balcony, and the warm welcome I would always get from his wife Vicki and their kids. Once inside, sitting on the sofa with Samir, it was like stepping into a parallel universe, and I would be transported to all the places he'd gone to in order to finally get away from where he was: over the border in the north to Lebanon while still a teenager, then to Tehran and Bombay, with the hope of returning to Baghdad, at the behest of his father's former business partner. After I'd left Jerusalem for good, he'd write me with an address in Manchester, or about the possibility of moving to Cairo. But nothing ended up working, and he'd always return to the spot so close to where he arrived as a child, as a refugee from Baghdad. This emotional and political status—that of a refugee—is something that Samir fought fiercely for throughout his life, as an emotional category for his characters and as an existential condition for himself and those who had undergone a similar experience. While all the outward trappings seemed of the time and place, there was something that always made me feel privy to some secret, that there could be no better place to be than where I was at that moment, sitting and listening to Samir's voice coming from other realms that he had traversed in both body and mind. While I can recollect everything as if I were right there now, it is hard to fully recapture the emotional texture of those visits, the oscillation of intensity, expectation, and human connection. Because of this, I am so grateful, as we should all be, to another Samir— the Swiss-Iraqi filmmaker, director of the masterpiece *Forget Baghdad*— for the loving portrayal of Samir Naqqash captured on film, in his own home, from that very sofa where we so often sat, talking for hours.

V.

Although their experience was bitter, these friends were each grounded in their own way. From his column in the *Iraq Times* in the late 1940s to the *Jerusalem Post* and the array of books that he wrote on

Middle East politics, Israeli society or the Jews of Iraq, Nissim remained a cosmopolitan among provincials. Absolutely steadfast in his allegiance to the language of his childhood, Samir went against all odds, writing incredibly layered and complex stories and novels in Arabic rooted in place, memory and uncanny flights of imagination. His books depict not only lost worlds but also lost languages, dialects forged by ways of being that reach far back in time and custom. Yet the record of these utterances and interactions between characters are never frozen in an idealized past but always reanimated through present consciousness, through that reverie of almost unparalleled concentration that I always felt in his singular speaking voice. Shimon reordered his own geography, working through layers of illusion to create seemingly realistic worlds that were anything but realistic. His particular and unique gift, one that he honed to greater and greater effect, was the ability to depict lives that no one else even imagined could exist, inhabiting worlds no one would think possible. I cannot overemphasize this last point because it has so much to do with the breadth of Shimon's humanity. When I say that the lives and characters depicted in his novels are unimaginable, this is literally true—due to racist attitudes, narrowness of vision, and lack of imagination or experience—the society in which his books were received had a difficult if not impossible time accepting the existence of the people he wrote about. All of this could as well be said about Samir, with a different slant. Of course, to actually create worlds that posit the existence of the people in them, has always been the most difficult job for a novelist and it is, unquestionably, a world-changing form of creation that is becoming that much more difficult, as our lives become more standardized and generic. I feel humbled and incredibly lucky to have had the opportunity to get to know these people, to spend time with them, and to count them as friends. But I want to emphasize—especially for younger people embarking on artistic or academic pursuits—that I took the time to be with them, to read their work, to come to an understanding of their worlds. I did this not just because we felt an affinity for each other as people but because I understood how important they were, how much particular history they carried, and how much of that history has been decimated and relegated to oblivion. And yet, it is precisely these tenuous threads that hold our world together, and they unravel unless we each act to find ways to reconnect them, and it is in that spirit that I think of them now.

Shimon Ballas

Exile by Choice

YUVAL EVRI

Shimon Ballas was born in 1930 in Baghdad into a middle-class Jewish family in the vibrant neighborhood of al-Bataween. He began writing in Arabic from a young age in Iraq and continued writing in Arabic during his first decade in Israel (mainly in the Communist newspapers) before gradually moving into writing in Hebrew during the 1960s. Throughout his many years of literary activity in Hebrew and Arabic, Ballas published more than ten novels, several story collections, children's books, a memoir and research books on Arabic literature. He also played a pivotal role in the development of the field of Arabic to Hebrew translation in Israel during the 1960s and 1970s and was a pioneer in translating Palestinian literature into Hebrew.

Baghdad of the 1930s and 1940s, with its unique tapestry of different sects, faiths, languages and ethnicities, left a deep impression on Ballas's upbringing and on the development of his political and literary work. In his memoir, *First Person Singular* (Begof Reshon) (2009), which was the last book he wrote, Ballas describes in great detail the importance of Arabic literature during the formative years of his youth in Baghdad. He was fascinated by the writing of Gibran Kahlil Gibran and Taha Hussein and tried to imitate their style of writing. Ballas would read and write in cafes, because "in the two-room house where we lived I had no quiet corner for writing" (20). Among other things he regularly read Egyptian newspapers. He also enrolled in correspondence studies at the Egyptian College of Journalism, studied for two years and published his first articles in Arabic in the college's journal.

In 1946, Ballas joined the Communist Party, after reading a French translation of Jack London's *The Iron Heel*. In his memoirs, he describes how the question of Palestine intersected with the anti-imperial struggle, following the signing of the Portsmouth Treaty between Iraq and Britain: "Precious memories remain with me from those days. These were days when I first took part in demonstrations, joining forces with protesters I did not know before, calling in full voice for the overthrow

Shimon Ballas, London 2007

of the government and for free elections." During the demonstrations he chanted together with the crowd: "We are brothers to the Jews, enemies of imperialism and Zionism!"

Emigration to Israel in 1951 had dramatic consequences on his life, radically changing his social and cultural landscape. Confronted with new political and social realities, the question of language and literary writing echoed ideological questions more than ever. Among the Israeli cultural and political elite, Arabic was marked as inferior culture and the language of the enemy. Ballas, like other Iraqi Jewish writers, was faced with a dilemma – to keep writing in Arabic or to switch to writing in Hebrew. Ballas was at first against the linguistic transition into Hebrew: "I was among those opposed. I said no, what, language, impossible. Language is a part of a person. Yes, it's the mother tongue, not just a mother's tongue, but the mother tongue." But gradually he changed his position: "I came to the conclusion: I live in Tel Aviv, I speak Hebrew. [After all] who is my audience?!" (Berg, 1996: 57).

Even after this linguistic transition, Ballas did not abandon his connection to Iraqi and Arab culture, nor to the Arabic language, as he declared in one of his interviews:

"I have never denied my Arab origins or the Arabic language, despite also having had a French education. The Arab identity has always been a part of me. And I have said and I say: I am an Arab who has taken up an Israeli identity, but I am no less an Arab than any other Arab. That's a fact, and I have nothing to be ashamed of about it. If Arabs are perceived as being inferior, then it seems as if I am doing this as a provocation. But there are Arab Jews, just as there are French Jews: How come a Christian can be an Arab but a Jew cannot? Why should it arouse such amazement, then, when I say that I am an Arab Jew? I am always told that I am Iraqi. Where is Iraq- on the moon?" (Interview in 1991 during the First Gulf War)

Ballas incorporated Arabic words and poetic styles into his Hebrew prose. He begins his first Hebrew-language novel, *HaMa'abarah* (The temporary immigrant camp), with Arabic words transcribed into the Hebrew, such as "Café *al-Nasr* [Victory]-Shlomo *Khamra* [wine], proprietor". The original version of the novel also contained entire poems in Arabic but these were omitted by the editor as unacceptable to the Hebrew reader (Berg, 1996:59).

Ballas, like most of his fictitious protagonists, operates in the borderlands between different languages, territories, identities and loyalties, moving across national and geographical boundaries. A central theme running through Ballas's work is the impossibility of writing a monolithic, uniform or monolingual individual or national narrative. His work emphasizes the contradictions and ruptures that form personal and collective life stories, the memories we seek to silence and repress, the road not taken and the missed opportunities. He emphasizes the different voices, languages and ideological possibilities, existing in multitudes rather than forming a monolithic story or narrative. In this way, his poetic strategy resembles a diasporic literature, where culture, border, time and space are resonant in the ideas of multiplicity – more than one homeland, identity, language and loyalty.

Ballas's own biography is interwoven with multiple languages and urban settings. His life story traverses three major cities: Baghdad, Tel Aviv, and Paris. The urban landscape—its cafés, alleyways and backstreets, cinemas, and parks—is found at the heart of Ballas's work. The urban landscapes of these three cities are brought to life as spaces of diversity and multiplicity of languages, nationalities and ethnicities, seen through the eyes of the "wanderer", the traveler, mostly via the prism of writers, artists, political exiles and intellectuals, who are both foreigners and locals in the city.

Like Walter Benjamin's image of the "city wanderer," the "flâneur" (Benjamin 1996: 41), Ballas also adopts the perspective of the outcast, who situates himself at the margins of society and urban life. From the margins, Ballas tries to uncover the borderlands, which are hidden from the eye and from the official maps of the city.

In one of his autobiographical stories "The Imagined Childhood", which appeared in the story collection *Downtown* (1979), Ballas describes an encounter with an Iraqi friend in Paris:

Do the two houses I grew up in still stand? A young Iraqi friend I made in Paris couldn't quite answer my question, however he was able to get me a map of the city; the kind they give out to tourists. On it, I found all kinds of streets and gardens, public squares and bridges, and housing estates on the city outskirts.

"I have a different map," I told him. "One of curved, intersecting alleyways like a tight-knit network of spiderwebs. I can sketch it out on paper, for I remember every twist and turn, every nook and cranny, every arch, every window, and every protruding house corner that stuck out at a sharp angle, where men used to hang about, relieving themselves."

[See below pages 32-39 for the English translation of the story.]

The tourist map that Ballas's Iraqi friend passes to him symbolizes the official logic of the urban space, as imagined from above, projecting the official, ordered and organized. As de Certeau puts it, the map symbolizes the panoramic city as organized by the designer of spaces, the city planner, and the cartographer, but it is a visual illusion that represses the daily practices of those who walk the city's streets (de Certeau, *The Practice of Everyday Life*, 1984). Ballas's writing reveals urban spaces that are not included on tourist maps. Instead of the division into well-laid-out streets and squares, Ballas concentrates on the alleyways, niches, and winding backstreets of Baghdad, Tel Aviv, and Paris.

Ballas's chosen strategy for presenting urban space mirrors the way he presents the biographies of his books' protagonists. His protagonists's life stories, like his own, are not organized into linear, coherent paths, but rather contain crises, contradictions, and multiple possibilities. In his stories, Ballas tries to tell the stories of the road that could have been taken from any given fork. The focus of the narrative shifts from a single, consistent story to a many-branched and multi-dimensional mélange of potential stories concealed behind the official story.

The subject of memoir writing and autobiography is a common thread found throughout Ballas's work over the years. Most of his protagonists are struggling with the task of writing memoirs. Ahmed Nissim Soussan, the protagonist of Ballas's 1991 novel *Outcast* (*Ve Hu Aher*) is based on the figure of Dr. Ahmed Sousa, an Iraqi Jew who converted to Islam and remained in Iraq after the departure of the majority of the Jewish community. The novel, narrated in the first person, is set during the Iran-Iraq War, when the protagonist, nearing the end of his life, decides to write his memoirs. In trying to sketch his life's path, he faces up to the options he didn't pursue but avoids the question which "writers of memoirs do, whether I could have acted differently" (Ballas, 2007: 23).

In Ballas's trilogy *Tel Aviv East* (2003), the main protagonist Yosef Shaabi recalls the words of Walter Benjamin writing about Marcel Proust: "Uprooting a man from his homeland does not mean that he is separated from it" (Ballas 2003: 472). Shaabi faces the dilemma of whether to publish the memoirs of his friend Shaul Rashti in the original Arabic or to translate them into Hebrew for the benefit of his potential readers. In the end, he decides in favor of Arabic, because he does not want to smooth over and straighten out the contradictions and fractures contained within his friend's identity, Rashti having lived most of his life in Israel while maintaining a connection to Arabic culture and language. "Satisfied with this formulation, he continued to describe his friend as a human being who, despite his engagement with life in Israel, never replaced the identity he was born into in his homeland with an acquired identity, but rather bore the two of them as one throughout his life, and even felt the need to express this duality in his personality in the difficult days he experienced after the death of his wife" (Ballas 2003: 472).

"I think that you're playing hide-and-seek with yourself. As if you're searching for a refuge in the biographies of others, and avoiding your own biography" (Ballas 2008). Thus, the friend of Yaakov Salem, protagonist of the novella *The End of the Visit* (*Tom Ha-bikur*, 2008), seeks to provoke him into writing his life story. Salem explains that his preference for writing others' biographies is in fact the only way for him to write about himself: "Seeking a refuge in the biographies of others? If what he writes has any connection at all to a biography, it is surely to his own."

Did Ballas, too, find in his literary work a refuge in the biographies of others? Was he also engaged in writing other people's biographies as different variations on his own life story? Did this provide a way to make sense of the many forks and multiple routes within the course of his own life?

Let's return to the story "The Imagined Childhood". Ballas decided to include this story in its entirety in his memoir, *First Person Singular*. However, he chose to leave out the final paragraph of the original story, as it appeared in the collection *Downtown* (1979). Reading the redacted paragraph may help us answer some of the questions above:

"A faded silhouette or polished reflection of an imaginary experience. I don't put much trust in childhood stories, just as I have equally little trust in dream narratives. I especially distrust authors' childhood stories; those who thrive in fiction have proven themselves the least reliable in relating things as they are; as they have been from childhood.

The house I grew up in, my neighborhood, my childhood – a wondrous dream, a flight of fancy, the most marvelous vision. No, I could not possibly put any of them into words."

The omission of this paragraph from the autobiography is not accidental. Especially in light of the reference to authors' autobiographical writing. Even when it comes to writing the story of his own life, Ballas disrupts the possibility of an orderly narrative based on a uniform and consistent sequence of events. Ballas does not believe in authors' childhood stories, and as such invites us to view his childhood story with the same suspicion, to read it as an imagined childhood, as a marvelous dream, which transcends the restriction of words and languages, opening new possibilities to imagine territories and identities beyond the national imagination.

SHIMON BALLAS

The Imagined Childhood

(EPILOGUE)

TRANSLATED FROM THE HEBREW BY ERAN EDRY

I grew up in Baghdad's Christian neighbourhood, al-Bataween, in two homes, with only a narrow lane between them. The first house, we left when I was six years old. It was in the second house that I spent all of my school years, from year 1 through to high school graduation. The first house was one of three in a cul-de-sac, wedged right in the middle; its walls brushing against those of the neighbours on either side. To our right lived a well-to-do Jewish family whose home was by far the biggest and most lavish on the lane. A cone-shaped streetlight hung at the front, made of colourful glass panels, and encased in this jagged tin that served as its crown. Come nightfall, upon hearing the street patrolman's heavy footsteps, I would dart towards the window to catch a glimpse of his silhouette in the dark, leaning a wooden ladder against the wall and climbing it to light the lamp. The wick's flame would dance across his scorched, gaunt face, making his dark eyes sparkle the most sinister shade. I would then watch him descend and carry the ladder on his back all the way to the top of the lane until he disappeared from view. I would wait for the ritual to recommence with bated breath, and when the long whistle finally came, ripping through the peace and quiet of the night, I would feel waves of chills shooting up and down my back. I couldn't say how old I was at the time; however, I do recall that long before we moved out of the cul-de-sac, the colourful streetlight had been replaced with a miniscule electric bulb which a mystery hand would switch on at the exact same time.

To our left lived an elderly Armenian couple – refugees from the Turkish pogrom. Their front door had an immaculately polished brass knocker affixed to it, and late at night, the door would open to the sound of its knocking. Foreign hymns were heard coming from inside the house – mournful tunes which, at times were accompanied by the sound of loud male chatter, and boisterous female laughter. The landlady – a short and stout, corpulent woman was the cul-de-sac's unofficial queen – revered by the older residents and referred to as 'auntie' by the younger ones. The children were particularly keen on her, for hers would be the place of refuge they would seek whenever they found themselves on the receiving end of their parents' wrath. She would serve them sweets, but would not spare them any admonishing words. However, her chiding was as tender to the ear as her sweets were to the palette. I was spellbound by her persona and the air of mystery that seemed to hang over her life. In summertime, she would sit outside her home, doing lacework. And when she noticed me watching her, she would beckon me to come over and sit at her side and tell me tales of another world. Her voice was crystal clear and would quiver ever so slightly; a gold tooth sparkled inside her mouth, and her laughter would ripple and roll like the splashing of spring water. She used to sing for the Turks and her photograph from those days, in which she wore a long, pristine white dress, stood on a square table, nestled between two wide settees in the front garden. Her husband, who was considerably her elder, would listen to her stories silently, sometimes getting up and stroking my head with his icy, emaciated hand. A host of eccentric guests frequented her home, speaking her language, whereas I – left unsupervised – would feel myself swelling with pride at the sight of her in the centre of it all, with all eyes on her, and all ears hanging on her every word. When eventually I was summoned back home, I would get up, ashamed, and drag my feet. Her husband would walk me to the door and deposit a sweet in my hand. He would then bolt the door shut. I never knew what went on behind that door and whenever I asked my mother, she would scold and condemn me to silence.

A truly extraordinary woman, that ageing chanteuse was – raised in exile and purged into exile when evil befell her people. Later, I would conjure her up in my story, Auntie Aouni.

Ours was an old house with a heavy, black door, which swung on wooden hinges that seemed to creak and groan every time I leant against the door, trying to get it to budge. There were two basements in our house – an upper basement and a lower one. The upper basement would don a festive cloak in the summer months, seeing as it was there that we spent the scorching afternoon hours: the room was always chilly, with the most blissful breeze coming through the chimney air vents. The lower basement filled me with dread. A great many stairs led down there, with the last ones all but consumed by darkness. From spring through to midsummer, it would become waterlogged and a nest of snakes would come fleeing from it into the house, in search of shelter. I would lie at my mother's side on a mat laid out on the floor as I watched the procession of snakes slithering about, under the wooden stool by the wall. In those days, the terror of snakes had yet to take root in my mind, and so I could still entertain myself, setting my eyes on this spectacular sight. I recall this one particular story that I'd heard from my mother time and time again, growing up. She had gone up to the attic that was used as a storage space for an assortment of old bric-a-brac, and as she was reaching for a wicker basket, a spotted snake leapt out at her. Overcome with such fear, she became petrified in place as the erect snake hissed furiously at her. The only memory she had of that hair-raising moment was the magic chant she had learnt at her childhood home from her parents, which their ancestors had bequeathed unto them:

"House snake, house snake, you shan't hurt us, and we shan't hurt you."

> You would never hear those fake cries of professional wailers at Christian funerals. That was the Jews' and Muslims' lot.

And indeed, it obliged her pleas and resumed its position curled-up on the floor in a large circle.

The tenants who took over from us had no fear of snakes. The family patriarch, a trained carpenter, was quite the adept snake hunter. In his teens, whilst working as a carpenter's apprentice, his Muslim employer gave him 'snake water' to drink; a concoction produced by dunking a venomous snake in a jar of water and leaving it in there for the next 24 hours. This water is a snakebite antidote and those who drink it shall be immune for the rest of their lives. He would hold the snake's head between his fingers whilst its body was wrapped around his arm as if it were a spring. He never killed any of the snakes he'd caught. The non-poisonous ones he would set free in the fields, whilst the poisonous ones he would defang. I watched him do it on the rooftop. He brought a piece of cloth to the snake's mouth and once it sank its teeth into it, he pulled the cloth out in one fell swoop, ripping out the serpent's hollow, venom-spewing fangs.

The second home we moved into was also a snake-infested den. They fed on mice and lived in the wooden ceilings. We would hear them slithering about above our heads, and their incessant, insipid hissing. A giant black snake took up residence in the kitchen and on hot days, it would come out of hiding in search of water. We memorised the magic chant and recited it in our prayers.

**

That said, my childhood days were also buzzing with other, far more pleasant sounds - the chiming of bells. There were a great many churches in the neighbourhood and their bells would chime daily, at regular intervals, summoning the worshippers for prayer services. I knew the chiming of those bells and could recognise each and every one of them. The big Catholic church bell's ringing was as heavy and lumbering as the priest's own march to the pulpit. In contrast, when the Armenian church's miniscule bell chimed, it just about managed a thin, timid ringing. At New Year's, Easter, and other Christian festivals, the chiming of the bells would cause the glass windowpanes to shake, leaving me feeling unnerved and elated in equal measure. Then there were the times when a single, solitary bell would chime sombrely at an unorthodox time of day. I would then know that a funeral procession was making its way to the church. Countless funeral processions passed by our window. The first to emerge, as they turned into the cul-de-sac were the teenage boys in their pristine white gowns, holding candles; behind them came the priests in their black robes, and in the very centre – the priest leading the procession. Behind them were the pallbearers, and behind them, the family, and their companions. All sounds of praying would cease the moment they entered the cul-de-sac and were not heard again until they had finished crossing it. They advanced in silence along the cul-de-sac; with the coffin, bearing the smallest statuette of the Crucified One on its lid, suspended in the men's arms. Passers-by stopped in their tracks, Christians made the sign of the cross on their faces, while Jews and Muslims watched the procession – their heads bowed.

You would never hear those fake cries of professional wailers at Christian funerals. That was the Jews' and Muslims' lot. On my way to school, I would sometimes cross paths with Jewish or Muslim funerals that bore an uncanny resemblance to one another. The coffin was carried on the mourners' shoulders, whilst the wailers beat their chests and pulled out their hair, as everyone rushed ahead in a great big commotion. I was drawn to the Christians' ceremonial grandeur. I loved their houses of worship and during the holidays, I would sneak in and stay throughout the course of incense-engulfed masses, watching the incense floating on the waves of pipe organ music.

I would often frequent this one French mission monastery. This particular monastery, that was used as a girls' school, held afternoon piano lessons. Several times a day, I would make a point of walking past the monastery, yearning to know the mystery piano that delivered such wonderfully mellifluous melodies into the world. However, I was much too afraid to step inside, seeing as how a stern-faced guard was permanently installed on a stool at the gates, forbidding any and all strangers from entering. Imagine my surprise then, when one morning as I accompanied our maid to buy some milk from the dairy at the far end of the neighbourhood, she paused at the guard's station and began conversing with him. I tugged at her sleeve, voicing my request in her ear, but she dismissed me with a smile and carried on chatting. I was unyielding, until she eventually relayed my petition. The guard smiled and promised he would let me in if I came back that afternoon. I promptly reported to him upon my return from school.

"You're early," he said, "come back later."

When I did, I found the Mother Superior standing at the entrance. Having been brought up to speed, she extended both her hands to me and pulled me inside. She then asked whether I was studying French at school, and when I confirmed that I was, she said:

"You are a clever boy."

She escorted me up to the second storey and led me into a spacious room that very much resembled a regular classroom, save for the black piano raised up on a stand, which stood at the front with a nun and her pupil at its side. They ceased their playing as we appeared at the door, and the Mother Superior said something, which I was far too flustered to take in. She then had me sit on a bench and excused herself. The teacher nodded at me and resumed the lesson whilst I was glued to my seat, awash with excitement and awe. From that day on, I would report to the monastery practically on a daily basis. The Mother Superior always greeted me with a smile and would ask me all kinds of questions. She was a beautiful woman, and the white veil that adorned her head gave her a saint-like aura. Everyone would address her as "Ma mère"; as did I. I was a shy boy, and my words were few and far between, however she would never let me get out of answering her questions. Sometimes, when she found herself with a bit of time to spare, she would invite me into her tiny chambers and deliver a long lecture that would render me utterly baffled and bewildered.

"You're only young," she would say, offering me a forgiving smile, "when you're older, you'll get it." Indeed, when I got older, I came to understand a great many things, however I would not maintain my interest in the monastery's day-to-day, nor did I continue to seek the elderly nun's company. I would become preoccupied by other matters that would determine the path I was to take in life.

**

Many Jewish families lived in the Christian neighbourhood, where signs of the Sabbath and high holidays were ever prominent in its alleyways. On Rosh Hashana, we all wore white – from head to toe; on Purim, we paraded about with our toy guns, shooting at everything, left, right, and centre; and at Passover, we unleashed our wrath at the gentiles. Having said that, we never did stop and look for any rhyme or reason behind the things we were doing. None of us knew, and I, for one still haven't a clue to this day why we should have been flying kites on Tisha B'Av. There wasn't a single Jewish child who wasn't flying a kite on Tisha B'Av. Granted, it was by far one of our favourite pastimes throughout the whole of summer but on that special day, the kite would take on an altogether ritualistic meaning. We would assemble it with our own fair hands, decorate it with a range of colourful tails, and compete amongst ourselves over who had the prettiest kite, and whose was the one that best "sat" up in the sky. On summer nights, the Baghdad sky would fill up with kites of all colours. We would tie the end of the string to a ledge, or a random lamppost and leave the kite suspended in the sky all night. On summer nights, Baghdad would slumber on rooftops, whilst the sound of kites fluttering under the stars was like a children's lullaby.

My personal favourite holiday was Passover. How I loved Seder night; sitting round the set table, reading the Haggadah, and sipping the sweet wine made by my mother's hands. However, in the run-up to the holiday, I would always find myself riddled with anxiety lest our father not be there with us and our Seder at home be cancelled. My father was a fabric retailer in southern Iraq and would only call on us once a month or every other month, when the shop was running low on stock, and he had to head up to the capital to replenish his supplies. Whenever he showed up, pandemonium swept over the house; already at the door, he was calling my mother and the maid over, whilst shouting warnings at the porter carrying his luggage, lest he damage anything. We would gather round him, and he would give us all a kiss, his rough stubble leaving us with severely irritated cheeks, and a thick smell of tobacco in his wake. Purebred, clucking chickens would come pouring out of his cases, flapping their wings, and depositing their excrement all over the place. Before long, our garden was overrun with parcels, boxes, and a huge pile of dirty laundry.

However, as great as our joy was at his arrival, as was our despair at his absence during the holidays. In his letters, he would name the date of his visit, however, on more than one occasion he left us hanging right up to the very eve of the holiday. My mother and the maid would spend the whole day slaving over the holiday meal, while I was glued to the window well into the late afternoon. There would be no miracle for us on such days and my heart grew bitterly resentful of him.

**

Do the two houses I grew up in still stand? A young Iraqi friend I made in Paris couldn't quite answer my question, however he was able to get me a map of the city; the kind they give out to tourists. On it, I found all kinds of streets and gardens, public squares and bridges, and housing estates on the city outskirts.

"I have a different map," I told him. "One of curved, intersecting alleyways like a tight-knit network of spiderwebs. I can sketch it out on paper, for I remember every twist and turn, every nook and cranny, every arch, every window, and every protruding house corner that stuck out at a sharp angle, where men used to hang about, relieving themselves."

"They've razed loads of neighbourhoods," replied my friend in a very fact-of-the-matter way, "yours could have been one of them." Whether razed or not, does it even matter? I daresay it will forever remain standing. The world of childhood is a timeless place that is far more rooted in the imaginary than in real life. It is a form of experienced perfection, the sum of which simply cannot be reduced to its parts, nor can it be put into words. We are accustomed to telling stories that make sense. The languages that we speak follow fixed sets of rules and adhere to concepts of time. For every effect there is cause, and that thread of causality runs through every sentence that passes our lips, for were it not so, we would be rendered unintelligible to all. How do we relate a dream? How does one recount an experience that transcends time? Childhood experiences cannot truly be shared unless one is willing to submit them to the confinements of time and bind them to the chains and shackles of cause and effect. Such are the childhood stories that we read. They are just that - stories. A faded silhouette or the polished reflection of an imaginary experience. I don't put much trust in childhood stories, just as I have equally little trust in dream narratives. I especially distrust authors' childhood stories; those who thrive in fiction have proven themselves the least reliable in relating things as they are; as they have been from childhood.

The house I grew up in, my neighbourhood, my childhood – a wondrous dream, a flight of fancy, the most marvellous vision. No, I could not possibly put any of it into words.

SHIMON BALLAS
He Loved Life
(Ahabba al-Hayat)*

by Adib al-Qass (the pen name of Shimon Ballas)

TRANSLATED FROM THE ARABIC BY
HANA MORGENSTERN

"And the little rabbit ran rapidly, fearing the wolf's teeth… but God had given her two long legs that helped her run so fast no one could catch her—"

Abu Harun stopped abruptly, turning his eyes towards his son Harun's hut, from which loud screams had begun to erupt. He had been squatting on the steps of his wooden hut, telling his grandson Said the story of the little rabbit.

"And what did the little rabbit do then?" asked little Said, looking up anxiously at his grandfather.

His grandfather rose to his feet and said, "The little rabbit? She kept on running—and now your mother's screaming because your father's beating her—"

He rushed into his son's hut. A large group of people had gathered to witness a scene that occurred repeatedly in this room. The wife

---

* "Ahabba al-Hayat" (He Loved Life) by Shimon Ballas was published in al-Jadid, the Israeli Communist Party's Arabic cultural journal, in 1955. It follows a day in the life of Yusuf 'Abid, a young Arab Jewish immigrant who is struggling with the unemployment and poverty that stand in the way of his marrying his girlfriend Salima. Yusuf undergoes a crisis when he is blackmailed by officials from the Histadrut (Israel's organization of trade unions), who promise to return his job if he accuses another communist worker of theft. In its didactic socialist realist style, the story exposes and condemns transit camp life, containing many common themes covered in later Arabic and Hebrew-language transit camp literature, such as depictions of substandard housing, poverty and unemployment, and the resultant drinking, violence and domestic discord. Harun's drinking and abuse of his wife and Yusuf's inability to marry highlight the unravelling family structures in which marriages deteriorate, children are neglected, parents move out of the natural order of rest and peace at the end of life, and young people fail to build their lives. The emblematic scene of frustrated workers at the unemployment office and the corruption of the Histadrut officials highlights the dissonance between the community and the Israeli regime, and is the central event of political revelation in the story.

rushed towards them, screaming desperately: "He wants me to work! How can I work with five kids? Where would I leave them? He works in the factory, but he wastes all his wages drinking and gambling! Yes, arak and gambling, that's what he loves!" She kept yelling and crying, beating herself. Her situation aroused pity in the hearts of those present, and they tried to calm and console her.

Yusuf 'Abid, who had rushed to Harun's hut along with the others, surveyed the scene with obvious disdain. He hated fights and yelling disgusted him, so he didn't stay long.

It was the time of the afternoon prayer, and the sun had begun to gather up its rays far away on the western horizon. A light autumn breeze blew, bringing tidings of the approaching winter. He left the house and plodded along, shoving his hands in his pockets and gazing out at the rugged road that stretched ahead of him. It wasn't nature with its constant changing garb nor that incident in the hut that preoccupied his thoughts; he was dwelling on issues that had been troubling him for a long time. He felt like someone struggling to climb to the top of a tree; he kept on climbing, doubling his efforts, but the tree kept growing and he could never reach his goal. He was headed to the labor office in the city. It had been two months since he had been fired, along with twenty other workers, under the pretext of diminishing output. The attempts of the workers to keep their jobs had been in vain.

Yusuf had proposed to Salima when he was still a soldier. He had met her at the transit camp over six months ago, when he still believed he might have a comfortable life after leaving the army. But as soon as he was discharged, life confronted him plainly and harshly, and his dreams dissipated like smoke on a windy day. The bare necessities of life consumed all the money he earned at work. He paid the debts his mother had incurred while he was a soldier, and bought some necessary items for the house, but he could not put aside a single penny towards marriage. Now two months had passed since he had been fired and he was once again drowning in a sea of debt. He arrived at the paved street, feeling his feet beat rhythmically on the hard, even ground. Every day he walked from the camp to the city, so as not to waste his precious pennies. The buses and cars would pass him by at breakneck speed, shattering his field of vision, their gurgling of engines turning into mocking laughter in his mind. He thought of Salima. A whole week had passed since he'd seen her.

He had decided not to visit her until he found something because he was tired of shaking his head wearily in response to her persistent question, "So have you found a job?"

He felt extremely embarrassed. His mouth and throat dried up, and he was unable to speak. He flushed with anger when he remembered the beautiful wristwatch that he had decided to buy her. Then he was sacked, making it impossible for him to realize this dream. He wanted to wrap her in his love and affection, and for hours on end he swam in a sea of daydreams, imagining times alone with her, moments of intimacy.

When he reached the city and headed towards the employment office, the sun had already risen above the horizon and the morning shadows had appeared. A few workers stood around talking in front of the office. Yusuf greeted them.

A tousle-haired man addressed him: "They haven't announced any work today. Yehuda hasn't even opened the window yet. Look!" He pointed to a piece of paper torn from a notebook, on which Yehuda had scrawled: "No jobs handed out today! —Yehuda"

The worker spat on the ground and swore: "To hell with them! They're all bitches, sons of bitches!"

A middle-aged worker standing next to him added: "What a racket! They're handing out jobs to their favorites."

"It's been a whole week since they've distributed any jobs. How is that possible? How are people supposed to live?" said Yusuf.

The middle-aged man laughed scornfully: "You think they care about your life? Your problems are not their concern."

A fat man in his forties with an eye patch approached them: "Oppressors, that's what they are! There's not an ounce of mercy in their hearts. They leave hundreds of families without work. How will they face God?"

The old man nodded. "Their hearts have no mercy," he said.

"I'm not even talking about myself," continued the one-eyed man. "I'm talking about young men like Yusuf, hundreds of them suffering unemployment. I've already had my youth. It was a happy time. But these poor kids, how are they supposed to face life?"

"Yes, that's true," the tousle-haired man said. Yusuf, however, kept his silence.

Then the office door opened and a bald man emerged. He held a bag in his right hand and threw wary looks at the workers.

"Greetings, Yehuda," said the one-eyed man, a stupid smile covering his face.

"Hello," replied Yehuda, as he approached them.

"How long are we going to be unemployed?" asked the old man.

"Yes, for how long? We're overwhelmed by debt!" added the tousle-haired man.

Yehuda smiled and looked at Yusuf out of the corner of his eye: "More work will be handed out soon. Don't despair, the situation will get better!"

Will there be work tomorrow?" the one-eyed man asked.

"I think so."

Then he turned to Yusuf and said: "How are you Yusuf? I have something to tell you!"

"To tell me? Of course."

Yehuda said goodbye to the workers and left with Yusuf. The road was almost empty, and a profound silence had settled.

"You need money?"

"Of course," said Yusuf with a startled smile.

Yehuda turned his eyes toward Yusuf, scrutinizing him: "I've been thinking a lot about your situation, and I think I can find a good job for you."

"Really?"

Yehuda patted his shoulder: "Yes, Yusuf, I'm doing my best. Meet me tomorrow at 4:30 in the afternoon at my house and I'll give you the final answer."

"Tomorrow at 4:30?"

"Yes, the matter is under consideration."

"Thank you, Yehuda!"

"No problem, I'm always ready to help you," Yehuda said, smiling. "And now, I have a meeting I have to go to. Goodbye, Yusuf, see you tomorrow."

"Goodbye," he said, turning towards Yehuda, but Yehuda was already walking quickly away.

When Yusuf returned to his hut that night he was agitated. The meeting with Yehuda had kindled his excitement, and he began entertaining his far-reaching hopes once again. His yearning to see Salima had grown, and this news about a job had set his worried soul aglow with hope and life. He thought and felt and worried and yearned; he whispered to his sweetheart who was waiting for him impatiently, he groaned and tossed and turned on his bed as if it was made out of thorns!

The next day he waited anxiously for the appointed time when he could leave for his appointment. On his way to Yehuda's only one thing occupied his thoughts: the feeling of triumph. He started to imagine himself working at a machine, making a daily wage, so that he could return happy to his mother and to Salima. He imagined himself on his way to the factory in the early morning, and the wonderful hours with his beloved Salima when he returned home.

But the flow of his thoughts was suddenly cut off when someone grabbed his arm, and he heard a gruff voice addressing him. "Are you going to Yehuda's?" It was Harun. "What time did he ask you to come? 4:30?"

The astonishment tied Yusuf's tongue and left him feeling confused. "Yes," he stuttered.

"I'm headed there, too."

But Harun had a job. He was the superintendent of the workers' committee at the factory. What business did he have at Yehuda's?!

"Yehuda is a good man. He wants to help you," said Harun. "And I've spoken to him as well. I told him about your problems."

He spoke as if he'd done something that deserved gratitude. So perhaps he was the one who had asked Yehuda to send him back to work? But wasn't he also the one who, as a representative of the head of the workers' committee, had accepted the dismissal of Yusuf and 20 other workers? It was truly strange.

"Did you talk to him about my situation?" Yusuf asked, in spite of himself.

Harun laughed and said, "I'm always trying to help you, Yusuf. But you have to use your brain!"

At Yehuda's, Yusuf met Manshi Hay, who had been fired along with him. Manshi received him with a smile and related the good news that the bad times would soon be over.

Yehuda began talking, starting with a report on the work situation, telling them about incidents that had happened at the employment office, how workers sometimes got angry, banged on the tables and broke the windows. He railed against them furiously but added that some destructive elements were working amongst them and pushing them to commit violent acts.

"Even inside the factory these destructive groups obstruct the work and create conflict between the workers and the employers!"

"They incite the workers against the elected committees, and they spread rumors that the committee doesn't serve the workers or care about their problems," Harun said.

"Yes, they are a fifth column within the national industries!" said Yehuda.

Yusuf didn't understand the significance of these words, and he was surprised to hear them talking about matters so far removed from what he had hoped to hear.

"We have to do whatever we can to defeat them," Harun said.

"Who are they?" asked Yusuf.

Manshi interrupted, laughing: "Don't you know yet? The communists!"

"Yes, Yusuf, we have to defeat them once and for all!" said Harun.

"But how?" asked Yusuf. Little by little he had begun to understand the meaning of the conversation.

Yehuda resumed speaking. "Listen, Yusuf, you know Shaul. He's not very sought after, always creating problems for the labor agency. He's a concern for the workers' institutions. He wants to turn the workers against their committee and stage a red coup in the factory!"

"He spreads lies and accuses the committee of lying!" added Harun.

Yusuf tried to compare this picture to the Shaul that he knew with the stern features and calm smile, but he couldn't combine them. The Shaul he knew was a diligent worker who loved his job, like the rest of the workers. He was known for his friendliness and gentle manners. He talked to everyone, criticized the boss and the workers committee, and demanded improvements to their conditions, but he had never carried out sabotage. When they were fired, Shaul stood with Yusuf and the other workers and demanded that they get their jobs back.

He felt disturbed and couldn't really focus on what they were saying as he tried to assess his role in this unsettling situation.

"You should make it known that it was Shaul who stole that money from Mr. Bernstein's locker," Harun was saying.

Yusuf awoke from his reverie: "What are you saying?" He shook.

"You're going to have to testify to that."

Bernstein's locker? What did Shaul have to do with that? The money was stolen and they hadn't found the thief.

"How can I testify? I didn't see him do it!"

Manshi laughed and said, "Don't worry, you won't have to go to court."

"Sign this, and tomorrow you'll be back at work." Yehuda took a piece of paper from his pocket and handed it to Yusuf.

Yusuf was bewildered, tongue-tied. He looked around in confusion at the assembled group of people.

"Don't worry about it, just sign this testimony," Manshi encouraged him again.

"He's signed too, and he's going back to work tomorrow," said Harun.

Just then, the door of the room opened and Frischmann, the secretary of the Histadrut, came in.

"Is the statement ready?" he asked, looking at the paper in Yehuda's hand.

"Manshi signed."

"What about Yusuf? Why hasn't he signed?"

"It's only been an hour. He hasn't decided yet."

"What's he supposed to decide? He signs it right now and gets his job back. I'm in a hurry!" he said, glancing at his wristwatch. He pulled the paper from Yehuda's hand and thrust it at Yusuf.

"I can't," said Yusuf.

Frischmann stepped back and looked at him sternly.

Harun shouted, "What did you say? Don't you want to go back to work?"

Anger showed on Harun's face and his eyes sparked viciously. Yusuf kept looking at him, remembering the incident yesterday, when Harun hit his wife in front of all those people, and his soul filled with disgust and hatred.

"Watch yourself. You have to do this," said Yehuda.

Manshi approached him "Listen, Yusuf, I signed! What do you care about this thing with Shaul? You should get married! Go back to work."

To live, yes. To marry, yes. But lying?

"I can't lie!"

"It's going to cost you dearly. You'll stay unemployed," Harun warned him.

"As a secretary of the Histadrut, I'm informing you that if refuse you will never get a job again!"

"Yusuf, think about your future… think about your life," Manshi said.

Think about the future? He thought about it all the time. He had built a palace in the sky. He had hung all his hopes on this meeting. He had planned to visit Salima this afternoon to tell her the good news that he was back in work. So, he would lose the job? Would he remain unemployed? Yes, he wanted to live. He wanted to get married just like everyone else! But why was there no honest way to get a job?

"But I didn't see it!" The sentence came out as if he were sick.

Harun got up, grabbed the paper and pen from Frischmann and jammed it between Yusuf's fingers. "Sign it right now, don't hesitate! Otherwise, you can say goodbye to Salima and to married life!"

How does he know Salima's name, the scum? Yusuf wanted to spit in his face. He wanted to him slap him, but he controlled himself and concealed his raging anger.

"Sign it, my brother… there's nothing bad in that," Manshi encouraged him.

"I can't."

Yusuf quickened his steps on the road to Salima's. He felt as if his head was going to explode from all his jumbled thoughts. Despite the cold, his body was dripping with sweat. The world was swaying in front of his eyes, and he couldn't discern people or things. He saw electric lights ahead of him through the thick fog and the bright pale spots burned his eyes.

Deep inside him a fire was blazing, and he felt the need to scream. He wanted to tell Salima what had happened to him, to reveal everything to her, about the stand he'd taken before the bared fangs of those mad wolves, about how he'd escaped from them. It was she who would give him courage and give him back his confidence! But Salima was in danger. Harun knew her name. Surely, he was capable of anything. He would hurry, hurry to her, hold her to his breast, protect her from any assailant. He would sacrifice anything for her, anything, even that which was dearest to him. The road he was walking was crowded with people, their voices ringing out, but he paid them no attention. He forced his way through the throng, to Salima.

DAVID SEMAH

Communism, Commitment and Humanity: David Semah

URI HORESH AND ORIT BASHKIN

Born in Baghdad in 1933, David Semah studied in the bilingual Jewish school Shammash, which offered excellent Arabic and English instruction. Like his high-school friend, Sasson Somekh, Semah had showed a great interest in Arabic literature at an early age. He was not politically active, but wrote a poem in honor of Iraqi martyrs who were killed in a series of grassroots demonstrations against the state in the winter of 1948, known as the Wathba. During the years 1949-1950, Semah's family found itself trapped in the situation which affected the lives of many Iraqi Jews. Right-wing elements in Iraqi society identified every Iraqi Jew as a Zionist, while the state of Israel pushed for their migration. The family had no choice but to migrate. Semah took with him one item to Israel – the diwan of the Iraqi poet Muhammad Mahdi al-Jawahiri, given to him by his Shi'i high-school teacher. Together with 124,000 Iraqi Jews who arrived in Israel with virtually no money, Semah found himself in Israel living in great poverty and suffering discrimination.

In response to these conditions, Semah, like other Iraqi Jewish intellectuals and activists, joined the Israeli communist party, MAKI. The party was an Arab-Jewish organization and a prominent cultural hub, which counted among its members many Palestinian writers and poets, such as Emile Habibi and the young Mahmoud Darwish. Somekh and Semah read Habibi's writings on Marxist literature with great interest and very much identified with what he wrote. The two

David Semah

addressed the literary journal of the party, *al-Jadid*, asking for permission to establish a club associated with *al-Jadid* that would bring them closer to Arabic literature. *Al-Jadid*'s editorial board responded to this call: Jabra Nicola, the editor, and Sami Michael came from Haifa and held a meeting in Semah's home with Somekh, Ballas, and other Iraqi Jews. Ballas, Somekh, and Semah also decided to publish in *al-Jadid* and invited more Iraqis to do so; they found in *al-Jadid* a home. *Al-Jadid*, for example, published Semah's poem, *al-Wathba al-ula* ("The First *Wathba*") in which the speaker yearned for a second *Wathba*, and more broadly, for a revolution.

Semah wrote poetry all throughout the 1950s and 1960s, and participated in the literary activities of *al-Jadid* and in the "Forum of the

DAVID SEMAH

Supporters of the Arabic Literature" in Tel-Aviv, which he cofounded with Somekh and Ballas. In 1959, he published his diwan *Until the Spring Comes* (hatta yaji' al-rabi') in the party's press. Semah then completed an undergraduate degree at the Hebrew University (majoring in Arabic literature), and in the mid1960s was sent by the University of Haifa to Oxford University. Semah's thesis was later published by Brill; it was the masterful *Four Arabic Literary Critics*, which analyzed the literary criticism of 'Abbas Mahmud al-'Aqqad, Muhammad Hussayn Haykal, Taha Hussein, and Muhammad Mandur. After his return to Israel, he became a professor of Arabic literature at Haifa University where he wrote extensively on Arabic literature, mainly in Arabic, English, and Hebrew, until his death in 1997.[1]

"He shall return"
(*Sawfa Ya 'udu*)

To the catastrophe-struck people of Kufur Qasim

TRANSLATED FROM THE ARABIC BY URI HORESH

I asked you, mother: where is my father?
So why won't you answer my question?
For I am startled by your dreadful silence
I asked you, where is my father?
Has he gone to travel the remote wastelands?
To bring me new clothes?
I have almost forgotten him! What color is he?
Does his eye glisten from grief?
Has he gone to hover above the clouds
And search for the light of the stars
To make a necklace and adorn my neck
For him to give me it on my birthday?

***

Yes, he will return
And in his hand a bouquet of roses
Anointing our souls with perfume
Yes, my daughter, he will return
And in his pocket a handful of coins
For quenching thirst and alleviating hunger
And for wiping the tears from our eyes.
For if there were bread and fortune at home
You would not have been in such bad a state
Weakened by chronic illness
And when the cough is gone
A question escapes your lips
Will he really return?

***

Indeed . . . he will return
But he . . . is in a distant place
Like the joyful dawn of salvation,
Like the day of freeing slaves.
And yet . . . he may return.
His hand is shackled in iron
Because he went to the village
To work there without a license.
Perhaps someday he will return
But only to leave us once again
As he suffers hanged, frozen
And glides into the darkness of the tombs.

***

I have trusted you, mother, not to lie
So why will you not tell me the truth?
I have heard our neighbor's children whispering:
"They have killed him!
Yonder, by the border."
My father will never return.

***

DAVID SEMAH

Indeed, my daughter, he will not return . . .
But will you not go to sleep?
You have asked enough, you have moaned enough
And the night has almost come to an end
As you keep a sleepless vigil in the darkness
Filling it with anguish, while all the people
Are covered in their sleep, dreaming.
I have promised you that salvation is near . . .
Do you not remember?
In the morning a huge crowd burst out
Preceded by a red flag
And they marched in files
Chanting:
"The day of the final struggle is near
And the storm has struck
Across the universe, furious and sweeping
Hurling away the oppression and the oppressors
And the thieves of the food of the poor
And jail and jailers
And the usurpers of the milk of the young
And the spillers of blood
To save their victims from loss.
So gather your strength, O hard workers
"For you have nothing to lose."
. . . And then he will return
A father, and a fond friend
And even your father, he still may return
And in his hand a bouquet of roses
Anointing our souls with perfume.[2]

A Poem, A Village

On 29 October, 1956, the Palestinian population of the state of Israel, already under a military regime that severely limited its movement, employment and labor rights, was declared to be under curfew from 5 p.m. till 6 a.m. (normally curfew started at 9 p.m.). The villagers of Kufur Qasim, who did not know about the changed curfew hours and were found outside their homes, were shot by the Israeli Border Brigades at close range. Forty-nine people were murdered. The state then tried to cover up the crime. The bodies were collected and thrown next to the police station away from the village itself. A media gag prevented any news from circulating about it; when communist Knesset members protested the murders, their comments were taken out of the minutes. Following the decision of an investigating committee, which was convened later, the Border Patrol brigade and its commander were tried and convicted for killing the victims in cold blood, but their prison sentences were later reduced (the last of the convicted was released at the beginning of 1960, less than a year and half after the trial).[3]

One of the individuals most identified with the struggle to uncover the truth about the massacre was an Iraqi Jewish journalist, Latif Dori, who lived in a Kibbutz close to Kufur Qasim. He collected the survivors' testimonies in the village itself and in a nearby hospital. Dori attempted to publish these testimonies several times, but his stories were censored, only to be published a month after the massacre, when censorship limitations were finally lifted. The evidence that Dori gathered was used in the trial of the border police. Dori is an honorary member of Kufur Qasim until today.[4]

Shortly after the media gag was lifted, David Semah published this poem, focusing on a young child and her mother. Indeed, many of the murdered were teenagers and children (22 of were under the age of 18). Some families lost more than one member: a forty-five-year-old mother and her seventeen-year-old daughter, a thirty-year-old father and his twelve-year-old son, and two teenagers, a brother and a sister, were listed amongst the casualties. While other Palestinian poets commemorated the women and children massacred, Semah chose to write on those who survived. The poem, constructed as a dialogue between a daughter and her mother, has three thematic foci: return, truth-telling, and being a child after the Nakba.

The theme of the Palestinian Right of Return was discussed in the communist daily *al-Ittihad,* which chronicled the attempts of Palestinians to smuggle back across the Israeli border and remain in their homeland. Sami Michael protested against the harsh treatment of these returnees by the Israeli border police. The theme also appeared in poems written in Iraq, in particular those of 'Abdel Wahab al-Bayati, whose works were published in *al-Jadid.*[5] The perception that the return should not be the return of individuals but should occur as the result of a political struggle is articulated in the mother's vision at the end of the poem, in which she imagines the crowd toppling the regime, allowing the dead and the living to return to the village both physically and metaphorically. At the end of the poem, then, a new dawn ends the darkness of the night with a vision a revolution and of return.

Telling the truth about the massacre occupies both mother and daughter. The poem opens with a series of questions posed by the daughter. The fear that the father would be forgotten, that his sight, his body, his remembrance, and the way in which he was killed would vanish from memory, shapes the dialogue between the two family members. As in other cases of trauma, the speakers do not know whether what has happened is indeed true, and both evoke dreams and visions. The important point, however, is not the hiding of the truth by the state. It is the fear that accompanies the survivors and silences them. The mother tries to hide the facts from her daughter: perhaps out of love; perhaps out of fear for what the truth would do to the soul of her daughter; perhaps out of unwillingness to come to terms with the horrible truth herself. The daughter's questions, nonetheless, force her to tell the truth.

At the time, many Palestinian poets, writers, and novelists wrote on the significance of coming to terms with the great loss and engaging in a struggle to change its results. Semah, like other writers of his time, believed in the commitment of the writer to his/her public, marked in Arabic by the word *iltizam* (commitment). The need to write poetry that would reflect the sufferings of the masses, galvanize them, and lead to political action further meant that Semah's role as a poet was not limited to the suffering of his own marginalized Iraqi-Jewish group but rather to all of the oppressed.

Finally, the poem sheds light on the lives of poor, Arabic speaking children in Israel. The daughter in the poem wants to lead a normal life. But in her oppressive conditions she too looks for a world beyond the shining stars above the clouds (or over the rainbow). Like any child, she wants material things, like a necklace, but also a refuge from a world of darkness; she yearns for the stars, for roses, and for a sense of family life, for all the things lacking in her life. The mother is also living in poverty, and needs "a handful of coins" to alleviate her hunger and anger, and to buy bread and medicine to cure a chronic cough. The miserable lives of Arab children in Israel are also reflected in the mother's speech, suggesting that those who would rebel confront "the usurpers of the milk of the young." The mother's words thus suggest that the father's murder was the last in the long list of crimes that affected young children's lives.

The lot of Palestinian and Mizrahi children in Israel was one of the major concerns of radical intellectuals during the 1950s. These children resided in great poverty, received poor education (if at all), and had to leave school to help support their parents. Works of literature, reports in the press, and accounts of Knesset members protested the children's hunger, the state's neglect of their health and wellbeing, and child and teenage labor. The sufferings of these children were depicted in many poems and short stories of Iraqi Jews at the time. In this poem, all of these pains, of Iraqi and Palestinian children, of their parents, and of Semah himself, are collapsed into a single poetic dialogue.

Notes:

[1] Orit Bashkin, "Arabic Thought in the Radical Age: Emile Habibi, The Israeli Communist Party, and The Production of Arab Jewish Radicalism 1946-1961," Jens Hanssen and Max Weiss (eds), *Arabic Thought against the Authoritarian Age, Towards an Intellectual History of the Present* (Cambridge University Press, 2018), pp. 62-85; Reuven Snir, "'Till Spring Comes': Arabic and Hebrew Literary Debates among Iraqi-Jews in Israel (1950-2000)," *Shofar* 24:2 (2006): 92–123. Sasson Somekh, *Life after Baghdad: Memoirs of an Arab-Jew in Israel, 1950-2000* trans. Tamar L. Cohen (Brighton: Sussex Academic Press, 2012)

[2] Da'ud Semah, "Sawfa ya'udu," Hatta yaji' al-rabi' (Tel Aviv: al-Matba'a al-Haditha, 1959), pp. 41–45

[3] Shira Robinson, "Local Struggle, National Struggle: Palestinian Responses to the Kafr Qasim Massacre and Its Aftermath, 1956–66." *International Journal of Middle East Studies* 35:3 (2003): 393–416.

[4] Orit Bashkin, *Impossible Exodus: Iraqi Jews in Israel* (Stanford: Stanford University Press, 2017), pp. 122-123, 164-165, 207-209

[5] Yaseen Noorani, "Visual Modernism in the Poetry of Abd al-Wahab al-Bayati," *Journal of Arabic Literature* 32:3 (2001): 1-17

Reading Sami Michael

RYAN ZOHAR

Sami Michael was born Saleh Kemal Menashe Eliahu to a Jewish family in Baghdad, Iraq, in 1926. As a young teenager in the early 1940s, Michael became involved in Communist organizing in Iraq and began writing and translating for political journals. In 1948, Michael fled Iraq after being sentenced to death in absentia by the government as a result of his activism. He traveled first to Iran and later to Israel in 1949, settling in Haifa. There, Michael wrote for the Israeli Communist Party's (ICP) Arabic-language journals *al-Ittihad* and *al-Jadid* under the pseudonym Samir Marid (meaning, "Samir, a rebel"). Michael's articles and stories appeared alongside the works of other Iraqi-Jewish writers, such as David Semah, Shimon Ballas, and Sasson Somekh, as well as prominent Palestinian men of letters including Emile Habibi, Tawfiq Zayyad, Jabra Nicola, and Emile Touma.

Many Israeli literary critics and cultural theorists have written at length about Michael's choice to switch from writing in Arabic to writing in Hebrew. Such studies often describe the painful dilemma faced by the first generation of Iraqi-Jewish writers in Israel regarding their choice of language. Michael's embrace of Hebrew in the years following his arrival in Israel is often contrasted with the decision of Iraqi-Jewish writers Samir Naqqash and Ishaq Bar-Moshe to continue writing in Arabic. Unlike Michael, their writing has remained largely marginal in Israel. Michael's Hebrew-language novels include: *All Men are Equal – But Some are More* (1974), *Refuge* (1977), *A Trumpet in the Wadi* (1987), and *Victoria* (1993). He has sat on the central committee of the Association of Writers in Israel and served

IRAQI JEWISH WRITERS

Sami Michael

as president of the Association for Civil Rights in Israel.

Despite his many accolades, Michael's work has not always been considered part of the Israeli literary canon. Instead, it is often reduced to minority or "ethnic" writing, precluding the possibility of its universality–a status often afforded to Ashkenazi-Israeli writers [1]. Some believe Michael's work is considered controversial because it raises the question of intra-Jewish inequality, in a state where all Jews are purportedly considered equal regardless of background. Critics also frequently note the multilingual landscape evoked in Michael's Hebrew works, subverting the dominant literary register. Yet, while Michael is now revered for his Hebrew-language novels, his earlier Arabic writing is often overlooked, and scholars rarely engage with his rich corpus of Arabic articles and stories published in ICP journals.

While it is Michael's Hebrew-language work which is noted for its use of multiple registers and languages, this does not mean that his Arabic work is characterized by an intransigent monolingualism. Michael often notes that upon arrival in Israel, at the age of 23, in 1949, he did not speak any Hebrew[2]. Even though Michael's 1952 short story *Tabarak al-Rabb (Blessed is the Lord)* was entirely written in Arabic, Hebrew still rears its head. Many of the more religiously-inclined phrases of the text, though written in Arabic, seem to echo Hebrew supplications. And while the frame story, narrated by Yemeni-Jewish street vendor Ezra to the "fellow Jews" of Haifa, is told in Arabic, one would imagine such a speech appealing for solidarity in the name of Jewish unity being given in Hebrew. In some ways, Ezra's speech can be read as being itself a translation from Hebrew.

Significantly, Ezra implicitly bases his call for justice on his and his listeners' *Jewish* identity. While this makes sense in an ethnonationalist polity, where loyal citizenship is evidenced by holding Zionist ideals, such appeals disaggregate Mizrahi[3] calls for social justice from any shared sense of struggle with Palestinians. It is against such strategies of disaggregation that many early Mizrahi leftists, including Michael, fought. Instead, these activists sought to highlight the hypocrisy of a state which purported to care for *all* Jews regardless of country of origin, while linking anti-Mizrahi policies to those which oppressed Palestinians.

The primary audience for Michael's *Tabarak al-Rabb*, in addition to Palestinians in Israel, was likely Arabic-speaking Jews in the *ma'abarot* (transit camps) who would have been familiar with the abuse Ezra faced at the hands of what was, at that time, a largely Ashkenazi police force.[4] While many of these Jews were likely not Yemenis themselves, they would have recognized that the Middle Eastern background of the narrator played a role in the way he was treated by the Haifa police.

The fact that Michael chose to write about a Yemeni protagonist also merits discussion. Michael did not only write about Iraqi Jews in Israel, but also Egyptian, Moroccan, and Yemeni Jews.[5] This choice both emphasizes the way oppression transcended country of origin and could only be conquered by shared struggle, and highlights the challenges faced in Israel by Yemenis in particular.

Yemenis were often stereotyped by Ashkenazim[6] as uncivilized, overly-pious, and exotic, among other conjurings of the Orientalist imagination. In fact, several of these stereotypes attributed to Yemeni Jews by Ashkenazim are reproduced by Michael only to be implicitly critiqued later in the story. Before celebrating his protagonist's triumphant resistance, Michael details how Yemenis are viewed as "all resembl[ing] each other," exotic in their submission to God's will, and meek like "house pets." At the base of the latter two stereotypes is the pejorative outlook on Yemeni approaches to the question of theodicy: In the face of real hardship, the Yemeni still sees the ultimate goodness of God.

In the eyes of secular Zionists who place emphasis on the primacy of man, such an outlook is weak, antiquated, and, as Michael suggests, even comical. This pejorative view is also indicative of the dissonance many Mizrahim experienced at having their Jewishness ridiculed or considered too traditional upon arrival in the Jewish State. Still, at the end of the story, Ezra's approach to theodicy seemingly vindicates him. When he finishes his speech and is arrested by the Haifa Police, we find one last, exultant, "Blessed is the Lord!" With this exclamation, Ezra defies the stereotypes earlier accorded to the Yemenis. Far from an indiscernible, meek body, he stands up and resists, drumming up solidarity for his cause and–in his own distinctly Yemeni way–proclaims the ultimate goodness of the Lord. But Michael makes it clear that Ezra's final gesture is an incomplete one; He may have won over the crowd, but he is still detained by the police and fails to secure the return of his donkey and cart. Even as his message is supported by the public, he still faces insurmountable odds.

The marginalization of Mizrahim by the Ashkenazi Zionist elite of Israeli society is also underscored by the story's symbolism. It is highly significant that Ezra is selling the cactus fruit or prickly pear– known as the *sabra*, the name of which came to refer to Jews born in Palestine. Sabras represented the "new Jew," devoid of any diasporic characteristics. Ezra decides to begin selling sabra pears only to be prevented from doing so by the state authorities. Similarly, he aspires to participate in Israeli society but is excluded from the cultural and political core of the state.

In Arabic, the word for prickly pear also contains the same trilateral root, *s–b–r*, as the word for "patience" or "perseverance". As Ezra details, the harvesting of the pears is a physically taxing process. It is also one which, Ezra seems to suggest, is the unique provenance of the poor. While Ezra notes that the pear is the fruit of the poor because it is a product of the natural environment, one could also conclude that it is because the poor know the true meaning of perseverance, or *sabr*. This same sense of steadfastness through hardship is conveyed by the "effective psychological weapon" that is the phrase "Blessed is the Lord!" Through his steadfastness and his conviction that God will rectify his lot, Ezra embodies the principle of *sabr*.

Lastly, in a moving passage towards the end of the story, a young boy decries the police brutality before his eyes by yelling out at the police "Gestapo!" The comparison of Israeli security forces to the Nazi Gestapo would have been highly provocative, as the story was written just a few short years after the Holocaust. When the young boy yells out "Gestapo" to the police, he at once casts the (likely) Ashkenazi officers as being the same as those who oppressed Jews in Europe, highlights the Jewish State's oppression of other Jews, and de-exceptionalizes and de-sacralizes the memory of the Holocaust as a uniquely European Jewish experience. It is an unsettling comparison, to say the least, but one that forces the reader to contend with the implications of the police's actions.

In recent months, we have seen an amazing wave of movements condemning police brutality gain traction globally. The common calls for anti-racist action among Black Lives Matter, Justice pour *Adama*, and Israeli and Palestinian activists decrying the killing of Iyad Al-Hallaq in Jerusalem, highlight important possibilities for transnational solidarity. Similarly, the writings of Sami Michael and others affiliated with *al-Ittihad* and *al-Jadid* both highlight the material conditions of oppression in Israel/Palestine and forge Palestinian-Jewish, as well as global, solidarities. Their stories, *Tabarak al-Rabb* among them, have much to offer our current times

(1) Ashkenazi: Jews of European origin, as opposed to Middle Eastern Mizrahi Jews.
(2) Nancy E. Berg, *More and More Equal: The Literary Works of Sami Michael* (Lanham: Lexington Books, 2005), 46.
(3) See note 1.
(4) Bryan K. Roby, *The Mizrahi Era of Rebellion: Israel's Forgotten Civil Rights Struggle 1948-1966* (Syracuse: Syracuse University Press, 2015), 22-36.
(5) Non-Jewish Palestinian characters also featured centrally in many of Michael's essays and stories in *al-Jadid* and *al-Ittihad*. See also: Orit Bashkin, *Impossible Exodus: Iraqi Jews in Israel* (Stanford: Stanford University Press, 2017), 217.
(6) Plural of Ashkenazi (see note 1).

SAMI MICHAEL

Blessed Is the Lord
(Tabarak al-Rabb)

TRANSLATED FROM THE ARABIC BY RYAN ZOHAR

Yemenis all resemble each other, just as the seeds of a pomegranate are all alike. They all have high-pitched ringing voices if they are still young and hoarse, throaty ones if they have been afflicted by the passing of years. What is more, their black eyes are all glazed over like sludgy tar and the folds on their weary faces bear the imprints of the years…years throughout which they have never once parted with their strange convictions.

But when their soft ringing voices hit your ears, and you hear them rushing to find comfort in the phrase: "Blessed is the Lord!" then, you realize that this saying is not a virtue they are left clinging onto, but rather an effective psychological weapon.

"Blessed is the Lord!" This expression attests to their assessment that life has been their mortal enemy and that they do not expect it to be anything more than a harsh, barren desert. For, if one of them were to stumble upon a few mere drops of murky water amidst the desert's burning sands, then blessed is the Lord! And, if one of them were to find himself under the shadow of the scrawniest little tree branch, then blessed is the Lord! And, so on. Where others would find themselves disappointed, the Yemeni finds this tenet beside him like a loyal friend.

This conviction elicits surprise for many people, whose enjoyment at hearing the sayings of the Yemenis never wanes—even though their sayings all resemble each other—just as one would never tire of the juicy taste of the uniform seeds of a single pomegranate. Thus, Yemenis' complaints and frustrations have become an amusing spectacle of sorts, like watching a house pet assume the role of predator.

SAMI MICHAEL

It is for this reason that a great crowd turned and looked from every direction towards Ezra and his family in front of the Haifa City Hall on one very hot day. Ezra was standing in front of a crowd, waving his open hand in their faces as if he were begging them to end the clamor and stop riling up the mob. He then turned behind him, towards his wife and their three children, and scolded her, saying "Calm her down, the baby! Calm her! And make her stop crying!" as if the child's screams were the only thing preventing him from speaking. The children and their mother shrank into a gloomy little ball, from which their eight obedient, dark little eyes looked out.

Ezra then looked out again towards the large crowd of people with sweat dripping down their faces, as the sun's hot rays beat down on the hair atop their heads. And Ezra said: "Listen to me, O Jews, O Children of Israel! Listen to the story of Ezra, son of Rafaeli the Yemeni!..."

Some in the crowd chortled, expressing their impatience with the man. Several even shouted out: "Speak already! Speak!"

"I will speak, comrades," the Yemeni replied, giving in to their resolve. "I had only one child in Yemen, but my wife here, sitting behind me, gave birth to another child at the airport, blessed is the Lord, just as soon as we had knelt down and kissed the ground in the land of our ancestors. Comrades! Fellow Jews! Block the cars from passing! Close the road! Ezra wants to speak to you about the catastrophe that has befallen him. He wants to tell you about how, on this land that God has blessed, a bunch of thugs have it in for him! I want to tell you all my story...it goes a little like this:

"Although they had told us about the many injustices in Israel, we entrusted ourselves to the care of God. So, we found ourselves a deserted orchard and we built ourselves a house of tin and stone beneath the lifeless trees. And, we went hungry, as if we were stranded out alone in the wilderness. Then, they fired me, telling me and the other men that there was no work left for us to do. I returned home, convinced that what I had been told was true. We ate only stale bread and green grass until my son fell ill—may God protect you from such hardship.

"So, I told myself, 'Ezra, you must find another path for yourself on this land, the land of the Lord!' My wife was wise. She told me, 'Ezra, let's borrow some money and buy ourselves a donkey and a cart so that we can begin picking sabra pears [1], and bring them to

Haifa to sell.' My wife's advice was sensible, and soon enough, two new souls joined the family: a daughter that the Lord sent us, blessed be His name, and the donkey that we bought with the loan we took out. Then, blessed is the Lord, we began to earn enough to eat, and even more than we needed to satisfy our needs. You see, Ezra, his wife, and his two children did not fear the thorns and did not care when they were pricked by them, so they picked the best and sweetest of all the fruits. All of Haifa soon learned the name of Ezra and came to eat his delicious cold fruit.

"Then came a dark day. A policeman approached the cart and asked me if I had a permit to sell the sabra pears. And so, I told him, 'We've never seen such a clever policeman as you!'

" 'Why?' he asked me.

"I replied, 'Because Ezra understands only a smidge more than his donkey. Blessed is the Lord! The sabra pear is the fruit that God gifted the poor because only their hands are rough enough to extract it from amongst the painful, prickly thorns. The pear is a gift from the Lord to the poor and one does not need a permit to become poor!'

"But the bastard yelled back at me as if it were the first time he had heard the name of the Lord. So, I said to myself, 'Ezra! Don't be stupid! This poor man is standing before you empty-handed, and so you must show some humanity and pity for him.' So, I asked my son, Youssef, to go peel one of the best and coldest pears and give it to the officer.

"As soon as the officer heard that, he went crazy, screaming at me, 'You want to bribe me?! You want to bribe me, you jackass?!' So, I told him that I just wanted to do him a favor. But his heart was harder than stone, and so my words never reached his ears. They took me from place to place, bringing me to this office and that office. By afternoon, I understood that they had confiscated the pears from me.

"I returned home and I told my donkey and my son, 'Those damn cops need fancy hats to protect their hard heads from the hot sun. All they know how to do is to go out and confiscate pears that are ready to eat, while we're out lopping off thorns, our hands and feet bloodied from the pears we've picked ... And they call me a jackass?! But it's all right, the Lord is still above us!'"

Ezra took a moment to gather himself silently, but kept panting wearily. His shirt clung to his sweaty chest. People had filled the street, blocking the cars in the road. The cars began honking angrily, urging the crowd to clear the streets. Ezra glimpsed a group of police officers trying to force their way up the road, but they encountered resistance from a group of men, the overwhelming majority of whom had been listening to Ezra and were drawn to his story.

Ezra proceeded to encourage the men resisting the police, shouting: "Yes! That's the way! Keep those damn cops out! Ezra does not want to see their faces…"

And he continued his story:

"The next day we went out, our cart brimming with cold, tasty fruits. The sabra pears sparkled like shiny, red eggs. Then, after only two hours had passed, the officer approached the cart looking as if he were death itself incarnate. As soon as his grisly mug caught my eye, I told myself, 'Ezra! Keep away from this man's wickedness and head to another part of this big city, where he can't see you and you can't see him.' I took the reins of the donkey, pushed away the hungry customers, and with one quick turn fled the scene. But the officer followed me… And why do I go on and on about all this? Because that very day they confiscated the fruit, the cart, and the donkey too! And just like that, they robbed us of our livelihood. I begged them to confiscate me instead and to release the donkey and the cart so that my wife and children could still find a way to live. But it was as if they were deaf… So, we moved from the deserted orchard to here in front of City Hall and we won't leave until they return our cart and donkey to us…I'm not even bothered about the pears!"

Just then, the police officers managed to break through the crowd and reach Ezra. When they placed their hands on his shoulders, the crowd called out with rage: "Let him go! Let him go!"

A boy who stood on the tips of his toes, craning his neck, cried out: "Gestapo!"

Ezra remained calm and with one expansive wave of his hand pointed to the large crowd and said to the police officers with satisfaction: "The people listened to me, blessed is the Lord."

---

[1] Cactus fruit, also known as prickly pears.

IRAQI JEWISH WRITERS

SAMI MICHAEL

Two Women
(Imra'ataan)*

TRANSLATED FROM THE ARABIC BY HANA MORGENSTERN

It was a Friday afternoon. I was watching the small troupe of actors rehearse in the closed room. Its members were new to acting and they worried that their actions and tone were artificial, which was making them even more nervous. Suddenly we heard sharp, repeated knocking on the door. The actors turned to look. A pair of wide eyes and trembling lips, and then a woman's body appeared in the doorway. Everything about the woman spoke of intense fear; her shabby green dress that looked like she had thrown it on in the middle of a chase, her quavering knees that seemed barely able to support her weight, her pleading look.

"They came again," she choked in a hushed voice. She seemed unable to control her sobbing. "They came to take me away."

Our necks froze involuntarily and we stared into the darkness behind the door, looking for the people who were chasing her. But we couldn't see anything because her trembling body filled the doorway.

One of the young people asked: "Who are they?"

---

* Imra'ataan (Two Women) by Samir Marid (pen name of Sami Michael), was published in September 1952 in al-Ittihad, the Israeli Communist Party's (ICP) Arabic-language newspaper. The story evinces many of the central themes found in other borderland stories of the period. It is much shorter and cruder than works published in al-Jadid, the party's literary magazine, most likely in order to render it more accessible to newspaper readers. Nonetheless, despite its brevity, the story tackles the theatre of institutional violence with some deftness. It captures the youthful callousness of the Israeli state, the terror and precarity of the borders, and the terrible vulnerability of the paperless Palestinians, accused of infiltration in their own land. As in similar Communist stories of the period, the border emerges as an encounter site where Palestinians are forced to seek Israeli Jewish support against Israeli government agents who seek to expel them, a relational mode made possible only when the discourses of the state and the security apparatus are rejected in favor of solidarity and the privileging of a humane form of community. Hana Morgenstern

"The police!" she snapped. "They came to arrest me and take me across the border. They're sitting in my house now, all four of them. They've got a statement from the Minister of the Interior."

I didn't understand why she had come here. "Who are you?" I asked.

"I am Awda al-Ashhab's wife. When they saw the baby they let me go on bail. But they're waiting at the house."

Then I realized that she must have been accused of infiltration. The day before, Awda al-Ashhab had said that his wife Maryam was angry with him because he was never at home. Party meetings were occupying all of his time. How repulsive. A wife and a mother, they would take her away from her own husband and two daughters by accusing her of "infiltration"?

One of the actors shouted resentfully: "But Israel was built for you. The government allowed you to stay—"

She raised her head but did not say a word. Another comrade and I went to vouch for her. She walked behind us, stumbling on the rough road, which was wet with rain. She walked deliberately slowly behind us because she was afraid to return home. The dark, overcast sky reminded her of the borders—of loneliness, hunger and tears. I felt the same way about the border. It was like a thin rope, fastened around my throat. How miserable is a state that surrounds itself with borders soaked in blood and catastrophe?

We arrived at the house. It was a narrow room into which two beds had been miraculously squeezed. On one of the beds lay a little girl covered in a tattered sheet, on the other a tiny, ruddy baby, no more than six weeks old. The room was crowded. Only two policemen fit inside. The other two waited outside the doorway, biting their nails.

We greeted the sergeant and he explained the case to us in a very apologetic tone as he watched the infant stirring on the bed. He then read to us the order to search the house of Awda al-Ashhab, who was known to be harbouring an infiltrator. He tried to make out the name of the judge who signed the warrant and shouted in relief: "It's a woman!"

"But this 'infiltrator' that Awda al-Ashhab is hiding is his wife!" I said angrily. "The Minister of the Interior himself knows that. She just gave birth to a child, here in Israel."

The sergeant held out his arms, looked at me, and apologized. "Believe me, I'm a father too. I have children, but these are my orders."

I believed him and trusted what I saw on his broad, honest face. It was Sabbath eve and he would certainly prefer to leave this filthy task and have dinner with his children at a table flowing with flowers and light.

The second cop in the room was very young. He didn't have any facial hair yet, and his face had a girlish softness. He tried to hide his nervousness behind a decisive tone, but he repeated the same apology that his sergeant had made: "We're only following orders, that's all."

"How binding is the Minister of the Interior's statement?" I realized immediately the stupidity of my question. It was only a promise, and promises in Israel were made and immediately broken. I told the young cop: "You might be a good person, but you are serving the worst cause, my friend!"

He shrank, and said in a faltering voice: "No, I'm not a good person," and there sparked in his eyes a base, primitive hatred.

Just then, people began congregating in front of the apartment. I recognized a lawyer, the wife of a Knesset member, one of the factory workers, and a government employee.

Maryam al-Ashhab joined them, and she seemed comforted by their stern looks and warm words.

The sergeant handed me the bail paperwork and said: "She can be bailed out for 100 lira if she comes to the police station next Sunday."

I grabbed the pen and signed, feeling that many mothers and fathers were signing with me – not only to stop Maryam's arrest, but to erect a wall between a mother and the police.

It began to rain again, drops that seemed like great tears dripping from the sky. The policemen left one after the other with their heads down, their heavy boots trudging through the puddles of rainwater and the darkness of the night.

I returned to the actors, thinking about the two women: the infiltrator and the judge. How would each of them spend that night? No matter how comfortable the second woman felt in her white room, with the security of her legal books and the gratification of her judicial orders, she would never feel the passion of the strong hands that would embrace Maryam tonight and try to spare her the rain, the judges, and the borders.

The Round Dove of Baghdad: The Poetry of Amira Hess in Context

TAMI ISRAELI

Baghdad-born Amira Hess (1943) is a descendant of the Beth-Adoni kabbalist and poet lineage which included, amongst others, poet and Torah scholar Hakham Harun Barzani, and Asenath Barzani, a renowned 17th century female poet and rabbi. Hess moved to Israel from Iraq in 1951 and initially settled at the Yokneam migrant transit camp. Her immigration experience would later become a fundamental, defining influence on her poetry – shaping, underscoring, and informing it. In 1984, Hess marked the publication of her debut poetry volume, *And a Madness-oozing Moon*, a dazzlingly beautiful, profound collection of poems that left Hebrew poetry afficionados positively entranced. Hess has since authored nine further poetry volumes, with the next one slated for publication in late 2021. The following translated excerpt of a poem from this new work offers a taste of her upcoming book, *How We Get Remade*:

> Buying a garment for the body on a new day
> random attire for your garden variety, ordinary day
> whose light comes with age.
> And all is crystal clear and as clear as day.
> that I have grown like a pea on a vast rooftop
> and things visible from the shopping centre here
> are not the things one sees from the Syrian-African Rift over
>   there –
> There, in the Dead Sea, all is broken
> and there are sinkholes
> whereas here, all is swallowed, all is absorbed,

Amira Hess

all is a different struggle, a different flow.
To the left, a red light towards the Sea of Galilee.
To the right, the dust of our homeland, wherever you are.
If your spirits are fallen,
we will place them on the pendulum of time
and an atlas shall hold the globe.

Throughout her career, Hess has been the recipient of many awards, including the 2015 Amichai Poetry Prize. In awarding her the prize, the judging panel wrote: "Hess's poetry is an unbridled strain of verse that deconstructs, and then simultaneously reconstructs and reshuffles all the cards in the deck that is body and soul, sacred and secular. Her musical poetry embodies a range of tensions and conflicts between interior and exterior spheres, the topographies of identity, Israel and Baghdad, femininity and masculinity."

Hess's poetry features an assortment of prophetic, mystical, and ecstatic elements, all of which are often in the throes of a range of physical and spiritual experiences, blending the sacred and secular, consciousness and dream states, and the religious and the prosaic in ways that are, simply put, unparalleled. Hess's genealogy links her to a range of rabbinical and kabbalist traditions that undoubtedly account for the centrality of dreams and madness in her body of work, as well as the ever-increasing presence of Arab Jewishness in her poetry book.[1]

If one were to attempt to place Hess's poetics along the continuum of Hebrew poetry, then the poetic model of Yona Wallach's verse would prove instrumental in positioning it. Much like Wallach's poetry, Hess's too is known to mix 'high' and 'lowbrow' content, to tackle nonbinary sexuality, and to engage in the tension between madness and sanity. That said, the thesaurus available to Hess is considerably richer and more multilayered – especially when it comes to mystical language, and Jewish-Arab vernacular. When asked about the presence of Arabic and Iraqi Hebrew in her poetry, Hess replied: "It's mental translation is what it is. You walk around, carrying with you the sum of your lineage's knowledge encoded into you." Moreover, as I shall demonstrate, her poetry is also very much entwined with the tradition of modern Hebrew verse in many more ways than has been acknowledged to date.

Take, for instance, the poem "Childhood", from Hess's eighth volume of poetry, *Tears Without Eyes to be Shed* (2014), which brings to light the poet's use of layering, signalled by the term 'childhood' and all the meanings it carries; an underlying premise is the pivotal role that social constructs play insofar as the concept of 'childhood' is concerned.

CHILDHOOD

I shall call on your dreams like an antidote to sadness
hailing from a rain-soaked mythical city
from a wondrous, resplendent jungle
and the glory of the hoopoe's call,
cranes too have said their piece.
Birds speaking their dialects, speaking their pain

and I, the warbler
my song on my crown
set alight and snuffed out
darkness, follow me, trickling.
Nest yourself in the round Baghdadi dove's
eyes, her solitude as great as her distance travelled.
You cannot touch the edge of the expanse
nor find her a nesting place in the present,
steer her unto her childhood.
In a flash, my wandering spirit is no more

At first reading, "Childhood" comes across as a lyrical poem that bids farewell to the childhood landscapes of the speaker's natural habitat before immigrating to Israel, through a confession in an elegiac, nostalgic tone that waxes reminiscent and seeks to revive it. "A rain-soaked, mythical city", "a wondrous, resplendent jungle", and the hoopoe's grace and glory all come together, lining the reader's consciousness, whilst distracting them from the poem's greater intricacies and complexities. Childhood emerges as a concept embedded in a cultural, historical context, with a deep affinity with the discourse surrounding it, and the imagery associated with it. And yet, the convention remains whereby a child is someone who ought to be paternalised; that is, an individual who may not lead their own life and make their own conclusive choices, independently.[2]

It seems that at the heart of the focus on the subject of the child's maturity is the formation of the trait which Kant viewed as central: the ability to exercise self-control. Lack of self-control, which is considered a fundamental marker of childhood, is described as the surrendering of oneself to man's primal instincts. Similarly, in the past, these same traits denoting lack of self-control were projected onto the working class and defined the West's Orientalist view of the East. According to Almog Behar, the leading scholar of Hess's lyrical oeuvre, Hess often does not distinguish between the Orient that is actually in the East, the Orient as it is perceived in the West, and Mizrahi (Jewish Middle-Eastern) identity as it was shaped in Israel by its devastating encounter with the country's socio-cultural Ashkenazi hegemony; or perhaps this is a distinction that is no longer viable.[3] However, particularly for Behar, her poetry has a magnetic pull, and as such, her lexicon often recurs in his own writings, appearing in a wide range of contexts.

Hess's "Childhood", which seems to have a personal, biographical aspect to it, and whose roots, as stated, are in the speaker's own childhood, also opens with a staple catalogue of imagery in Hebrew poetry, and gives a brief tour of its modern chronology, starting with an allusion to Bialik to represent immigration; or as it is more commonly referred to amongst Jews, the act of "making Aliyah" ('ascension') to Israel. In the spring of 1892, a then-19-year-old Haim Nahman Bialik published his debut poem, "To the Bird", in the literary publication, *Pardes* (Orchard). The longing for an imagined, resplendent Zion alongside the vivid account of the Jew's trials and tribulations in exile all unfolded in a musical dialogue between a young speaker and the bird at his window. Bialik's poem, amongst other things, established a model by which the bird is one of New Hebrew poetry's most central figures and is often used, owing to its migratory habits, as a double agent negotiating the migrant's two homelands.

Four species of bird are mentioned in "Childhood": the hoopoe, the crane, the warbler – the speaker's focaliser – and the dove. The hoopoe has been dubbed 'Israel's national bird', and its image has been commemorated with a series of postage stamps. The crown on its head, no doubt, helped to cement this image, as did the bird's status in culture and literature, and particularly, in Bialik's body of work.[4] In his lyrical folk poem "Twixt Euphrates and Tigris", which first appeared in 1906, Bialik unfolds a bawdy Eastern European tale of the sexual coming of age of a teenage girl who seeks out the goldcrested hoopoe to ask it to find her a handsome groom. The girl's explicit desires end in disappointment and disaster. Bialik places the lustful girl in a mythical Orientalist setting, thereby transposing urges and desire onto the East, where the river that keeps this Edenic paradise hydrated has since split up into four separate rivers, two of which are found in Iraq.[5]

The hoopoe in this poem, playing the role of the matchmaker, also has its own intercultural affinities. It is a fixture in Arab fables, and plays a pivotal role in the Qur'an story of King Solomon and the Queen of Sheba. Shortly after its publication, "Twixt Euphrates and Tigris" was set to music to the song "Qadduka-el-Mayyas ya 'Umri" (Your sexy body my life) by Arab composer Uthman al-Mawsili. The pairing proved immensely successful and Bialik's poem shot to fame.

The mixing of Orient and Occident gradually made the two that much more inextricably tied, whereas the origin, meanwhile, was only drifting further and further away. Literary scholar Ziva Shamir argues that Bialik concocted a one-off blend in which the foreignness of the various compositional motifs was no longer evident.

At the start of "Childhood", the speaker in Hess's poem revisits the dreamscapes that are located in a Bialikan mythical-lyrical landscape and claims them anew. Instead of an Orientalist fantasy pining for the wholesome origin, she highlights the presence of that origin as a site of division and pain; of wandering and of multiplicities. She offers up her poem as a possible response to that ill-fated matchmaking, and in the Hebrew source text, taps into the double meaning of 'Etzev' (which can mean both 'sadness' and 'nerve'), and the linguistic affinity in Hebrew between lamentation ('kinna') and nesting ('kinnun').

The cranes also feature in these dreamscapes. They have previously recurred as a major motif in the poetry of Yocheved Bat-Miriam (1901-1980), one of Hebrew poetry's foremothers, who would use them to reference her childhood and recalled freedom in Eastern Europe's nature, forests, and fields. Each bird's language in the poem becomes the conduit of the pain of splitting languages and tongues, and in doing so, also takes us back to Leah Goldberg's famous poem, "Pine."[6] In the course of "Childhood", the speaker identifies herself as a warbler – a tiny, somewhat dull and greyish songbird – certainly next to the hoopoe's conspicuous grandeur, or the cranes' formidable size. And yet, its song packs quite the potent punch; as such, it awards the warbler its crown. The poem can, once more, bring us together with the wholesome, round dove of Baghdad. What is particularly interesting is the finely woven thread between the dove and rabbi Asenath Barzani from whom Hess, as previously stated, descends. In a 1664 letter that appears in the Mosul Jewish community's book, Rabbi Pinhas Hariri refers to her as "my dove, my lamb, my faith, my crest, and my splendour." Except that the round dove no longer has a place to rest its wings in the present, and its loneliness is as vast as the geographical distance between Israel and Iraq.

The poems included throughout this essay offer a glimpse of Hess's later poetry, and are taken from the volumes *Tears Without Eyes to be Shed* (2014), *Amira's Zodiac Sign Book* (2018), and her forthcoming book.

AMIRA HESS

How Long Must We Be Remade

How long must we be remade.
How long must the body be made a home
under the cover of tents on the verge of collapse.
What might give shelter from the tears
a realisation,
the heavens' descent.

The torrent of rain has buried vast aeons.
A man underwater emerged whole
a shepherd unto himself
and he is but a lamb.

What did we know?
A vision swiftly looted us here in Zion?

Hush, we mustn't weep
that it is no dream
a thousand nights of pitch black ferries.
We have wandered through a searing darkness
and I, pregnant with my self.
As my wife, I was a son unto myself.

Skies have fallen on my head
never scorching with flames of love
the abyss that burnt within me.
I, myself, am women led
to the gallows of realities.
I am a child lost to the illusion.

*

Salima, you're still tearing up there by the fridge with the block of
   ice over
my eyes.
This was in the tin hut.
No great and terrible guiding wizard comes for me,
   my spirit nailed in, lest it flourish.
I stood next to you, Salima, and a night at the migrant camp flew
   by us like a heavy shadow.

There are nights when the memory of cacti pricks at the tongue
   and the body
for I have tasted the forbidden sabra fruit.

Oh, that intoxicating smell of daffodils
tugging at a child's legs to run deep in the Kishon River swamp
with bouquets in his hands –
A dreamy morning run into the swamps' magnificent mouth.
I rose to a wholly intoxicating morning, and the most majestic
   twilight time
cupped into its folds a slender girl breathing in the vistas
of every exile's world, stretched out before them.

I was made of pure silk and muslin
and my spirit brushed in the blossoms of a Venus' comb.

What pains you, Salima? Perished into hard times before you were
   born and you're yet
a bud, changed into a man-owned woman, a girl orphaned of her
   father
with no one to hold her. And only I stood there for you at a
   distance, on the banks of the Nile
taking you into me, an alien, a waif.

Your eyes so small and so piercing, a dead-end emotion
like a spearhead
like a polished diamond
amongst ruins, your joy
persists, palm trees and the date's nectar.

Buying a garment for the body on a new day
Random attire for your garden variety, ordinary day
whose light comes with age.
And all is crystal clear and as clear as day
that I have grown like a pea on a vast rooftop
and that things visible from the shopping centre here
are not the things one sees from the Syrian-African Rift over there

—

There, in the Dead Sea, all is broken
and there are sinkholes
whereas here, all is swallowed, all is absorbed,
all is a different struggle, a different flow.
To the left, a red light towards the Sea of Galilee.
To the right, the dust of our homeland, wherever you are.
If your spirits are fallen,
we will place them on the pendulum of time
and an atlas shall hold the globe.

Poems translated from the Hebrew by Eran Edry

Notes:
[1] In her article, "The Cloven Spirit: Two Horses Along the Light Line," Pedaya highlights the prominent place Arab Jewishness occupied amongst Baghdad's intelligentsia, pre-Arab nationalism (26).
[2] See also Even Zur's reading of the concept of 'childhood' in the lexical journal for political thinking, Mafte'akh 13 (Hebrew for 'key').
[3] Almog Behar, "Identity and Gender in the Poetry of Amira Hess," published in BGU Review – Fall 2013.
[4] For instance, Ziva Shamir explores the place of the hoopoe in Bialik's poetry at length in the chapter, "Who Put the Hoopoe in a Golden Crest" – taken from her book, *The Fusion of New Ideas and Ancient Myths: A Study of Bialik's Adapted Legends* (2012).
[5] "And a river went out of Eden to water the garden; and from thence it parted and became four riverheads… The name of the third river is the Tigris; it is the one that goes toward the east of Assyria. And the fourth river is Euphrates" (Genesis 2:10, 14).
[6] "Perhaps only migrating birds know / suspended between earth and sky / the heartache of two homelands." (Poem by Leah Goldberg, English translation by Rachel Tzvia Back).

Maryam al-Mulla as an Iraqi-Jewish Feminist Activist

BY REUVEN SNIR

Since the late nineteenth century, intellectuals throughout the Arab world struggled for women's rights. Prominent among them were the Egyptian Qasim Amin (1863-1908), whose books Tahrir al-Mar'a (The Liberation of Woman) (1899) and al-Mar'a al-Jadida (The New Woman) (1901) were significant landmarks in that struggle. In 1923, his compatriot Huda Sha'rawi (1879-1947) established al-Ittihad al-Nisa'i al-Misri (The Egyptian Feminist Union). In Lebanon, Nazira Zayn al-Din (1908-1976) published al-Sufur wa-l-Hijab (Unveiling and Veiling) (1928) and al-Fatat wa-l-Shuyukh (The Young Woman and the Sheikhs) (1929) that caused a great uproar among Islamic clergy leaders. In Iraq, Bulina Hassun (1895-1969) established in 1923 the first Iraqi feminist periodical Layla, and fourteen years later, Maryam Narme (1890-1972) published Fatat al- Arab (The Arabs' Girl). In Iraq also came the breakthrough of Jewish women's involvement in Arabic literature – among the pioneers, we can mention Istirina Ibrahim (1914-1996), Esperance Cohen-Moreh (1930-2019), and Maryam al-Mulla (1927-2013), with whom the present essay deals.

She was born in 'Abbas Afandi neighbourhood in Baghdad.[1] Her father, Ibrahim Ya'qub Rahmin Mulla was known as a poet in the vernacular and he inspired her to compose such poems herself. She studied at the governmental schools Mutawasittat al-Rusafa and al-I'dadiyya al-Markaziyya li-l-Banat but could not complete her studies following the death in 1940-1941 of her father and two of her three brothers. In the mid-1940s, al-Mulla started to publish short stories in magazines such as *al-Musawwar* (The Illustrated), *al-Fatat* (The Girl), and *al-Siyasa* (The Politics). She worked at the schools of the Jewish community, especially at Frank 'Ayni and Shammash schools. In 1948, she married the journalist Salim al-Bassun (1927-1995), who shortly after their marriage was expelled for some months to the town of Badra on the Iraqi-Iranian border after he published an article against the government. As Arab-Iraqi patriots identifying with Iraqi national causes and Arab culture, they were by no means Zionist and refused to join the mass emigration to Israel during the early 1950s. They considered themselves an integral part of the local Arab society and tried to improve that society as part of universal civilization. In October 1973, however, the political situation in Iraq following the escalation of the Israeli-Arab conflict left them no option other than leaving their homeland and emigrating to Israel. After their emigration, al-Mulla continued to publish her literary works in Israeli Arabic journals and newspapers as well as for the governmental radio in Arabic. During the last years of her life, she republished most of her stories and poems on the internet.[2] According to her daughter Niran Bassoon-Timan (Niran al-Bassun, b. 1958), presently the Director of the Iraqi Cultural Forum in London, a collection of the stories will be published in the near future.

One of al-Mulla's most well-known literary works is the story

"Ma'satuhu Mathal" (His Tragedy, a Proverb), translated and published below, which deals with the relationship between the sexes in traditional Iraqi society. The story, written in *fusha* (standard literary Arabic) with dialogues sometimes in *'ammiyya* (colloquial language), starts with a popular Iraqi proverb that the protagonist, 'Amir, used to recite tens of times every day: *illi yidri yidri willi ma yidri hafnat 'adas* (He who knows, knows and he who doesn't know, a handful of lentils). This proverb, known in various versions, is generally used when something significant is concealed behind something trivial or less important. It reflects the folk sources from which Arab-Jewish authors drew inspiration, including its style from the traditional *hakawati*, the itinerant storyteller who until the mid-twentieth century used to appear in coffee-houses and squares where he would present stories inspired by hoary folktales and legends. This story, however, is not a folktale; it contains the basic elements of the modern short story, such as the organization of the action and interaction of the characters into an artful pattern. And because the main aim is to reach a totality of effect, the principle of selectivity is preserved; it has a plot which has a beginning and develops through a middle to some sort of denouement at the end.

The story starts with the aforementioned proverb that 'Amir used to recite while children teased him – knowing nothing about his past, they considered him a madman. But he was a newcomer to the village, along with his family, after his madness had set in. In their old village, his family was part of the poor working class and totally subjugated to the whims of the land-owning class. He had three daughters, the oldest, Nahiya, was seventeen and beautiful and the object of matrimony for many young men. Zahi, the landowner's son, tried to seduce her, but she always rejected his advances. One day, when Nahiya was gathering firewood alone in the orchard, Zahi attempted to rape her. 'Amir heard her screams and rushed to her aid but it was too late: Zahi had taken her virginity by force, and fled for fear of the dagger 'Amir was waving about in the air. Managing to catch up with him, 'Amir stabbed Zahi but when the police arrived, Zahi claimed that all he had wanted to do was to hang out with 'Amir, bringing him a handful of lentils to share with him. But 'Amir did not want to publicly declare in any way that Zahi had profaned his daughter's innocence. Consequently, 'Amir was arrested and sentenced to a number of years' imprisonment. On the day of his release from jail, Nahiya was not amongst the members of his family that received him – she had died after his being jailed. He struck his face, tore his clothes as a sign of mourning, and began to shout: "Nahiya is dead while the criminal wanders about free." When his wife asked him who the criminal was, he replied: "He who knows, knows, and he who doesn't know, a handful of lentils." And from that time on, he used to recite that proverb and was considered to have lost his reason.

Interestingly enough, the title of the story refers to the tragedy of the father alone – the story was published in the beginning of the 1950s when Arab society was not yet fully ready for any such feminist struggle; the writer had to present the tragedy of the young woman through the tragedy of her father. Also, the story implicitly refers to the purity of women as a benchmark for the entire family's honour. The narrator emphasizes that 'Amir does not want in any way to expose that Zahi had profaned his daughter's innocence. The option of murdering his daughter never occurs to 'Amir although such a practice has been employed by several communities in the Arab world, even when woman is entirely blameless. On most occasions, the victims are women perceived to be "misbehaving", mainly when they violate the sexual norms; by murdering their daughters and sisters, the fathers and brothers reassert their control over the women in

The Monument to the Unknown Soldier, Baghdad 1950s

their families and wash off the disgrace attributed to the family.

The complex attributes of honour killings delineated in Arabic literary works can guide us to have a better understanding of honour killings as a social phenomenon. As literature vividly conceptualizes the complex web of relations between individual and society from multiple points of view while narrating actions in their social context, it is an important tool in terms of understanding the dynamics of such a phenomenon. It is no coincidence that only a few years before al-Mulla published her story, the Iraqi poet Nazik al-Mala'ika (1923-2007) wrote one of the major literary cries against honour killing in Arab societies. Her poem "Ghaslan li-l-'Ar" (Washing Away the Shame) (1957) tells the story of a young woman, aged twenty, killed by her brother, the "executioner", in order to "wash away the shame". The poem encapsulates the liberal cry among Arab writers against the issue of family honour; this view was shared by Arab-Jewish authors such as Ya'qub Balbul (1920-2003) in "Sura Tibqa al-Asl" (True Copy) – two brothers murder their own sister because she is pregnant. In Shalom Darwish's (1913-1997) story "Ba'da Suqooṭ al-Basra" (After the Fall of Basra), Jamila is raped by Farid, and as a result of losing her honour, she prefers to let people think that she has become mad. She blames herself for an act for which she is not responsible. In al-Mulla's story the father actually loses his mind following the rape of his daughter – the option that Nahiya is to blame for her tragedy never occurs to him. While murder for family honour has never been practised among Iraqi Jews, the fact that these writers dealt with such a negative practice only proves that Iraqi-Jewish authors felt themselves, at the time, to be an integral part of the Iraqi nation and society.

---

[1] According to information from her family, one of her grandfathers used to visit the neighbouring towns and villages to sell his merchandise and help the locals in writing letters and petitions which caused them to call him Mulla (Mullah), which literally means, a Muslim scholar and teacher.

[2] Particularly on www.akhbaar.org (accessed on 25 July 2020). For a list of her works, see Khalida Hatim 'Alwan, *Hafriyyat Unthawiyya: Dirasa fi al-Qass al-Niswi al-'Iraqi al-Yahudi al-Mughayyab* [Feminist Diggings: A Study of Hidden Feminist Iraqi Jewish Fiction] (Baghdad: Dar wa-Maktabat 'Adnan, 2016), pp. 31-34.

[3] The story was published in *al-Musawwar* (Baghdad) in 1951 (precise issue and date are not available); republished in Shmuel Moreh, *al-Qissa al-Qasira 'Inda Yahud al-'Iraq* [Short Stories by Jewish Writers from Iraq]. Jerusalem: Magnes Press, 1981), pp. 176-178.

MARYAM AL-MULLA

His Tragedy, a Proverb

A SHORT STORY TRANSLATED FROM THE ARABIC
BY AVIVA BUTT AND REUVEN SNIR

He who knows, knows and he who doesn't know, a handful of lentils.

'Aamir would recite that popular Iraqi proverb or that saying tens of times every day. The children used to stand around him and tease him: "You buy lentils, 'Aamir?" He would run after them and throw stones at them, sometimes hitting one of them and sometimes missing. Those children knew nothing and didn't understand why 'Amir's mind was unhinged. This wretched man, who never harmed anyone with his madness, was a new person to them. He had arrived at their village together with his family, after he had gone mad. They hadn't known him when he had lived in his village!

'Amir was a religious, God-fearing man, serious-minded and amiable toward all mankind. In his village, he was an energetic fellah, who sowed, reaped, and worked from morning until evening. Back then he was thirty-five years old and was contented with his family, which included a loving wife and three daughters. The oldest was seventeen, and her name was Nahiya. She was beautiful, astute, and courageous; she feared neither night nor men. Many young men in the village loved her, and each one of them wanted to take her as his wife. Zahi, the landowner's son, tried to seduce her, but she always rejected his advances. Many times he threatened her, but she abhorred him and poured biting and insulting words into his ears. She detested him because of his being an unruly boy, who spent most months of the year wandering about European countries, surrendering himself to his pleasures at nightclubs and lavishly spending monies that his father, the landlord, earned while the farmers are bearing the burden of his cruel attitude.

One day, Nahiya was gathering firewood in the orchard. When Zahi saw that there was no one around, he jumped on Nahiya from behind and threw her to the ground. Nahiya began to scream and cry out for help; her father, on his way to the orchard, heard her screams and rushed to her aid. He supposed that a wicked beast had attacked her. But when he arrived, it was already too late. Zahi the brute had carried out his scheme, taken her virginity by force, and fled for fear of the dagger Nahiya's father was waving about in the air. 'Amir found his daughter thrashing about like a slaughtered lamb, chased after Zahi, and shouted: "I swear by God I'll kill you, you coward!" When he managed to catch up with him, he stabbed him with the dagger which penetrated his shoulder; Zahi fell upon the ground bleeding profusely.

A gathering formed around them, and soon the police arrived and escorted the two men to the police station. The police interrogator asked Zahi the reason for the brawl, and he claimed that all he'd wanted to do was to hang out with 'Amir. He brought him a handful of lentils, and all of a sudden 'Amir had run after him threatening to kill him. The interrogator turned to 'Amir and said: "Aren't you ashamed, 'Amir? You wanted to kill the landowner's son, who was kind to you, and brought you a handful of lentils from the harvest that in fact belongs to his father." The interrogator didn't let 'Amir reply, and 'Amir himself did not want in any way to expose the affair and declare publicly that Zahi had wounded his honour and profaned his daughter's innocence. And perhaps he planned revenge and wished to conceal the scandal until he could undertake measures for revenge.

'Amir was arrested, put in jail and sentenced to a number of years' imprisonment. He couldn't bear the disgrace, and the years of imprisonment were very hard for him and his family. On the day of his release from jail, the members of his family received him, but Nahiya was not amongst them. When 'Amir asked about her, his wife said that his daughter had died a number of months after his being jailed. He smote his face, tore his clothes as a sign of mourning, and began to shout: "Nahiya is dead while the criminal wanders about freely." When his wife asked him who the criminal was, he replied: "He who knows, knows, and he who doesn't know, a handful of lentils." And from that time on, he recited that proverb.

This short story "His Tragedy, the Proverb", Arabic title "Ma'satuhu Mathal", was published in *al-Musawwar* magazine (Baghdad) in 1951 (precise details unavailable). It was republished in Shmuel Moreh, *al-Qissa al-Qasira 'Inda Yahud al-'Iraq* (The Short stories of Iraqi Jews), Jerusalem, Magnes Press, 1981, pp. 176-178.

Exploring Ronny Someck

BY ALMOG BEHAR

It would seem that Ronny Someck may well be one of Israel's most popular and best-read, living Hebrew poets of the last two decades. His popularity of course, has nothing whatsoever to do with any prominent literary critics' verdict on his body of work (quite possibly, owing to the glaring absence of any such critics with sufficient gravitas or king-making abilities in the last two decades), or the musical adaptations his poems have had (two, "Solo Arak" and "Rice Paradise", had beautiful music scored for them by Israeli musician Yair Dalal); both are factors that previously would have carried tremendous weight in determining a poet's popularity. Ronny Someck's popularity, however, has that much more to do with the poet's willingness to act as a "travelling agent" – whether for his own poems, or for poetry as whole – wherever it is required: in a library, school, café, prison, or care home, and no matter the audience. Above all else, Someck's wide appeal is inextricably tied to his deep-seated belief that poetry is an art form that must maintain a state of constant dialogue with as wide-ranging an audience as possible, as opposed to the same, niche 300 to 400 poetry devotees.

For instance, "Left Foot Goal", written in memory of Hungarian footballer Ferenc Puskás, first appeared in a newspaper's sports supplement rather than its literary section, before being part of his collection *Algeria* (2009). Another in the same collection, "When you Find me Stuffed in a Suitcase", was inspired by the harrowing disappearance and murder of four-year-old Rose Pizem, and read out on national television whilst the search for her was underway. The poet exists in his own time, and in conversation with his contemporaries; in the poem "Cellular Gunshot Blues on the no. 30 Route", also in *Algeria*, Someck quotes a fellow bus commuter, juxtaposing her words with *Song of Songs* verses whilst dialoguing with other poets including Sargon Boulus and Max Jacob.

In his earliest writings, Someck's use of pop culture was nothing

IRAQI JEWISH WRITERS

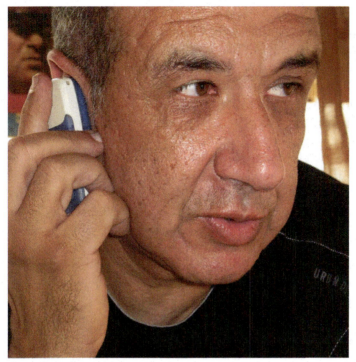

Ronny Someck

short of groundbreaking, essentially heralding the arrival of a new generation in the world of poetry, one whose members would dedicate whole poems to Marilyn Monroe. Of course, 1976 Marilyn Monroe-referencing pieces such as "For Marilyn Monroe" in Someck's debut collection *Exile* (1976) are worlds apart from any of his twenty-first-century poetry about the late icon, as in *Algeria*.

One of Someck's earliest poems, "Poem of Longing" (*Exile*, also available in the bilingual English-Hebrew *The Fire Stays in Red,* 2002), demonstrates the poet's extraordinary capacity for infusing a sense of longing with irony and a lack of any and all pathos, writing about "Grandpa's acrobatics" and how "Grandpa talked / and dreamed, dreamed and talked". Much later, in *Algeria*, Someck's longing moves on from his grandfather and father to the end of his daughter's childhood, as he is faced not with the end of his own childhood but that of his daughter's, who is now on the cusp of adulthood.

Music has always underscored Ronny Someck's poetry – whether Arab tunes from the likes of Umm Kulthum, Mohammed Abdel Wahab, Fairuz, and Salima Mourad or Western pop hits from Elvis,

The Beatles, Bob Dylan, and various blues musicians. Someck dedicates the poem "Taqsim" to the memory of Iraqi oud player, Yousef al-Awad (aka Yosef Shem Tov) who was a musical legend in life, and who had passed away just outside Tel Aviv in the city of Ramat Gan. In earlier poems, such as "Secret" in *The Revolution's Drummer* (2001), Arab music was a secret which he knew how to explain.

When Someck revisits Iraqi poet Sargon Boulus's poem *Insomnia*, set in the city of Lodève, south of France, he concludes by saying how "*The petrol that set dreams alight carried on coursing / through the engines of the aeroplanes that were bombing / his father's tomb, / there on the ground from whence / his life took off*". Of course, one cannot forget that Someck's life also took off in Iraq, which he describes in the poem "Baghdad" from *The Milk Underground* (2005), and is featured below. The memory, from which the poet extracts the events worthy of commemorating in verse, is steeped in scars, haunted by the violence of a knife in a poem that began with murder and gunfire.

Someck writes how "*I am the world champion of inconsequential details / therefore I will not write about how I was there*" (in "On the Eye of the Storm"), therefore one can envisage that this is how he defines both the poet and the poetic act itself: the poet knows all the irrelevant details, and realises that what others, i.e. the historian, news anchor, military commander, or prime minister, might dub as 'inconsequential details', may very well be the most crucial details concerning life itself. The poet will not uncover a scientific truth, nor will he write about major events, or decide whether thousands get to live or die – instead, he will only turn his verbal torch onto those seemingly trivial details that someone may or may not have left in the shadows, thereby rendering them inconsequential. He may also mix up timelines, events, and characters in the name of reviving those so-called irrelevant details as symbols, or reimagined possibilities for his readership. The poet, unlike the author and politician, knows how to tame the urge to elaborate, to win every last dish, treat, button, and word; for it is when one sifts through and streamlines them that a poem is born. Therefore, poets who "*hang line headers off pillars of foliage*" ("Sonnet of Those who Make Do with Little"), know that "*One tree is enough to narrate the whole wood*" (ibid).

The full version of this article is available on
www.banipal.co.uk/selections/

RONNY SOMECK

Eight Poems

TRANSLATED FROM THE HEBREW BY ERAN EDRY

EVE OR EVENING

"You do know," our Russian neighbour said to my dad,
"that Umm Kulthum you're always playing at full blast
said she would come and sing in Tel Aviv when Abdel Nasser
has captured it."
I stood next to him and in my seven-year-old mind
a dilemma ran rampant:
Was I in favour of the woman's blonde coiffe and turquoise eyes
who was also Eve's mum and who, in my heart, I had crowned
migrant camp neighbourhood Beauty Queen,
or the chanteuse who longed to live in the evening's eyes
and beckon the sun "come hither, come hither."
"We," the words left my father's lips, "love her,"
and in my eyes I saw him wishing he could only say that
"If that is the case, then have at it, Nasser,
Do your worst, and if only for a moment.
Save me a front row seat,
and don't let me miss the second her voice
blows even the bowties
right off the violinists' necks.

RONNY SOMECK

SAND

To the sandbag Ali Farag brought me from the banks of the Tigris.

If this sand had hands, they would paint
arabesques of the first words to leave my mouth
across my lips.

If it had a brain, it would recall
a baby's feet running round its face.

If it had eyes, they would notice that
the Tigris waters suddenly stationed
ambassador tears in the State
of my eyes.

Milan, May 2019

GAZA. WINTER 1968

To Ayman Hasan

In a restaurant by the sea,
my mother and father were having fish.
"That's what," they were saying, "the restaurants were like
on the banks of the Tigris in the city where you were born,
and in that Abdel Wahab song you're hearing right now,
not one lyric has changed."
The smell of coffee crept in like smoke from a flame
that once swirled on the gold chests of kings' concubines,
the monarchs of this place.

And I, who felt the prick of the surviving bone
from that fish's heart,
already knew that the wooden legs of the table
on which a white tablecloth had been laid,
shall never recover from the saw's teeth
that bit into them.

SECRET

It might not bear repeating,
but my mother wept when she suddenly heard
Cleopatra.
So who are you, Mr. Abdel Wahab to lift an Egyptian queen
off the history books and translate her into tears in my mother's
diarised memories.
And you, Cleopatra, breaking hearts in nostalgia's
game of poker on a small Ramat Gan side street,
do you recall the musclebound slaves
who had dived for pearls with which to glorify your throne,
the throats you had choked up in Bagdad cafes
and the wind that lashed at the doors
whose hinges creaked against a belly harbouring a secret?

It's been a while since I last wrote the words 'nostalgia'
'tears', or 'memories' in such close proximity,
but these words are the teeth of a comb with which, I,
in lieu of an Egyptian mistress, stroke your hair.
May you be beautiful, Cleopatra,
May you be worthy of melting once more
the tip of the iceberg below which goldfish
spell out the word 'sun'
from memory.

UNCLE SALIM

In the days when train tickets
still commanded some respect,
and were printed on green cardboard paper
and nothing less,
Uncle Salim would pull out of his jacket pocket
a small pile he'd collected at Haifa Railway Station,
and help us imagine a steering wheel
in the round space
between one hand and the other.

RONNY SOMECK

We would close one eye, hold the punched ticket hole
up to the other, and through it we saw
the razor-sharp red tie he wore to hide
the sad state of the rail workers'
khaki shirts.

He would then exhale the memory of locomotives
that he once ran along the rail tracks of another land,
and the carriages heaving with tales
from the Tigris and Euphrates
would breathe air that much cleaner than the mothballed scent
that clung to the new immigrants' memory baggage.

"This train service to Heaven," he heard just before he died,
"will be departing in three minutes,"
and that was exactly the right time for him
to load up his 99 years onto the carriages,
the top hat he loved pushing to and fro,
and also traces of the cheers
he always had saved for the sound of
Abdel Wahab's voice.

BAGHDAD

With the same chalk, a policeman marks a crime scene corpse
I mark the boundaries of the city where my life was shot.
I interrogate witnesses, squeezing drops of Arak
from their lips, and mimicking the dance moves of
pita bread over a hummus bowl with some hesitation.
When I am caught,
they will take one third off my sentence for good behaviour
and incarcerate me in the hallway of Salima Mourad's throat.
In the prison kitchen, my mother will be frying the fish that her
    mother
had pulled out of the river waters whilst recalling the word 'Fish'
emboldened on a massive sign in front of this brand-new
    restaurant.

Whoever ate there would be served fish no bigger than a pin
that is until one of the customers asked the owner either
to make the sign smaller or the fish bigger.
The fish would prick with its bones, drowning the hand
that had descaled it, and not even
hot oil in the interrogation pan
could get so much as an incriminating word
out of its mouth.
Memory is but an empty plate, scarred with a knife's
scratch marks on its skin.

SEE-THROUGH

Tayeb studies Literature at Tel Aviv University.
He has a rucksack with a grammar textbook
and a Mahmoud Darwish essay inside.
It's a see-through rucksack because this summer,
any other kind in the x-ray eyes of every officer
would flag him as a would-be bomber.
"Inshallah," his father says, "even that
will soon come out in the wash," as he hangs out
clothes that have had shame stains rinsed out of them
on the washing line of time.
But life too must go to the marketplace,
and he goes with it
to buy some olives in Spoken Arabic, about which he
will write poems in Arabic fusha*.
Meanwhile, Tayeb remains visible.
The skin stretched across his arms
does not hide the sinewy muscles,
the pliable cartilage in the space between the bones
and the blood vessels in which despair's
own swimmer could row drunk
all the way to the tower where lifeguards have flown
a black flag.

                                          Summer 2001

* Modern Standard Arabic

MONA YAHIA

Matches

A SHORT STORY

"Matches" and *When the Grey Beetles Took over Baghdad*

Initially "Matches" was meant to be a chapter in Yahia's novel *When the Grey Beetles Took over Baghdad* but at a certain point she felt it was a digression and removed it. When she recently reread it, she was taken by the question: what do you pick up from the world around you as a child, and to what extent do you understand it? Growing up in Baghdad in the 1950s and 1960s, she would overhear snippets of adult conversations with graphic descriptions of torture prisons. As she later explained, those scenes haunted her childhood and teens, and sometimes they catch up with her even now, fifty years after she left Baghdad. That is why, when revising "Matches", she put more emphasis on the play element to create a safe distance from the brutality involved, whether physical or verbal. In retrospect, however, she says that the idea of a game was inspired by Jean Genet's play *The Maids,* which fascinated her as a student of French literature twenty years before she started to contemplate writing about Baghdad.

The interrogator orders the sergeant to blindfold the bound prisoner. Although taken by surprise, the prisoner meets his tormentor's gaze with defiance. You can't fool me, mummy's boy, the interrogator's lopsided smirk returns. You'll crack as instantly as a china figurine. The sergeant covers the prisoner's eyes with a chequered keffiyah. The girl ties his legs to the chair, for good measure. Not too tight, the interrogator remarks, almost softly, and ruffles the prisoner's glossy black hair. He does not really want his prisoner to break that soon. The interrogator prefers longer sessions. The sort of games his cat does not tire of playing with its prey before finishing it off with a bite to the neck.

– What a shame we can't find an electric chair, says the girl.

The three boys hoot with laughter. Suha, who's the youngest, laughs along pretending she understands.

– I told you she's too stupid to play with us! Nuri groans, trying without success to move his legs – tied by his sister with excessive devotion.

– Enough, let's get on with it, Ghassan, the oldest of the four and the only boy with long trousers, says in a brisk tone, at ease in his role as interrogator.

Undaunted by the glaring sun, Ghassan and Kamal spend the long summer afternoons playing on the shadeless rooftop of their two-storey house, away from adult supervision. The place is bare, except for an iron bed, no longer in use, and a clothesline stretching from one side to the other on which freshly washed bed sheets and towels are hanging. The roof has a view of the street and the neighbouring front gardens and a partial view of the main road, which has been festooned for the upcoming anniversary of the Ba'ath Revolution. For two days, the men from the municipality have put up banners and flags and posters of the President, and served as perfect targets for the brothers' guerrilla and sniper games. When their cousins, Nuri and Suha, came over this morning, the now reinforced gang moved to a tougher and more daring game: prison.

The sergeant positions himself behind the prisoner, swinging a length of rubber hose back and forth. The interrogator hoists himself up to sit on the footboard of the bed ten feet away, watching, ready to interfere. The girl stands halfway between the bed and the chair, her back against the wet laundry, feeling it, soaking up its coolness.

The interrogator snaps his fingers, signalling the sergeant to pick up where he has left off.

– I repeat my question: in what shithole do you think you are, Brigadier? The sergeant bellows.

– The Rashid Camp prison I suppose . . . How the hell would I know when I can't see a thing, he lies, too complacent to suppress the mockery in his voice.

– Wrong! The sergeant lashes the back of the chair.

The prisoner throws his head forwards, groaning, pretending to be in pain.

– Where did you say you are?

– Abu Ghraib?

Wrong again! The chair receives another blow. The prisoner lets out a louder, more affected, cry of pain.

– For the last time, and you'd better get the right answer – for your own sake . . . The sergeant roars and glances at his older brother for approval.

His head slumped, the prisoner starts speaking mechanically, as if reciting a list of plant species.

– The Central Prison, the Army Intelligence Prison, al-Fursan, al-Fadhiliyah, al-Hamidiyah . . .

– Al-Hamidiyah's a *suq*, you shithead! Suha corrects him.

– Shut up or you're out! Kamal snarls at her.

The interrogator pulls the peak of his pilot's cap over his forehead.

– I'm bored, he grumbles.

– But Ghassan, I swear I don't know what he wants me to say! Nuri

---

Mona Yahia was born in Baghdad in 1954, and escaped with her family to Israel in 1971. She studied psychology at Tel Aviv University and fine arts in Kassel, Germany. Her first novel, *When the Grey Beetles Took over Baghdad*, (Halban Publishers, London, 2000) won the *Jewish Quarterly* Wingate Prize for Fiction in 2001 in London, and is published in German and French translation. Her latest publication, *Snapshots: Istanbul Behind Closed Doors* (Binooki, Berlin, 2019, in English, German, and Turkish) consists of a series of photographs of a historical khan in Istanbul, the architectural structure of which is transported into that of a short story. She is currently working on the last stages of a new novel, *Four Days*, a family saga of four generations of a Jewish Arab family that spans the 20th Century and is set against the backdrop of the changing map of the Middle East. Mona Yahia lives in Cologne, Germany, and writes mainly in English.

raises his head, suddenly serious and alert.

— Kasr el-Nehaya, Suha whispers.

— Kasr el-Nehaya, the prisoner repeats nonchalantly.

— Right! The Palace of No Return, where scum like you meet their rotten end. Now that we've settled this, are you ready to confess, Brigadier?

— Confess what?

— That you've been an American agent all the way, you traitor! The sergeant brandishes his hose.

— That you've been a Zionist agent all the way, you criminal, the interrogator adds, listening with delight to his deep, recently broken voice.

— That you've been an Iranian agent all the way, you animal! The girl strides forward and screams passionately in the prisoner's face.

— You're bathing me with your spittle, you foul-breathed parrot! He fires back.

— It's no fun playing with him, she complains.

— No, it's not, Kamal agrees and rights his fake moustache. He's not playing, he's just fooling around.

— Want to replace him? Ghassan asks.

Kamal shakes his head. Not for the world would he put himself in his brother's hands, game or no game.

— Me, Ghassan, me! Suha implores, thrusting out her forefinger as if in a classroom.

— It's not fair, Ghassan, we haven't started yet, Nuri objects.

Ghassan takes out a cigarette from his pocket and sticks it between his lips.

— All right, it's your last chance, Nuri! Be serious or I'll have you replaced, understand?

Reluctantly, the girl recedes to the washing line. The interrogator motions the sergeant to continue.

— You've sold our military secrets to the enemy, you dirty crook! Be a man at least and own up to your crimes.

— That's not true! You haven't got a shred of evidence against me.

— *Ibn el-haram*, bastard! We've got enough evidence to hang you ten times! Kamal, running out of threats and accusations, strikes the rubber hose on the chair with frustration.

— I'm innocent. *Wallah,* I'm innocent, the prisoner yelps.

The interrogator yawns demonstratively. The girl imitates him, the braces on the teeth of her upper jaw glinting in the sun.

– Hey, chick! A light! The interrogator snaps his fingers and indicates his cigarette.

The girl races inside, returns in a flash, gasping, and hands him over the matchbox. The interrogator reminds her, almost scolding, that she is expected to light his cigarette. The girl strikes a match and holds out the flame to him, shielding it from imaginary wind with her other hand. Ghassan is about to slap her buttocks, the right thing to do for a man in his position, but is thwarted by a beginner's coughing fit as soon as he takes the first pull.

– Good! He says, still coughing. Now I want you to show the traitor what fire is.

It takes her a moment to get it.

– But *Khala* said I had to return the matches right away!

– Fine by me, he flatly replies. Be a good girl and do what your aunt says.

Just as her little hand encases the door handle, he adds:

– You might as well stay in the kitchen and help *Khala* with the cooking.

Kamal and Nuri guffaw. Suha lets go of the handle, hangs her head in shame.

– For God's sake, Suha, don't be a baby! Ghassan growls.

– For fuck's sake, get on with the game, Suha, or I'll never let you play with us again, Nuri hollers.

The girl narrows her eyes, squares her shoulders, and struts towards the prisoner.

– Look at him, Mr Corruption has the nerve to speak! You can't blare out orders anymore, Brigadier. You're nothing but a piece of shit. Even your little sister can pee all over your face, you vile servant of imperialism.

– I'll break your braces and all your ugly teeth as soon as my hands are free, you worthless cow.

In a reflex action Suha covers her mouth with her hand.

– Don't be afraid, the interrogator reassures her. He's bound and blindfolded, don't you see? All he can do is talk, talk, talk. Nothing but hot air. It's your chance, girl, go and give it to him!

The girl simpers, strikes a match. Hesitantly, she inches the flame above the prisoner's shoulder, half way under his earlobe.

– Feel the fire, Brigadier?

Her jaw drops in disbelief when he jerks his head to the side and blows out the match with two puffs.

– For your information, I can see everything through your lousy keffiyah, he blurts out. Even a donkey would do a better job!

– Let me do it! The sergeant, who takes the insult personally, begs the interrogator. Let me teach this vermin a lesson.

The interrogator silences him with a sweep of the hand, orders him to withdraw to the corner.

– Listen to me, girl, you shouldn't let this son of a dog confuse you. Go and stand behind him. He can't blow out the match from the back of his head, can he?

From her new position, the girl strikes a second match and edges the fire to the prisoner's ear. He starts up, cranes his neck away. She keeps her hand steady. The prisoner's face contorts. He writhes, stamps his feet but does not utter a single groan.

– The truth! Out with it! She barks, her voice quavering.

And drops the match with a shriek, shaking her burnt fingers.

The prisoner bursts into gleeful laughter. Suha grabs his hair and pulls his head back with all her force. Startled by his scream, she immediately lets go. The sergeant shoots forward to snatch the matchbox from her hand.

– Take off his blindfold, Sergeant, the interrogator forestalls him.

The sergeant does what he is told, after which he angrily whips the keffiyah across the prisoner's face. A sharp cry of pain escapes Nuri.

– We've said no hitting, Suha protests.

Ghassan stares at his brother blankly before he stubs the cigarette out against the iron bed leg.

– It doesn't count, he decides to Kamal's relief, rights his cap and jumps to his feet.

Kamal chucks the keffiyah over the washing line. The interrogator snatches the matchbox from the girl's hand and gestures his two subordinates towards the iron bed.

– Look at you, a Brigadier in the Iraqi Army – pride of the nation, he circles around the prisoner, fencing him in. If only you'd resisted the urge to be a brigadier in the CIA, too. Don't you dare to contradict me, *ya kunderah*, you stinking shoe! We know all about your bank accounts in Switzerland.

– By my honour, I've served my country with utmost loyalty and devotion. Every *fils* I've earned is *halal* money.

– Now he sounds just like Baba! Suha giggles, sitting next to the sergeant on the footboard, swinging her legs with mirth.

– Served your country? Among how many others, you imperialist whore? The interrogator turns around and scowls at his aides, as if to remind them of something.

The two dutifully double up and cackle.

– By the life of my children, I've never met with foreign agents.

The interrogator strikes a match.

– Every source burns itself out, sooner or later, he says evenly.

Watching the fire crawl down towards his fingers, he deftly picks the stick from its burnt end with the fingertips of his other hand.

– So where did you say you sold our military secrets? In Tehran? New York? Tel Abib? The interrogator crushes the dead match in his palm.

– Nonsense, I've never leaked any military secrets.

– Do you really expect me to swallow this horseshit? If so, why have you applied for a visa to Switzerland, Brigadier? And why have you bribed the clerk in the embassy to keep quiet?

– I was . . . I was going on holiday, the prisoner falters, taken off guard by the new turn.

The interrogator grabs his prisoner's ear and twists it.

– It was a private matter… nothing to do with the army, I swear. Just a woman . . . I had to keep it secret, because . . .

– Because, because, because of what? The interrogator twists his ear further as if to tighten a leaking water tap.

– Aaaaa, . . . Because of my wife!

Suha titters. Kamal glares at Nuri. His cousin has no right to blab about that ugly old story. No right to know about it even. In Kamal's version, his father had moved out of the house – for weeks or months he can no longer recall – only to turn up at the door again one day, all smiles, his arms full of overpriced gifts as if he had just returned from a business trip abroad. The rest was kept back from him, the youngest son, the sensitive one.

– So, you're going all the way to Switzerland just for a screw? But why, Brigadier? What's wrong with our belly dancers? Don't you fancy them anymore?

Nuri drops his head, trying in vain to stifle a fit of laughter.

– *Ana 'l abu abuk*, a curse on your father's father, the interrogator bellows, experimenting with the power of his new voice. What the fuck do you take me for? – Juha, or his donkey?

Suha is laughing till she cries. The prisoner raises his head again, collected, ready to give an amusing quip. A quip Kamal has no wish to hear. He hurls the rubber hose in his cousin's direction. Suha shrieks. Nuri ducks down just after the hose has swished short of his head and hit the tan brick wall behind him. Ghassan charges at his brother, grabs him by his shirt and flings him to the concrete ground, calling him all the names under the sun. Terrified by the scuffle, Suha jumps off the footboard and scuttles over to the safety of her brother's side.

–You all right, my love? What's happened? What's got into Kamal?
– God knows! He needs his head examined, I guess!

Kamal lies face down at his brother's feet, inhaling the smell of his leather sandals, sensing an army of unwashed toes close in for the bullying. Behind them, a pink bed sheet hanging down to the ground curtains off the roof from the street, the cars, the flags, and the government's men with whom he tirelessly exchanged fire the day before in a brave but abortive attempt on the President's life. Either way he is a condemned man. The interrogator tucks his foot under the prisoner's face, as if poking a dead bird, then tips his chin up to look into his eyes. Kamal does not resist, unsure what his brother has in mind. If the brute orders him to kiss his stinky foot, he will spit on it instead and die with honour.

– Rise to your feet, Sergeant. Iraqi soldiers don't lie idly on the grass.

The sergeant obeys, his forehead throbbing with pain.

–What the fuck did you think you were doing, barging in on a high security interrogation?

The sergeant reaches out to feel the welt above his right eye.

– Keep your hands to your sides, you turd, and straighten up!

His lips trembling uncontrollably, the sergeant braces himself for the imminent blow, not knowing from which side it will come. All eyes are fixed on the interrogator. The girl steals towards the washing line, for a better view. Nuri watches with less enthusiasm, annoyed by the prolonged digression. Neither suspects that Ghassan is having qualms. That the sight of his brother, humiliated and reduced to submissiveness, does not feed his scorn but rather fills him with pity – the last thing that befits a senior interrogator.

MONA YAHIA

—You're demoted to private! He reaches out and plucks a bristle off the fake moustache.

The soldier blushes. With solemn ceremony the interrogator puts a match to the bristle. The girl stops her nose with her fingers.

— It stinks! She complains.

—That's how it smelt in Germany when Hitler burnt the Zionists, the interrogator points out, informatively.

Missing the attention he had enjoyed until his imbecile of a cousin stole the show, Nuri drops his head and lets his tongue loll.

— Water! My throat's parched! Have mercy, I beg you, get me a glass of water!

— Let's get him dirty water from the washing machine! The girl suggests.

— No, from the loo, the soldier caps that, back on the job. If he's really thirsty, he'll drink anything!

— From the loo! From the loo! The girl applauds, full of mirth.

Tahrir Square, Baghdad, in the 1970s

– Good idea, Sergeant! The interrogator says, with stress on the Sergeant.

Kamal brightens up as if he has been promoted to general. The prisoner continues to act as if he is half-dead. The interrogator beckons the girl over and whispers at some length in her ear. She nods radiantly. It is his moment to deliver that overdue slap on her butt, but the girl has already sped inside in her eagerness to carry out his instructions. She returns in no time with a glass of water wrapped in layer upon layer of toilet paper. She passes it on to the interrogator, then wipes her hands on her skirt, twisting her face in disgust. The prisoner clamps his mouth shut, fearing the worst.

– What's the matter, Brigadier? I thought you were thirsty! The interrogator swaggers over towards him.

The prisoner fidgets in his chair, fighting back tears, trying to wrench himself free. The interrogator sniffs the glass then draws it away from his nose with a grimace.

– Granted, it's not rose water! But we're not in a position to pick and choose, are we?

He grips the prisoner's lower jaw and pushes the brim of the glass between his lips. The prisoner tosses his head about, struggling frantically until his nose or chin hits the glass and spills water on the interrogator's hand.

– Coward! The interrogator backs away. Even latrine water's a waste on you!

He wipes his hand with the toilet paper, crumples it and flings the wet ball angrily at the prisoner.

– Let me force his mouth open, the sergeant begs.

Both sergeant and prisoner let out a howl of revulsion when the interrogator throws back his head and takes a swig. Nuri darts a searching glance at his sister who returns his silent inquiry with a poker face. The interrogator rinses his mouth at leisure, gargling unrecognisable melodies – anything from *MoonWalk* to the national anthem, entertaining his audience and setting the stage for the inevitable finale. In the middle of *El hawa hawaye*, suddenly tired of his performance, the interrogator lowers his head, turns to the prisoner and spits the contents of his mouth straight into his face.

Nuri's rage and distress and humiliation gush out in a torrent of abuse at his tormentors, who cannot stop laughing their heads off.

A woman peeks out from the door, her head in curlers. She has a colourful dressing gown on and carries a red plastic bucket.

– I can't believe my ears! Your tongues are fouler than the sewage! Ghassan, Kamal, what on earth are you doing to your cousin? Why is he bound to the chair? Are you mishandling the poor boy?

– Oh, no, *Khala*, I'm teaching them tricks how to untie knots, Nuri hastens to say, acting bold and in charge of the situation.

– We're just playing, *Yom*, Kamal confirms, scanning the floor for the rubber hose, praying it does not give the game away.

Ghassan walks over to his mother, takes the bucket from her hand.

– You look tired, Mama darling, why don't you go and have a nap? He kisses her hand. We'll be quiet, I promise! And don't you worry about the laundry, we'll take it down for you and bring it downstairs.

She studies her firstborn mistrustfully, the way she did the day he suddenly towered over her. The youth speaks with a man's voice and wears long trousers, and yet there he is still messing around with the children. She cannot see through him anymore. All she knows is that soon, very soon, he will start shaving and stop playing.

– All right, you may go on, but stop swearing, do you hear me? Aren't you ashamed to use such street language? And be quiet for God's sake, you'll wake the dead with all this noise!

No sooner has she shut the door than Suha steps out from behind the washing line, waving the rubber hose with a triumphant grin. Kamal gives her a conspiratorial wink. The interrogator snaps his fingers, summons his two aides to take stock.

– What now? What do we do with him? Sergeant?

The sergeant snatches the hose from the girl's hand, adjusts his moustache and stands to attention.

– Every word that leaves his mouth is a lie, *ya sayyidi*. Why waste our time when thousands of others are waiting to be interrogated? Let's show the nation we mean business and execute him!

The interrogator turns to the girl.

– And you? Anything to say?

Like the sergeant, she stands to attention.

– We won't get the names if we execute him now, *sayyidi*.

– Go on, the interrogator nods approvingly.

– So let's extract the names first . . . and then we put him on TV, and only afterwards . . . she draws her forefinger across her neck.

– That's a smart girl! The interrogator exclaims.

Kamal hurls the rubber hose to the ground.

– It's the last time I'm playing with her . . .

Ignoring Kamal's outburst, the interrogator breezes towards the prisoner.

–You ever seen anybody keep quiet while his moustache's on fire?

–What moustache? Suha asks. Nuri hasn't got one!

– Of course he has, are you blind or something? He snaps his fingers. Sergeant, step forward.

The sergeant obeys. The interrogator grabs for his fake moustache and hands it over to the girl.

–There you are, the Brigadier's bushy black moustache!

The prisoner does not put up any resistance when the girl applies the moustache under his nose and secures it with the rubber band around his head. Her job done, she cocks her head, studies her bother's new face and tries not to giggle.

– For the last time, Brigadier, the interrogator says, toying with the matchbox. You either reveal the names of your collaborators or your glossy moustache goes up in flames.

–You don't scare me! I'd rather die than please rabble like you!

The interrogator strikes a match and directs the flame towards the prisoner's face.

–You're right, Sergeant. It's a waste of time with him.

–Wait! The girl calls out.

–What now?

– Let's gag him! In case he shouts . . . to make sure *Khala* won't hear.

The interrogator whistles in wonder and puts out the match.

–You've heard her, Sergeant! He points to the clothesline. Go and pick up the keffiyah and stuff it into his mouth.

– But how can he confess if he's gagged!

The interrogator stares hard at his sergeant while he racks his brains for a way to counter his argument.

–That's his problem! He finally replies, unblinking.

– His problem, the girl repeats imperiously.

Kamal eyes his brother in disbelief.

– But we've said . . .

–We've said no hitting and no spitting, Ghassan interrupts him. Have we ever said no burning?

Kamal turns to Nuri. The prisoner, who has assumed an air of martyrdom, averts his eyes, refusing the alliance.

– You're insane! Kamal raps out with horror in his eyes.

– He's breaking, he's breaking, Suha sings out. Kamal's the first to break . . .

– Shut up Suha, we're still playing! Ghassan hushes her with murder in his eyes.

– Do you refuse to gag him, Sergeant? Are you with us or against us?

– You make me sick, all of you!

– Come on, Sergeant, we're not pulling out his fingernails, we're not shooting electric shocks up his arse, we're not seating him on a scorching stove and that kind of thing. God forbid! All we're talking about is a fucking moustache, it's hardly worth the fuss.

– Oh yes? And what if the keffiyah catches fire and you can't put it out in time? He might burn his face. He might be maimed for the rest of his life. It's a sick game, just count me out!

– Hurrah! Nuri shouts, almost leaping from his chair. I won! I won! I'm the winner!

– Kamal's lost! Kamal's lost! Suha claps her hands.

Ghassan unties Nuri, slaps him on the nape of his neck.

– Congratulations, Cousin! You've gone much further than I'd expected!

– Let's have another round, Nuri says, stroking his arms and flaunting the red lines imprinted by the hemp cord.

– Oh yes, another round, another round, Suha sings out.

Ghassan removes his pilot's cap and jams it on Nuri's head.

– Nuri's the interrogator this time, I'm the prisoner. I'll be a university professor, I'm tired of fat-bellied officers. Nuri, pass the moustache to Suha. She'll play the sergeant. Kamal, you've lost, you'll be her assistant.

Suha puts on the moustache, drunk with joy.

– Quickly, Ghassan, sit down, she gasps. Where's the keffiyah, I'll blindfold you myself. Kamal, you tie him to the electric chair. Where's the cigarette? Nuri, don't you forget the cigarette. Please hurry up, Brother darling, let's have another game before Mama comes to take us home.

Reading Samir Naqqash

LITAL LEVY

> "In this place, words were more important than food and water. Words were a link, *the* link; they were knowledge, and knowledge was guidance."
> – *Shlomo the Kurd*

Samir Naqqash was a perplexing figure: an author who wrote in a language almost no one could read, and who was seemingly at odds with his own time and place. Nevertheless, over the course of three decades, Naqqash produced a unique and impressive literary corpus illustrating a bygone era of Iraqi life, a legacy that culminated in his accomplished final novel *Shlomo al-Kurdi wa-ana wa-l-Zaman* (Shlomo the Kurd, Myself, and Time) in 2004.

Born in Baghdad in 1938, Naqqash arrived in Israel in 1951 as part of the mass emigration of Iraqi Jewry. Like many others, his family had traded a middle-class, professional life in Iraq for an unknown future in Israel. For the Naqqash family, that future held great disappointment and loss, issuing from the shock of resettlement in a squalid tent camp and followed by the death of Samir's father and brother within the first years of arrival. These traumas profoundly shaped Naqqash's adult outlook. He completed his education in Israel and acquired fluency in Hebrew, yet throughout his literary career he wrote exclusively in Arabic, the language of the country he had left behind – a country with which Israel was still at war. Moreover, he wrote in a unique idiom that captured the colloquial richness of the once pluralistic Iraq, but that was difficult or even inaccessible

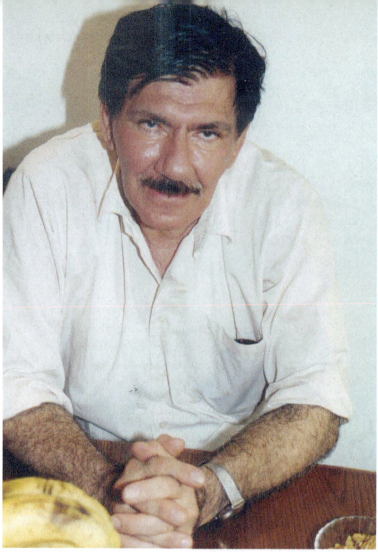

Samir Naqqash

to the majority of his readers.

   Rejecting the advice of mentors and colleagues who forewarned that a Jewish writer of Arabic would never find readers, Naqqash persisted in what could be seen either as a doomed, quixotic mission or as an uncompromising, heroic act of linguistic fidelity and cultural preservation. In so doing, he set himself apart from other Iraqi-Israeli writers of his generation such as Shimon Ballas, Sami Michael, and Eli Amir, who adopted Hebrew and achieved both commercial and critical success. Naqqash, by contrast, made himself into a scholar's writer: esoteric and fascinating in equal measures. He won Israeli governmental prizes for Arabic literature, and later in his career he received recognition from Arab intellectuals and writers, especially in the European diaspora. But as Mati Shemoelof notes "beyond the accolades, he lived with a sense of deprivation".[1] His career ended prematurely with his death from a heart attack at the age of 66, mere months after the publication of *Shlomo the Kurd*.

In interviews, Naqqash traces his writerly path back to his formative years in Baghdad. In particular, he locates it in the vibrant social milieu of his family home, which was a meeting point for Iraqis of different religions, ages, classes, both men and women. As an attentive and precocious child, he absorbed visitors' distinctive speech styles, as well as a multilingual wealth of proverbs and idioms ranging widely from archaic Ottoman Turkish and Persian words and sayings to traditional Kurdish and Hebrew expressions. The young Naqqash was also an avid reader. In a 1996 interview with Ammiel Alcalay, Naqqash notes that his schooling in Iraq exposed him to "all of world literature" in Arabic translation, from which he drew inspiration.[2] All these influences found their way into his work. His prose style was distinguished by his harnessing of Iraq's many ethnic oral dialects, which he fashioned into a literary tapestry that required the use of footnotes as a reader's aid; yet in his work, he often attempted to explore more universal, philosophical questions.

Naqqash obtained a degree in Arabic literature from the Hebrew University of Jerusalem, and began publishing his own fiction in the 1970s. Between 1972 and 1980 he published four short story collections, mostly on themes of Jewish life in Iraq and Iraqi-Jewish life in Israel, and often with folkloric elements. These early works were self-published and underwritten by donors. Early on, Naqqash was drawn to polyphony, recreating the voices of a colorful cast of characters from across the spectrum of Iraqi-Jewish society. Several of these early stories are miniatures of individual figures or events, often underscored by irony or black humour, while others take on more philosophical dimensions, sometimes verging on existentialism. The stories as a whole are vivid, evocative, some sometimes quite dark.

In the 1980s, Naqqash moved into longer and more complex genres – plays, novellas, and novels. His breakthrough 1986 novel *Nzula wa-khayt al-shaytan: riwaya 'iraqiyya* (Tenants and Cobwebs: an Iraqi Novel) won him critical acclaim, and was published in English translation by Sadok Masliyah in 2018 with Syracuse University Press.

SAMIR NAQQASH

The Arabic cover of Shlomo the Kurd

This linguistically complex novel depicts the intertwined lives of Jewish and Muslim neighbours in an apartment block in Baghdad during the period of growing ethnic and political tensions that preceded the mass emigration of Iraqi Jewry. Each character narrates their thoughts in their own native dialect, Jewish or Muslim. Over the course of the 1990s, Naqqash gained increasing recognition among Arab readers abroad. *Shlomo the Kurd* was published by Manshurat al-Jamal/Al-Kamel Verlag, an independent Arabic publishing house run by Iraqi exiles in Cologne; the same press also reissued his 1987 novel *Fuwah ya dam!*

Concerning his decision to write in Arabic rather than Hebrew, Naqqash explains that "A Jew who writes in Arabic presents all kinds of problems to everyone, yet I am simply continuing to write in my own language."[3] He elaborates: "In Arabic, you can convey various levels of spoken language in a way that you cannot in Hebrew. There are also personal obstacles and reasons why I went into the Arabic language in such great depth and these are connected to the new reality here and the trauma we underwent. This resulted in a kind of roadblock between me and . . . everything that is Israeli which has lasted until the present."[4] That "roadblock" had many implications. Throughout his life in Israel, Naqqash identified as an Iraqi Jew in exile. From his teen years onward, he tried repeatedly to leave Israel, starting with failed attempt to cross the border by foot into Lebanon. During 1958-1962, he sojourned in Turkey, Iran, and India and acquired knowledge of Persian and some Hindi. In 2002, Naqqash moved his family to Manchester to start a new life working at *Al-Mu'tamar*, a daily newspaper published by Iraqi dissidents in London. After Saddam Hussein's fall in 2003, the editorial board relocated to Iraq; Naqqash stayed behind in Manchester for another year without work and then returned to Israel in 2004. Ironically, according to family members, just as he began to make his peace with life in Israel, that life was abruptly cut short; he died two months after his return.

In some cosmic sense, Naqqash's life seems almost to converge with that of his creation "Shlomo", culminating in the close timing of the novel's 2004 publication with Naqqash's passing. Shlomo is a Kurdish Jew from a remote mountain town, a traveling merchant who has seen it all. Unlike his creator, Shlomo does not speak Arabic, but is conversant in Persian, Kurdish, and other languages. Like Naqqash, Shlomo's peregrinations lead him from Baghdad to Tehran and Bombay, and finally to Ramat Gan, a suburb of Tel Aviv populated largely by Iraqi Jews. From there, the elderly Shlomo narrates his lifetime of memories, recalling episodes from the First World War to the late 20th century. These memories unfold as two-way conversations with Shlomo's younger self and with the persona of Time. Through them, we are drawn into the merchant's journeys, his family life, his loves and losses, his interactions with a diverse array of humanity; we see history in motion, the vagaries of human nature, and the devastation wrought by violence and war. In the excerpts presented here, we find Shlomo at sea on his way to India, reflecting on alienation – the sensation of exile – in light of his inability to converse with those around him. The sections that follow this return us to Baghdad of 1951 just prior to the vast outmigration of Iraqi Jewry that included the Naqqash family. These excerpts offer a glimpse of Naqqash's unique writerly style, at once sensual, culturally allusive, and introspective. "Seek, Shlomo! Seek! Search for those who can understand you" could serve as a final epitaph for Naqqash himself, who throughout his adult life sought understanding for an impossible situation through his writerly craft.

Notes:
[1] Mati Shemoelof, "With New Translation, Samir Naqqash's Place in Israeli Literature Should Finally be Celebrated," *Mondoweiss*, August 17, 2020
https://mondoweiss.net/2020/08/with-new-translation-samir-naqqashs-place-in-israeli-literature-should-finally-be-celebrated/
[2] Ammiel Alcalay, ed. *Keys to the Garden: New Israeli Writing* (San Francisco: City Lights Books, 1996), p. 102.
[3] *Keys to the Garden*, p. 110.
[4] *Keys to the Garden*, p. 108

SAMIR NAQQASH

AN EXCERPT FROM THE NOVEL

Shlomo the Kurd, Myself, and Time
Shlomo al-Kurdi wa-ana wa-l-Zaman

TRANSLATED FROM THE ARABIC BY ZEENA FAULK

Baghdad-Bombay 1924

I walked around in tattered, loathsome garments and clutched a donkey pannier jam-packed with a change of clothing, some food, and my sack![1] I certainly was not disguising myself as a beggar, since Time had turned me into a true nomad. Nor was I a hoarder, as my home in the town of Siblakh[2] was always wide open to relatives and nonrelatives alike. I spent – or rather depleted – my wealth by helping my brethren and my townspeople during the years of war.

Now, I have nothing save my sack of money, which I miraculously amassed from cleaning faeces, and from Asmar's jewelry. My humiliation burst out in the sweat of my brow and wiped my dignity dry. My one and only sack had thus become my spirit, since I could not tolerate living in any way that wasn't dignified. From that point onward, I would begin to gather the bits of my broken pride, and from there I would wield my fractured bones. I tied my sack with a thousand knots, and, with the dishevelled demeanour of a beggar, I pressed onward.

No, I would not pamper myself and sit like a king, cross-legged on his sack. With my appearance, I could not even pretend to be second-class.

I flung myself down on the ship's deck, among the poor, rogue beggars, and those who sold the land under their feet and the roofs over their heads to finance a pilgrimage to Iraq to visit Najaf, Karbala, and the shrine of the Hanbali mystic Sheik Abdul Qadir al-Gilani in Baghdad. Mumbling Indians, light-skinned shepherds, nomads, and the humidity, the stench, the mice, and the cockroaches! And there I was – a merchant shoved into a large hole behind which lay a merchant's memory. Before my eyes stood the prospect of a trading project, mixed with my other thoughts, which never knew the art of calming. The ideas buzzing in my head were already bargaining and trading. It was here when alienation, that feeling of estrangement, began.

Was the eternally honest Asmar correct? In this filthy, wretched, pitch-black corner all I could hear was the sound of myself. My head was a storage depot, or a resting place for stowed memories that were equal to the size of our destination, the Shatt al-Arab and its estuary.

We sailed the Arab Gulf. With just a soft strike of my magical cane, I thought, water would spring robustly upward and fragments of memories and chaotic events would come rushing through. But the only recollections I retained were those that fit my state of mind. I was drowning in loneliness, thinking mostly of the prison cell in Tehran into which Shah Qajar[3] had thrown me before the eruption of the wretched war. Meanwhile, I was drained. But I went on clutching my sack, my unconsciousness, and my crushed bones – not to mention the taunting pain that came and haunted me after I regained consciousness. My aches intensified with every movement I made. That Shah inflicted all that pain on me before he travelled and forgot me.

Silence was over there, and loud turmoil was with me. I spoke Arabic with great difficulty, so that I often had to cackle in order to make a statement of sense. The languages around me sizzled like fatty butter in a frying pan: harsh, fiery languages that zinged with curry and spices. Yes, spices! Would I return to spices to find my lost dignity? Spices! And here began the feeling of "alienation".

Had Asmar, the mother of my boys, been right all along?

Here, surrounded by Indians, suddenly I was unable to speak. How long would this last? They said that, if we were lucky, it would be two weeks before we arrived in Bombay. Should I abstain from speaking for two weeks?

"Yes, you could do that, Shlomo. You surely could."

Indeed, during the long days and nights of the war ordeal, you were alone in the deserts and wastelands, and on the mountaintops. These were the frenzied days of human folly that began after all languages ceased to exist. Snow piled up so high that it buried pathways and froze people's tongues. The perils of war could be sensed everywhere, and an abstinence from everything, including from speaking, had begun. But then what?

Could any other person know who they were as much as you did? Deep down, you were filled with opposites and contradictions. Did you forget the horribly bright human blood that was splashed all over the piles of icy snow? Did you remember? Or did you forget these sorts of details from all the chapters of your life?

Reticence lies in silence, in sorrow, and in confutation. The noise and hope around you were like a pigeon's hatchling trapped inside an egg. Yet it must make its way out. You were never like an "Indian" recluse, isolating from life in a hermitage, turning away from all things.

"Seek, Shlomo! Seek! Search for those who can understand you."

In this place, words were more important than food and water. Words were a link, *the* link; they were knowledge, and knowledge was guidance. If you were guided, then you would arrive at what you sought after most, and you would attain your wish. Stand on your feet and stroll among the people. Was it a Kurd you were looking for? Impossible, I should say! Have you ever heard of a Kurd sailing the sea from Basra to Bombay?

None, except for me – the only Aramean on this boat. To expect another Kurd on this vessel would be like searching for an Indian who wore a Bedouin keffiyeh and agal!

These Arabs from the Gulf examined me with animosity and suspicion. I gazed back at them, but coyly. Had I opened my mouth, things might have become complicated – a stammering, nasalised hybrid; a Kurd, a Jew, a Persian, an Azerbaijani, a Baghdadi, all travelling to India. I was all of that – an emigrant, a wanderer, a merchant, and an adventurer. I alone was the Sindbad of the twentieth century.

Was I truly unable to converse, and all the languages that I spoke were merely a monkey's squawking and rumbling amongst all these people on board this ship?

Snippets of memory and the remnants of broken languages rushed through, like gifts carried by the wind over this ocean, or like its rising waves that, at times, resembled mountains.

"I worry about you," Asmar had said. Then she added: "I'll marry you to Aster." Aster then died, along with the two children. I was hurting when I delivered the news to Asmar.

My father said that the Aramaic of the mountains "had been the language of the Jews since the Assyrians took us captive". "And Hebrew is the language of our Torah," he added. "You won't leave school before you've learned it well."

"*Shalom aleichem, Hakham Nahum.*"

The rabbi was simply resting there. His beard and the falling snow were the same colour, so similar that you couldn't tell which was which. On that day, the Hebrew language was stabbed in the heart and pushed to its death. I didn't hear the rabbi's response, but, on one of the morning tours in Siblakh, I told Mir Ali in Kurdish: "Rest assured that I delivered the entire house's furnishings to you without leaving a single trace. And they stole nothing from your house either – not even a horseshoe!"

There had been around ten soldiers and, by taking small sips from a bottle of vodka, they found the strength to resist the pouring sleet.

"Would you like more bottles of aged wine?" I asked in their language. "All you need to do is help me move some furnishings out of this house." They all jumped to their feet to help, not really believing what I'd said.

Shah Qajar, who was surrounded by his entourage, said to me as he sipped wine from a gold cup: "Choose between fifty lashes with a soft stick, or double that with a firmer stick." He spoke in Persian, offering me one of two deaths. When I answered his bravado in Persian, he punished me with both. My determination and soul remained steadfast. However, it was my sack that saved me.

It was indeed the sack that gave me back my slaughtered pride. It protected me in Bombay, and it helped me return to you, Asmar, the mother of my boys, just as I once used to return to you in the days of old – all loving and gracious. On that day of punishment, my soul did not budge. It remained unwavering, like a sublime mountain with a bright white cap at its peak.

When I was near Tabriz, I shouted in Azerbaijani: "Come out, Jaafar and Hussein Akbar, and let's talk." With great trepidation, the two emerged from behind a boulder, each carrying a firearm. Birds of prey hovered above, but my heart remained robust, like the mountains in Azerbaijan. The birds of prey could be seen wherever the two Akbar brothers settled.

"You shouldn't do that. You owe your necks to my father," I told them. They might have nodded in acknowledgement of the unmerited favour my father had bestowed upon them.

After we had been forced to flee Siblakh, a generous Jew from Baghdad told me: "The English have jobs. You wouldn't mind working as a shit cleaner, would you?

"I wouldn't," I replied. "The son of a turd wouldn't mind working with shit."

And now I was cackling like a hen and kicking the plate away from me. In front of the waiter on the Indian ship, I cackled like a chicken. First, I put my hand on my backside, then I brought it back curved, and raised two fingers to imply that I wanted two eggs.

"I'd like two eggs," I exclaimed. Then I pointed to the bread. "And bread, I won't eat meat." I could never even think of eating food served on these plates. I was a deeply religious man, and I only ate kosher. I wouldn't think of touching a plate that had ghee and meat side by side. In my faith, we separated the plates of meat and dairy. Of course, I was saying all this to myself, for how could an Indian waiter understand?

The waiter was indeed smart. He nodded to show he understood. He smiled and rushed off to bring eggs and bread.

"I also want grilled fish on a sheet of paper or wrapped in bread and that mango pickle concoction called amba," I asked when he returned.

I thought that I suffered from vision and hearing impairment, and that I was only able to converse in monkey signs and chicken cackling. I then walked into a corner filthier than filth itself. And with my wary, nomadic look, I triggered peoples' fears and aroused their deep-seated revulsion. I ate and then wiped my mouth with my sleeves before reciting the long prayer of the "blessing of food". My juicy lips quivered as the repressed whispering began. Folks whizzed around me swiftly, exchanging prying looks.

"Strange, this man is. Truly bizarre!"

Of course, I did not understand what they said, but I read it on their faces, which betrayed a curious shock. I swear they were more likely asking, "Who is this man, and what is he mumbling?" They were gazing at my donkey pannier basket in surprise, and, in the morning, their eyes followed my hand as it dipped in to retrieve another yet smaller basket. I opened the latter wide to spread out a triangle-shaped cloth, and, like a shawl, cloaked myself in it. I then rolled up my left sleeve and wrapped the ends of that black cloth around my arm. At this point, I could no longer see anyone. I had plunged deep into my prayer and vanished into the essence of a higher power through supplication.

"O Elohim! You have bestowed upon me your care in the most critical moments and swathed me in your compassion in the most difficult times. Direct my steps and help me overcome and keep Asmar and the boys safe."

When I finished, peoples' eyes were a hunter's net, in which I was caught. I was pulled back again to the shores of alienation on this foul-smelling wooden boat, which was thoroughly weather-beaten and damp. The more they whispered, the more I felt the net tightening around me. My spirit had to hide this "unseen" that transpired in front of me. An undetermined existence was theirs. As for me, the pressing question I had to ask was: "Was Asmar, the mother of my boys, truly right?"

Yehuda Bahr

Wait. That tanned, fat man who hid his genitals with the Indian wrap was heading towards me. His body was bare to his navel. It was still a bit chilly and just thinking about baring one's body made me feel cold. Of everyone, this man showed the most curiosity about me. His looks had haunted me ever since I'd turned into this corner three days ago. I hadn't left my spot since, except when it was absolutely necessary. He approached me, squatted at my side, and then said: "*Shalom aleichem.*"

Hurrah! With certain features in our faces – and in our genitals – we could recognize one another in this life and in the next.

"Are you from Baghdad?" the man asked.
"In a sense. An Iranian Kurd flung into Baghdad by compelling circumstances years ago." I replied.
We both nasalised the Arabic Baghdadi dialect we spoke. I knew where my nasal twang came from. What about his?
"Decades ago, my family left Baghdad for Bombay, where I was born and where I have been living since," he started. "But no matter how far from Baghdad we lived, we were still Baghdadis. My extended family is in Iraq," he added proudly.
"Were you visiting?" I asked curiously.
"A visitor and pilgrim," came his answer. "I made the pilgrimage to Prophet Haskell, Ezra El Soufir, Priest Yehoshua, and Prophet Yona." He paused a bit before adding: "Yes, we live there, but our hearts are forever in Iraq."
Despite the two different accents, we connected. The guts of alienation hurled me into the arms of this man, Yehuda Bahr.
"My family named itself after this very sea.[4] My grandfather crossed this sea for the first time on his way to India," he explained.
Yehuda Bahr was relaxed, gentle, and calm! Nothing like this turbulent sea – its infinite breadth made me feel as if I were a grain of sand. I felt I was diminished compared to the size of this mysterious sea. Dread crept over me from an ambiguous source as I watched the waves rising high, like the mountains of Iran and Kurdistan. Yehuda, meanwhile, was laughing at my ignorance of seas.
"You chose the right time. It's early spring, which is when the sea is relatively calm." He then asked: "Haven't you heard of the days of "seizures" in the summer?"
He was talking about the days when the sea rose in a grand revolution at these edges of the world. Was it calm now? Perhaps! We used to think that the day when ten women and children had been slaughtered in Siblakh as not too disastrous. Azrael, that Angel of Death, had, on such days, recruited all his aides to reap people's spir-

its during that vile war in Siblakh, plucking out lives simply and without accountability!

But relativity shone through to light up the true essence of matters and nature's phenomena. Killing and destroying remained the truest forms of realities – phenomena unchanged in the night and the day, in the cold and the heat, and in the fall and the spring.

"Calm," he called the sea!

We made a connection and through it my perceptions expanded. I learned many things when I became – and remained – as close as a heartbeat to Yehuda Bahr. I suddenly became a very large child clasping his "father's" tail, following him wherever he went. Like a child, I went with him even to the toilets. I remained with him, and with me were Asmar and the boys, as well as my donkey pannier, my sack, and my great hope.

Yehuda helped me with heaps of information, but he didn't encourage me to attach myself to hope. I hid the story of my sack from him, and I restrained my wild dreams when I recounted the secret of my ride across the sea to Bombay. I was merely a nomad seeking work throughout God's vast world. That was all!

In truth, it was good to talk to him about the past, rather than about the future, which is obscured from all but God. Here, an adventurer was speaking to a "poor" man about things that made the hair on his naked chest and abdomen stand on end. I talked with him endlessly, and painstakingly tallied up what was for me in his responses.[5] I fired my questions at the right moment, and, with my long experience, worded them precisely. In this way, I did not direct him to the doors of scepticism. And I did not embarrass him when it came to things about which he was likely ignorant. This man lived with his wife and six children in one room inside a shared house where no sunlight entered, and where the hallway was flooded year-round with filthy water!

Yehuda described "Nekbara", the Indian shelter where the poor Iraqi Jewish migrants lived in Bombay. The shelter undoubtedly seemed like our quarter and the Kurdish immigrants' neighbourhood in Baghdad, except that its vile nastiness might have made it much worse.

Two days after we made a "connection", Yehuda Bahr said: "I wish I were able to welcome you in my home! But . . ."

I knew everything that he might have strung along after that "but", and after the enormity of information he shared, another "but" came through bearing a brighter tone.

"But what about those "Sassoons", the offspring of Daoud Sassoon, the well-known philanthropist?" he suggested enthusiastically. "Whoever turned to them would not be disappointed, and they would never go hungry or be homeless again," he said.

That was how I should take care of my expenses in Bombay, I immediately thought. In the past, it was I who fed and sheltered visitors. But this was a must, and necessity knows no laws. I had now secured my food and would not be sleeping on the side of the road with a thousand homeless men and beggars. I could have all that without harming my sack. I should not lose sight of the goal, the reason why I sailed the sea. This sack was predestined to restore my glory, and to reach the dream. I must do that, by your eyes, Asmar!

There I was, making a friend and a guide while I was still at sea. I should make more as soon as the ship was moored at the Sassoon Dock . . .

No, no! The ghosts of the past had been resurrected unexpectedly, and its devils danced over the fragments of slain angels. The surprises that were forming every second were a deterrent. What would the next minute be like? A surprise? Damned be that past and its memories. A surprise or a deterrent? Don't pre-empt events, Shlomo.

What would happen after my first steps on the Sassoon Dock?

I placed my trust in He who had never disappointed me in the most critical moments of my life: My Lord, my refuge, and the giver of blessings.

At Sassoon Dock!

Shlomo and I glimpsed the piers of Sassoon Dock. But we saw that port through the prism of a forty-year difference. At the time, I had just returned from Bombay a month before, it was in 1964. We met in Tehran where Shlomo told me about Sassoon Dock. That was on a Saturday evening in my room, which was cosy with rugs, curtains, and the bluish flames of an Aladdin kerosene heater. I was shaking with cold when, on a Saturday night, Shlomo was hogging the heater between his legs and holding out his palms over its flames. Outside, creamy and frosty snowflakes were falling, and it was a Saturday evening, Um Aziza and her daughter were outside. They were bathing, washing clothes, and doing their hair. He was still hogging the heater and wishing death on me because I inhaled the smoke that puffed out from the heater. Saturday night in the life of the Sassoon Dock!

Sassoon Dock was the pier of a port that had been abandoned a month ago. It was at the farthest end of the Byculla region of Bombay. Rusted metal and black, brittle, worn wood panels! Nothing but filthiness, nastiness, and rats! An effaced remnant! Even the water at the port had become stagnant, algae-choked, and lifeless. Death permeated everything that had once made that concrete pier teem with life.

Forty years ago, Shlomo came down from the ship into the crowded, noisy concrete port. His sack was in the donkey pannier, his body and soul that he kept close to his heart. And his heart began to throb in panic.

Was it in the middle of this sea of white clothes and black heads that Shlomo would find his prize? Amongst this unintelligible, feverish noise? In this horror? This was the Day of Judgement in the flesh! There was neither beginning nor end to the deluge of people, and a person would shrink in size, fade, and then melt into this throng and completely vanish.

Where did Yehuda Bahr go to? The "Father" to hold Shlomo's hand, for he had wandered off. Shlomo never felt such fear before this, not even in the most precarious moments in Siblakh. This was a terrifying crowd. He lost his way in the suffocating sea of people. Take him back to the other sea. "The other sea?"

Wait, which of the two seas was the original? And why had Yehuda Bahr become like a father to him when he himself used to be the father of the frightened, the distressed, and all those whose hearts were troubled with fear?

Now he was looking for warmth like the warmth emanating from the dung in the stable at his splendid home in Siblakh. The dung back then saved his frozen feet when he was neither short of expertise nor of self-confidence. But here at Sassoon Dock, in the presence of his absent words and his deafened ears, this sea lifted its head up high and boastful. Fear occupied the feelings of strangers in this sea of people, who sauntered unhurriedly in an awe-striking funerary manner. No one would rescue Shlomo from this sea, save Yehuda Bahr, he was the only straw to rescue him from drowning.

"Yehuda Bahr! Yehuda!" Shlomo shouted as loud as he could.

But his voice was swallowed up into the guts of the Great Noise that fed on the torrents of voices coming in from all directions. Currents of voices combined tens of dialects and languages – mutterings in Hindi, Urdu, Amharic, English, and so on.

"Shlomo! Shlomo!" he suddenly heard.

Shlomo's ears spared him from going astray. He had roamed the mountains of Kurdistan, the deserts of Russia, and the wilderness of Azerbaijan, and he learned how to determine the direction of sounds. He infiltrated this compact human wall while he leaned over the donkey pannier as people pressed on his chest. He breathed painfully and fitfully, but saved his soul from slipping. His spirit now returned to his body as he broke through the waves of people, slowly, but with one foot in safety and the other searching for his lost identity.

There he was – Yehuda Bahr – standing at the curry vending cart on the other side of the street. He was waving and inviting Shlomo to join him. Idol-worshipping Bombay was no longer a strange place for a believer like al-Kurdi. There, he returned and found God. Here in the land of idols, he found Yehuda Bahr – Yehuda the Saviour, and the resurrected hand of God.

Baghdad in late 1951

My heart was like winter in Baghdad: cold, bleak, forlorn, and barren. Flashes of gleaming hope occasionally visited me, but they were like the screeching carts selling beetroot on the asphalt streets that were washed by rain in the middle of the night.

They "skimmed off the finest of the milk" and threw the frothy scum out of the butter pouch. Most of Baghdad's Jews had left, even Meriam and Sayyoon. With their husbands and children, they packed only the important of their life's possessions. And they left me with the cursed wife, Um Aziza, and her daughter. They chose another fate in Israel.

The obvious features of my storeroom in the caravanserai did not change, but the customers became different. Credit-based businesses with our cousins, Baghdad's merchants, increased. The cash flow in the caravanserai stagnated, and frustration nested in my soul. Being in the same house with Um Aziza was hell. Don't ask me how this misfortune happened. But know that only smart men stumble. I was already in deep trouble and marrying Um Aziza was a lifelong open wound.

Um Aziza was foul-mouthed, wily, and malevolent. I stuffed her with blessings and was myself bloated with her curses. If I put my hand on her back in kindness, she would shove my hand right up my backside. She always raised her hands in my face in prayer, wishing I would die and disappear. I blamed myself, feeling I was just receiving what I had coming to me. How could I allow another woman in my house after Asmar? Even after her death, Asmar remained righteous and faithful. She had never blamed me. Once, I saw her crying in a dream. She was sad because I had to put up with Um Aziza.

"I'd give my life to you," Asmar said. "I wish you'd asked for my help in a dream so I could have pointed out a good wife for you after my departure."

When I woke, I prayed for Asmar. Repeatedly, I said aloud to myself and with all my senses: "What has been done cannot be undone."

I then fled to the Haydar-Khana coffeeshop. Oh, how I miss the past! I used to drown myself in work in the caravanserai! I lingered in the office too late at night, simply forgetting myself and burying myself in the piles of ever-renewing work.

After they left, work decreased, and the money shifted to the clients' pockets. Debts and debts only! The names of those who bought on credit weighed down my books. Thousands and thousands of dinars. In the coffeeshop, I smoked hookah and listened to its gurgling. I gazed at the wide-open parrot cages that dangled from the coffeeshop ceiling. The parrots emerged from their cages to climb up and down the "chains". Long, thick, metal chains that connected the cages to the ceiling. I looked closely at what was happening and tried to discover some wisdom or meaning in it.

Wisdom changed each time, I should say, for I tried everything in my life and exhausted all its wisdoms.

No – but this was one fatal mistake because, notwithstanding all the wisdom that was saved up in your head, you were still ignorant no matter how long you'd lived. It was like filling a ripped pouch with water: life surprised you at every turn.

I learned from my life's miseries that fate had thrown mankind on a landmine, and he had to feel what was under his feet before he could take any step forward. The next step might surprise him with a misfortune. And since no one knew what the next step might hold, he must remain there in his spot or move forward constantly, mindless of the risks. An equation of contradictory ends! But my faith in the old saying "what befalls you was only your own share" settled the paradox between the ends.

The fact is that you cannot know your future, and life is like a magician's hat from which something unexpected shoots out every minute to surprise you. This fact remains unchanged – regardless of wisdom, theory, experience, and your preferred philosophy of life.

On a bed-like seat in the coffeeshop, I stretched out my legs while I still clutched the hose of the hookah. I blew out the smoke of frustration and the divine. Fragmented memories of several colours disturbed me in moments of fantasy! That was the rundown of human life, moments of fantasy. The latter you recalled nostalgically and prayed they would not end until Death rolled you down. Only then would other people pray for you while you would've joined your God, leaving your mortal body behind along with these bygone fantasies.

The ramshackle nature of all these things was flickering through my head on that ominous day in the Haydar-Khana. I was reliving the past and was ignorant of the next booby trap. I felt nostalgic, tortured, and hurt. I felt I was sensing my way through the most pitch-black of nights, which could not even compare to the peak of the war in Siblakh.

I suspected that whatever was coming would be worse than the Farhud, the violent dispossession of the Jews of Baghdad in 1941, which happened when I was hanging out with a bunch of my friends at Rabbi Michael's house.

While I was thinking all of this, I prayed for Asmar, who had been lost in the Farhud. I felt sorry for everything that had been taken during the Farhud. I then cursed Um Aziza before cursing the sham of life. I tried to see the bottom line of my bountiful experiences, but I realized straight away that they were simply dust in the wind.

During all these mental battles, and in a half-asleep state, I replied to a greeting from what at first seemed to be the apparition of a man. His appearance and identity were not immediately evident to me. Quickly, I shook off my thoughts and my lunacy onto the shore of the past and future. He was a policeman, and he was calling my name – the new surprise coming out of the depths of life's goddamn magician's hat.

> Selected from Samir Naqqash's novel
> *Shlomo al-Kurdi wa-ana wa-l-Zaman*
> (Shlomo the Kurd, Myself, and Time),
> Manshurat al-Jamal, 2003, Pbk, 360 pages

Translator's notes:
1 A traditional draw-string sack to keep money in, made of fabric, whose owner might knot it a hundred times to make sure that it wouldn't be easy to steal from. Used by older generations of Iraqis.
2 Siblakh is a Kurdish town located on the Iran-Iraq border. It was under the administration of the Shah of Iran and was exploited as a battlefield between Russia and Turkey. The town was attacked several times during the war and its people were killed, displaced, or forced to leave.
3 Ahmad Shah Qajar ruled Iran as the last member of the Qajar dynasty from 1898 to 1930.
4 *"bahr"* is Arabic for "sea".
5 Naqqash uses an elaborate, metaphorical expression that is common in spoken Iraqi Arabic. The expression has several versions but the common one is something like *ihki bil qintar wa ihid bil mitqal*, which roughly translates as "speak through a quintal but measure what you take with a gold scale". A quintal is equal to 100 kilograms in most metric systems, while the mithqal is the unit of measurement for gold.
6 Another popular adage in Iraq: *waqa'a al fas bil ras*, or "the axe had already fallen on my head." The likely meaning is that "it is already too late" or "too late for second-guessing."
7 Karrada is a district in the southern tip of the peninsula of Baghdad where upper-class Iraqis from different religious faiths and cultural backgrounds live.

Read more from
Samir Naqqash's book
Shlomo the Kurd... online at
www.banipal.co.uk/selections/

The Quest for Home, the Quest for Identity:

The Jewish-Muslim Prospect in Eli Amir

HADAS SHABAT NADIR

The theme of 'home' and one's quest for it stands at the very heart of Eli Amir's oeuvre. Born in 1937 in Baghdad, Iraq, Amir, who moved to Israel at the age of 13 chronicles in his novels the search for a sense of belonging and a home that would accommodate his complex, multifaceted identity: someone who is part of Arab-Baghdadi culture on the one hand, but who is also seeking to carve out a place for himself in the hegemonic, Israeli sphere. In his novels, *Tarnegol Kaparot* (Scapegoat) (1983), and *Na'ar Ha'ofanayim* (The Bicycle Boy) (2019), Amir describes the immigrant's gruelling experience of integration and assimilation in Israel in the face of the local establishment, and his sense of alienation and foreignness. At the same time, Amir never relinquishes his Arab identity. In his novel, *Mafriach Ha'yonim* (1992, *The Dove Flyer*)[1] that was later made into a film (2013), Amir returns to Baghdad, its streets, and the Arabic language. It appears that critics have taken to describing the theme of one's quest for home in Amir's body of work as a chronological narrative of migration, settling down, and belonging. In this essay, I set out to explore the 'quest for home' theme as a mode of looking back; a regression to a past that has gone, never to return. It seems as if any sense of home and belonging was consigned to Jewish-Arab-Muslim life back in Baghdad – a time capsule of sorts that can never be revisited.

The question of home and the Jewish community's place in Iraq is at the very centre of Amir's novel, *The Dove Flyer*. In this book, Amir

Eli Amir

traces the life of Baghdad's Jewish community between 1949 and 1950 (in the immediate aftermath of the founding of the State of Israel) and on the cusp of Iraqi Jews' mass immigration to Israel. The novel captures, with poignance and sensitivity, the vast network of tensions, anxieties, and questions that arose with regards to the ongoing existence of Baghdad's Jewish community specifically, and to Iraq's as a whole: between the Zionist movement that was prominent at the time in Iraq, the rise of communism, and the desire to further sustain Jewish Iraqi existence and presence in Baghdad. This constellation of tensions proliferates after the events of the Farhud (the 1941 pogrom against Iraqi Jews).

In his novel, Amir recounts Iraqi Jews' loss of their sense of safety and security in those fateful years, and their quest for a place to call home: whether that be Iraq or Israel. The hitherto safe and protected Jewish neighbourhood is transformed into a dark, alien crime scene when the local community finds itself hounded by two restless figures whose fate is neither understood nor known, and who will not allow normal life to resume. One is Shafiq 'Addas, a wealthy Jewish businessman who was falsely accused of collaborating with the Zionists and is subsequently hanged in the town square – an innocent man. The other is Hezquel, leader of the Zionist movement, who is locked up and tortured in an Iraqi prison, and whose fate remains

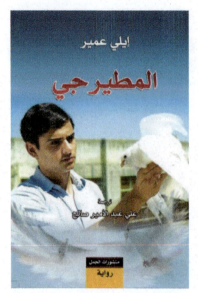 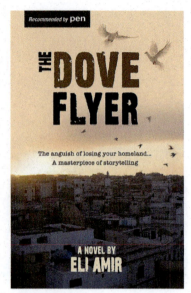

The Arabic and English covers of al-Mtayyrji *and* The Dove Flyer

unknown. These two figures turn the Jewish sphere into a violated, vulnerable, alien, and menacing space. 'Addas's body creates a secret-centric sphere where the corpse has no voice, and where there is no opportunity to present a logical explanation for what has happened. Justice cannot be served by laying the body to rest, which would restore the peace that had been disturbed. The body swinging on the noose in the town square before frenzied crowds not only rocks the whole community, demanding justice for itself, it turns the whole city into a would-be crime scene, a monstrous sphere that cannot be contained within the inner domain of the tragedy and is instead frequently projected outwards – into the streets, the alleyways, the labyrinths, and the city's entertainment and leisure centres. Therefore, for instance, a perfectly casual night out at the cinema for two teenagers almost instantly turns into a public lynching: "*and from somewhere in the theatre, through all the screaming, a faint, dream-like shriek rose: 'Jew, dog!'*"[2] *[. . .] and like a nightmare made manifest, the blows came down on us.*"[3] The city is becoming a thousand-limbed monstrous beast.

In the face of the threat to the local Jewish population, the Zionist movement continues to brew beneath the surface, with the imprisoned Hezquel at its helm. It appears as though there is constant tension between Hezquel's prison and the Jewish neighbourhood, as created by the Zionist movement. It is a metaphorical system that enables direct correlation between the prison and the Jewish neighbourhood: in the aftermath of the pogrom and the Shafiq 'Addas affair, the movement turns the Jewish sphere into a universe of small, compartmentalised spaces; a cluster of closed-off, secret spaces where caches of weapons are hidden, where target practice sessions take place, and where the movement's leadership and its men meet. An arms cache is hidden under Abu Salah's shop where meetings and training are held. It is a system abundant with layers upon layers of alternative Jewish existence that exist alongside the communist leadership's hiding places, as it, too, has been banned in Baghdad. It is a whole bustling world, in and of itself, that thrives under the veil of ordinary life whilst at the same time striving to maintain the current order of things as a way of keeping up appearances, thereby creating a ruse that hides and obscures what is actually happening under the surface. The function of Hezquel, imprisoned in the Iraqi jail, and his tortured soul is to create a panic-stricken sphere, pining for disaster.

Meanwhile, alongside the Zionist movement and the Iraqi government's coordinated system, beneath the surface another, almost imaginary, narrative of potential Jewish-Muslim coexistence appears, that weaves continuously throughout the entire novel. Already at the start of the novel, and in tandem with Hezquel's incarceration, the protagonist recalls his own life in the Muslim neighbourhood. His recollections paint a clear picture of Jewish-Muslim coexistence:

Back in the days when Jews and Muslims lived together as good neighbours. [. . .]When papa came home from work, she [mama] would bathe me in the tub, dress me in a dishdasha, a gown as white as Ismail's, and get me ready for candle-lighting [. . .] sometimes Ismail's would stay at ours for Sabbath, sitting with us and listening to papa making kiddush, and all those chants and hymns in a strange language, to the sound of the Iraqis' maqamas and Abdel Wahab's tunes, wearing a white skullcap on his head [. . .] I would wake up to the sound of the Muezzin's prayer which was when I learnt that there were in fact two Allahs, our Allah and their Allah. And yet, papa loves hearing the sound of the Muezzin's prayer, at the end of which he says in a deeper voice, just like a Muslim: 'Allah speaks the truth, the gospel of Allah the Great.' Suddenly, something came to pass and I didn't know what.[4]

The home with the open rooftop symbolises the potential mending of Jewish-Muslim relations and their melding into one living fabric.

ELI AMIR

The majority of scholars have focused on Jewish-Arab identity; however it appears that part of a Jewish-Arab existence also holds the prospect of a Jewish-Muslim category, where a layer of Muslim existence is retranslated into Jewish customs and vice versa. Amir portrays an alternative life system where the difference between the secular and the holy is delineated by both Jewish and Muslim practices. It is a way of differentiating between the categorical divisions forced upon man, and a form of religious existence that holds the potential of bridging these divides: for instance, the mother dresses Kaabi in a dishdasha[5] ahead of Sabbath Eve whilst the lighting of the candles symbolises the transition from secular to scared. At the same time, Ismail, the neighbours' boy, is there on the Sabbath listening to Jewish chants, hymns, and melodies performed to the tune of Abdel Wahab's music. The sphere of Muslim existence is interpreted into a Jewish-Muslim religious mode of existence. Meanwhile, Kaabi's father, too, enjoys listening to the Muezzin and is described as praying just like a Muslim at the end of the prayer. The open rooftop looking up at the heavens signifies not only the actual Jewish-Muslim coexistence but also the imagined, fantastical one, as if it were an opportunity to mend and put the world to rights. That said, the open rooftop equally also stands for the Jewish-Muslim prospect being a strictly Edenic one that cannot be realised; the flaming sword at Heaven's gate also exists on an earthly, corporeal plane: World War II has broken out and anti-Jewish voices soon infiltrate the area, forcing the family to flee their home to the Jewish neighbourhood. Khairia, the Muslim mother looking after the family's home during the pogrom, stands out as a final flicker of the memory of an erstwhile coexistence no longer tenable.

Allegedly, the exodus of Iraqi Jews marks a realisation of the Zionist narrative: the journey from exile to salvation at last completed. However, soon enough it becomes painstakingly evident that Jewish existence in Israel has far from lived up to the coveted salvation experience one has longed for. The father's sense of oppression at the hands of the Iraqi regime is replaced by the exact same feeling, only this time at the hands of the Zionist-Ashkenazi establishment.

Through the Zionist-hegemonic from-exile-to-salvation narrative, one discovers another underground narrative that ties siblings Hezquel and Abu Kaabi umbilically to each other whilst reversing the Zionist tie, i.e. from Israel to Iraq, from exile to salvation. Like his incarcerated brother back in Baghdad, Abu Kaabi is likened to a mad prisoner, hovering between life and death in Israel. The demise of his dream of growing rice crops sends him over the edge and he attempts to take his own life. His suicide attempt very much echoes the threat of hanging that his imprisoned brother faces back in Baghdad. The two siblings are suspended between life and death, between dream and insubstantiality, between salvation and exile. The system of coordinates between the brothers not only fails to realise the exile-to-salvation vision, it goes so far as to amplify the desire to return to Baghdad, echoing the only prospect for salvation and mending[6]: Jewish-Muslim coexistence that had been the norm until World War II.

Whilst in *The Dove Flyer*, the protagonist realises that a sense of home, identity, and security only exist in his Baghdadi past, in the place where he was able to successfully merge the Jewish-Muslim patchwork of existence into a cohesive whole, in *The Bicycle Boy* (2019), Amir brings readers the story of Nuri, who had emigrated from Baghdad to Israel with his family, and whose journey of assimilation and integration the novel traces. Amir describes Nuri's struggles to integrate in his adoptive country in the face of the Israeli establishment and the kibbutzim – neither of which will accept him. Nuri becomes 'the bike boy' – a postal courier for the Prime Minister, cycling around delivering important post. However, in the course of his assimilation, time and again Nuri recalls life in his native Baghdad and is overcome with longing for it.

Translated from the Hebrew by Eran Edry

Notes:

[1] *The Dover Flyer* was published in English by Halban Publishers in 2010, translated from the Hebrew by Hillel Halkin. An Arabic translation, *al-Mtayyrji*, was published by Manshurat Al-Jamal, Beirut-Baghdad, in July 2018.

[2] 'Yahudi, Kalb!' in the Hebrew of *The Dove Flyer* has the Arabic for 'Jew, dog!'

[3] Ibid, 44.

[4] Ibid, 93-95.

[5] A dishdasha is a traditional long gown for boys and men in the Middle East, also called a galabiya or jellabiya.

[6] Known as 'Tikkun' in Judaism

ELI AMIR

The Bicycle Boy

AN EXCERPT FROM THE NOVEL

TRANSLATED FROM THE HEBREW BY ERAN EDRY

Even after Abu al-Wazir had been to see his son on several occasions and had got himself better acquainted with the relaxed pace and style of kibbutz life, he once again turned up in a smart suit, a tie, a grey felt hat with a black hat band, a pair of two-tone brogues, and a flower on his lapel. Abu al-Wazir was reluctant to embrace the local khaki fashion; holding on to his suited pioneer chic and turning up at the kibbutz looking the part of an Old World patriarch who had just been ejected into the beating heart of this brave new world. He pulled a pocket watch with a gold fob attached to it out of his waistcoat pocket, popped the cover open, glanced at the dials, stuffed it back in his pocket, and resumed his tour of the great kibbutz outdoors, as if he were a local landlord paying a visit to one of his mansions.

Nuri felt quite embarrassed by these visits. He knew full well what the other kibbutz members and their children thought of his father and his dress sense. At times, he would take pride in him, though he mostly felt shame. And as if his outfit weren't bad enough, his father would often hum those Arab songs that made up the soundtrack of his soul, and would speak to his son in Arabic – in this place – where Hebrew is effectively canonised, and where everyone is expected to check their native tongue and culture at the gates and adopt this new Israeli way of life. There was the patriarch, out and about in the kibbutz, exploring the area; his fingers rolling some misbaha beads behind his back as if he were there on behalf of some Baghdadi Rothschild-esque baron, or the actual baron himself who, somehow, had wandered off and ended up somewhere unbecoming of his stature.

Indeed, Nuri dreaded his every visit. Every day, he would be put to the test and failing was not an option. He could not disappoint and had to prove himself with every challenge thrown at him. He shared general tales of kibbutz life with his father and would volunteer just a little bit more information when discussing his own day-to-day life, his studies, and the local social and culture scene. Today, too, he was telling his father how, even after three years of living in the kibbutz, he was still learning to wrap his head around this new world he has discovered, and of all his efforts to find out more and more about it, getting to know the people who had left their colder climates to move to this valley which, in the summer, becomes a proverbial furnace. When his father replied, he spoke in broken, half sentences and odd, random words that would not coalesce into a coherent statement. It seemed as though he were trying to articulate some things that had been weighing heavy on him. Nuri, too, was reluctant to let his guard down and share what was in his heart, keeping his doubts and dreams close to his chest.

On every visit, his father made a point of going up the hill where the abandoned Arab village of Abu Shusha stood, as if the place were Al Kifl – his home village on the banks of the Euphrates. It was there that the prophet Ezekiel is said to have been buried, and numerous times every year they would go and stay with his grandfather's brother – a strict and austere old man who would give them cucumbers, hard feta cheese, and the most incredibly rich and delicious barley pita bread. His father made a life for himself there until he decided it was time to relocate his family to Baghdad so that his sons and daughters may have a chance at an education. Now, at Abu Shusha, he wandered about the derelict homes and abandoned plots of land whilst the prickly pear hedgerows and groves continued to blossom and bear all kinds of fruit of all scents and flavours. He could almost imagine catching a fleeting glimpse of Al Kifl's Shiite farmers who would also make their bread from the soil, like the people of Abu Shusha; how they, too, would listen to the Muezzin's calls to prayer and would also get down on their knees five times a day and pray. He would recall the colourful cockerels that used to wander around; how he would hear the sound of their clucking, and the jingle jangling of the goats' bells, and the donkeys' braying as he took in the scent of laffa[1] bread baking in the heaving ovens.

Nuri's father continued exploring the ruins on the deserted hill. The grapevine canopies seemed on the verge of collapse; the waterholes abandoned; and the heart couldn't help but ache for a place orphaned of its people. He looked over the valley that had been conquered and tamed, sown and reaped by Muscovite Jews who had planned and plotted what they would plant and grow in every last plot; where and when they would interfere with nature, creating hybrid fruit and vegetables and making their shape and taste infinitely superior. Except Abu Shusha wasn't enough for his father, and he also asked to see Ghubayya al-Fawqa and Gubhayya al-Tahta – the other two villages by the kibbutz that had also been abandoned. There, too, he stood in his patriarchal garb, looking out to the horizon, as he enquired about the villagers who had lived there before the war. Nuri, on his part, told him everything he'd heard and learnt from the other kibbutz members. Every so often, his father would grab a fistful of earth from the land where the deserted village stood, which he then rolled in the palm of his hand, just as he would his misbaha beads that praised and lauded the great Allah's name with each and every one of its 99 beads.

Nuri watched his father as he picked up the soil, stroking him with his eyes. He grabbed a fistful of soil himself, so as to show his father the newfound bond he had formed with the land. His father then seemed overcome with a sense of compassion for his son and for himself – realising how difficult, if not altogether cruel it would be to tear Nuri away from his life here and to take him back to what, for him was 'home', and for Nuri the abyss.

The apparent thought of it made Nuri's shoulders slump. His father, standing behind him, took hold of him and began massaging his shoulders, straightening Nuri's posture, and not even realising that he himself – his son's progenitor – was the heavy load on his shoulders, weighing them down. Nuri, who was absolutely dreading his father's visit this time, was trying to mask his embarrassment over his father's mannerisms and kept expecting him to tell him the reason for this latest visit. He didn't like it when the kibbutz children mocked his father's appearance, and it was doubly painful watching his father failing to acclimatise to the rules of the new place and, evidently, showing reluctance to acknowledge them. He was careful not to say anything and was worried his father would need only to take one look at him for the expression on his face and his hand gestures to then betray it all, anyway. For that reason, he donned a severe, blank expression and waited until nightfall when he could finally release his shame and sorrow-tinged tears into his pillow. It wasn't hard for him to guess what his father had to say to him and why he found it so difficult to articulate it: surely, he had to have realised there was nothing he wanted more than to stay here.

[1] Iraqi style oven-baked wraps

IRAQI JEWISH WRITERS

NAEL EL-TOUKHY

Complete but Unfinished
— on translating *Chahla and Hezquel* from Hebrew to Arabic

TRANSLATED FROM THE ARABIC BY JONATHAN WRIGHT

On the bus from my home in Heliopolis, going downtown to meet Malak, my girlfriend at the time and later my wife, I was reading *Chahla ve-Hezquel* (Rachel and Ezekiel) by the Israeli writer Almog Behar. Suddenly I took the decision to translate it into Arabic.

I had recently posted on my Facebook page my translation of a passage from the novel that says that Gamal Abdel Nasser's dream of Arab unity came true among the Arab Jews in Israel. Drawing on the shared experience of Jews from Iraq, Yemen, Egypt, Syria and North Africa, the narrator, an enthusiastic activist for Mizrahi identity, comes to this startling conclusion: "We, the oriental Jews, are the real Nasserists."

I had translated this passage as soon as I read it the first time, maybe even while I was reading it. I imagined that, because of its oddness, it would interest Arab readers, and especially Egyptians. This was an extremely fresh and unusual point of view for us as Egyptians and Arabs, and even, I expect, for Israeli Jews who read the novel.

Now, as the bus drove through Abbasia Square towards downtown and my girlfriend, I came to a chapter that explains the phonetic differences between Ashkenazi Hebrew and old Hebrew, which is close to Arabic. The passage revived my old passion for the letters in the scripts of the two languages I know best and how they are pronounced – a passion that dates back to the time when I began to study Hebrew twenty years ago and that planted the seed for my fascination with linguistics in general.

In that chapter, Hakham Ovadia, a Jew of Iraqi origin, explains how words are mispronounced in modern Hebrew compared with the original Hebrew. The passage poses quite a challenge for translators: how to explain all these subtle differences to people who don't know Hebrew in the first place. But it was precisely that challenge that I was inspired to accept.

I had mixed feelings about the passage, but in the end the call was so powerful that blocking my ears would not have saved me. I knew with certainty that whatever excuses I might come up with, I would end up translating it anyway.

No one in the cultural elite, which is basically Nasserist in Egypt, objects to translations from Hebrew to Arabic. Although this elite is committed to the slogan "No to Normalisation", it has rarely described translation from Hebrew as a form of normalisation. Cooperation with Israeli publishers might be described as normalisation, but the act of translation in itself would not be, though the elite might view such a translation as an unnecessary act of stupidity. The downside is that anyone who translates from Hebrew into Arabic faces an endless flood of polemics over what normalisation means, without of course anyone taking the trouble to discuss the work itself. So in the end the work gets buried under the dust of debates that we have rehashed many times over, and we do not give ourselves a chance to be surprised by new ideas.

But the call came to me on the bus and it was pointless to resist. I met Malak at the Tak'iba Cafe downtown and told her I was going to translate the book. I didn't say, "I'm thinking of translating it." I said, "I'm going to translate it."

I didn't find the translation easy in the least. The many Talmudic references in the book complicated my task, since in the previous few years I had concentrated on modern Hebrew literature and hadn't devoted the same attention to Jewish religious writings. The exchanges between me and Almog and the texts that went back and forth between us over two years show that I asked him about one hundred and fifty questions. Sometimes I wonder how he found the time and patience to answer them all.

* * *

Egyptian readers have various expectations from Israeli literature. Some of them want biographies of the founding fathers of the Zionist movement. Some of them want spy novels, and some want science fiction. Others want sex, lots of sex. But *Rachel and Ezekiel* doesn't provide any of this. It just tells the story of a poor, confused man with his wife in Jerusalem, waiting for Passover and the birth of their first child.

Many Arab readers of the novel wondered about the plot, which is in general a very simple plot, if we can call it a plot at all. But the essence of the novel lies in the characters, who are characters that literature rarely deals with, let alone examines in depth.

My decision to translate the novel arose from a passionate interest in the similarities and differences between the two cultures and languages, but I ended up somewhere else entirely. Ezekiel himself, the devout hero of the novel, is of Iraqi origin, lives in Jerusalem with his wife and is trying to write poetry.

In his failure and his haplessness despite his intelligence, Ezekiel opened a window through which I could understand many of the people around me in Cairo – people called salafists, Islamist groups linked to each other by their enthusiasm for Islam and their desire to follow the example of the Prophet Muhammad. They come across as slightly foolish: it's hard for me to write the word salafist without adding "sheep", a word often associated with it. We see them as mindless flocks of sheep that proliferated after the Egyptian uprising of 2011.

Unlike the Muslim Brotherhood, these people don't have any organisation that holds them together. They don't have a programme, a strategy or an aspiration other than something vague called "Islam". They are just individuals who have resorted to religion because they wanted to give their lives meaning – poor, feckless people, this is what helped me to understand Ezekiel, with his fear, his silence and his uncertainty, which is so candid, about matters that someone from outside his world might consider to be extremely esoteric.

* * *

Reading a draft of the translation, Malak said: "I like Ezekiel, but he's very annoying. He keeps going to see Hakham Ovadia to ask him about questions of religious law that are of no interest to anyone but the two of them. This might irritate readers, and they might sometimes want to give Ezekiel a whack to free him from the fantasies in his head."

But Ezekiel would no longer be Ezekiel without these fantasies, without his ingenuous and very honest and sweet faith, which he shares with the rabbi closest to his heart, Hakham Ovadia, who is another gem I chanced upon in the novel.

Throughout the novel Hakham* Ovadia is preparing for a big sermon he is going to give on the need to unite all the pronunciations of modern Hebrew in one standard form. Like an artist preparing his immortal work, he keeps tweaking his sermon. But when the day comes, almost no one attends. The people in the audience have to go out into the street to persuade other people into the synagogue to make up a quorum for prayers and the sermon.

After that the rabbi lies in bed, hallucinating and rambling unconnected thoughts, in what turns out to be one of the finest chapters in the book, if not the finest of all.

"But I tell you, Ezekiel my dear, my beloved, my consoler," the rabbi says in his delirium, "by the law given to Moses in Sinai, it's fine by me if you go on the way you are. If you asked me for freedom I would give you freedom, but it seems to me that you are not asking for freedom. You want me to subject you to His will and tell you what His will is, and I don't yet know what His will might be."

The discourse about revolution and freedom in Egypt was still fresh at the time, in 2013, and you can imagine how this sentence affected me, how it reminded me that for some groups of people freedom was a heavy burden because it forced them to do something they had never in their lives even thought of thinking about: to think.

As soon as President Hosni Mubarak stepped down, I had to laugh when I saw how confused the Egyptian media were about who they should pay homage to. There were the young revolutionaries, the Supreme Council of the Armed Forces and Prime Minister Ahmed Shafik. The broadcasters didn't know who was the real ruler of the country, the one to whom they should grovel. It hadn't been that way in the pre-revolutionary period, when the situation was clear, since there was only Mubarak. Freedom confused the Egyptian media, and everyone else as well. Hakham Ovadia's delirious ramblings helped me to understand this.

Throughout the translation process, I learnt things about what was happening in my country and my city, and sometimes about myself, troubled as I was by questions that didn't trouble others, and confused as I sometimes was by freedom, so I often kept silent, because only silence was likely to conceal my lack of confidence in myself.

"Now you can leave. I'll resume the conversation with the God of my forefathers, if he's listening." That's how the rabbi finally brings an end to his ramblings to Ezekiel, after lengthy references to his own silence, to Ezekiel's silence, to the silence of men in general, and to the world that would sink into silence if it weren't for women.

* * *

On the same day as my first daughter was born, more than five years ago now, *Rachel and Ezekiel* was published in Arabic by the Cairo publishing house Kotob Khan.

This was no more than a coincidence but, like Ezekiel, like all believers, in fact like everyone, I wanted to see it as more than a coincidence. Like Ezekiel, I like to give great meaning to the events in my life.

The novel ends with a phrase borrowed from Jewish literature: "complete but unfinished", or *tam velo nishlam* in Hebrew, a phrase that leaves a very beautiful impression both in Hebrew and in Arabic as *tamma wa lam yaktamil*.

With help from the expression "complete but unfinished", I now understand that there are endings. The novel was published on January 19, 2016, and while my daughter, born on that day, continues to grow and mature, she still, while I write this article for example, raises in me questions that I know will not soon stop.

Note:
* 'Hakham' is the traditional title in the Middle East for a Talmudic scholar/teacher rather than 'Rabbi' ('al-Rab'), which might be misunderstood as referring to God, though the two have virtually synonymous meanings.

ALMOG BEHAR

Chahla and Hezquel

AN EXCERPT FROM THE NOVEL CHAHLA VE-HEZQUEL
(RACHEL AND EZEKIEL)

TRANSLATED FROM THE HEBREW
BY DAN CERN AND ERAN EDRY

Per Halachic law imparted unto Moses at Sinai, Amnon[1] hates Tamar[2], and Sarah hates Ishmael. Hezquel took in the rabbi's words that had been drummed into his ear at length for the past hour, knowing full well they stood to go on for yet another equally lengthy hour, tugging and pulling at his thoughts. In his heart, he tried to summon the memories of past loves and hates he had experienced and in the process, his head slumped forward ever so slightly as his eyes closed in sweet sloth.

Without warning, his body suddenly felt that much heavier and he found himself drifting off into a semi or rather, quarter slumber state as the dozing sensation that began in his squinted eyes filled his head with the most pleasant fog. Meanwhile, the rest of his body started to gently tremor and vibrate and vibrate until he had tipped over and crashed into one of his peers in the audience, or into one of the stools piled high with scripture textbooks. He was then jolted wide awake and straight into the rabbi's next sentence whose words found their way directly into this thoughts.

"A man must not wear women's clothing and the woman must not wear that which pertaineth unto a man." The words of the great Torah scholar, Hakham Ovadia, wove themselves into his thoughts, wriggling and worming their way through them as Ezekiel recalled how, as a child, he would wait all year for Purim to roll in again when he could once more slip into women's clothing. He also remembered how his mother came up to him one year and said: "Why not dress up as a rabbi, or cantor, or magician, or an insurance agent?" And how he had wept and sobbed, pleading with her for a dress and a long, straight-haired wig he could stroke, seeking her joy and approval at his desire to dress up as her.

Almog Behar, Jerusalem, 2011.

"Why always go for the same costume every year?" His mother demanded. "One would think you spend the whole year in fancy dress and that only in Purim do you slip out of it and into your own skin." In his restless sleep, he wondered who Amnon was and who Tamar was and why this Amnon should have hated Tamar. And from somewhere in his head, as his lesson with his mentor, the Hakham, was still in session, his mind conjured up the image of a grieving Tamar, donning sackcloth and ashes over her head, wearing Joseph's savaged technicolour coat, wandering about, crying out and siting all by her lonesome; and he recalled her tale, joining her in mourning over Ammon's love of yore that had turned to loathing. And he despised Amnon, as did Absalom, his brother, who was known for his luscious curly locks and was horrified as his spirit, unyielding, demanded that he not turn out just like Amnon and all other men. That he not say" "Come lie with me, my sister"; that he not trade love in for hate, nor hate for love, that he not command "Put now this *woman* out after me"; that he not lay a hand on the fair maiden Tamar, nor that he feign illness.

And his mentor, the Hakham, explains the following: Amnon hated his sister whilst his heart was merry with the pancakes she had made him, whereas Absalom hated his brother Amnon, with his heart merry with wine. Neither had Tamar in mind, but rather honour. Hezquel wanted to ask: "And their father, David – did he love Tamar? And Amnon? And Absalom? And Jonathan? And did he have any love in his heart for five-year-old disabled Mephibosheth, son of Jonathan, the son of Saul? And who was Rizpah[3] Bat Aiah[4] whose name alone hung like the threat of a truly woeful fate?

"Such is the reward of Torah studies," the Hakham explained as he took on the questions of angels with his answer: "The Torah is what it is, and it is for me to study." It's for me to study, Hezquel thought, recalling all his years of studies, and how both his parents would sit with him in their narrow flat on the terraced housing estate on Bar Yochai Street in the 8th or 9th wards of the Katamon borough of Jerusalem, demanding that he dedicate himself to his Bar Mitzvah studies in the run-up to his 13th year, and how he went up to his teacher, a redheaded Kurd, when he was 14 and informed her that, "my future hasn't worked out for me; I won't be continuing with my studies; I've had my fill." And how he loved shul as a child, where he held the edge of his father's prayer shawl and sang songs to 'Lijah the Prophet'[5] and Bar Yochai, that wretched saint who never once walked the streets. And, hand on the Torah, he loved his father fiercely. And how devastated was he when he died, a fortnight after his Bar Mitzvah, when he had stood there, and placing a heavy hand on his head, recited: "Thank the Lord I am now unburdened of this one." And indeed, so soon thereafter, he went and unburdened himself of this world, as if he had just shed a weight so heavy that his role in this life was now well and truly completed, and so he literally went and unburdened himself of the whole thing. And how Hezquel wept and wept when he died, to the point his mother intervened and said: "Enough! I've buried a husband. I've cried for him; Lord knows how I've cried for him, but you, my boy, should eat, and study, and paint pictures with lots and lots of colours. Enough of this incessant crying. You also have a mother." And he went quiet, facing her, and in his heart he echoed unto himself over and over: "I also have a mother, I also have a mother, I also have a mother."

"Moses imparted the Torah from the smashed pieces of the Tablets of the Law," the teacher exclaimed and stamped his feet as if to remind his audience of the shattering sound of the stone tablets, and of the panic and tumult of the people who had been worshipping the golden calf. And Hezquel thought, Moses taught the Torah from the smashed pieces of the tablets whereas I can't even find respite from my own thoughts. And he tried to count how many things in his life had smashed to pieces; and how many of those he'd picked up and how many had scattered everywhere, and he realised that the task at hand was far more daunting than anything Moses might have faced. He then thought back to this one moment three years ago as he was walking along King George Street when he caught his reflection in the shop windows and realised how he was gradually becoming the image of his father over the years – noting his hands' propensity to join together behind his back as his father's did; his slow, cautious gait far behind his mother that was no different to his father's; and how, like his father, he'd spent the last four years in a state of silence. Whenever he shaved, he would leave a moustache identical to his father's, and would stand in front of the mirror for minutes on end, his eyes fixed on his father, his maker's face that was staring right back at him from the looking glass. And only when his eyes began to well up did he press the razor to the moustache whilst repeating in his father's voice: "Thank heavens I am now unburdened of this one. Thank heavens and good riddance." And he would place his slender hand over his head but try as he might, it just didn't carry the same weight. And afterwards, he sometimes would burst into tears, though not always.

Meanwhile, the teacher continued to go through lists with great restraint: "Hadassah is Esther, Iscah is Sarai who is Sarah, Job is Moses, Kohelet is Solomon, Jacob is Yeshurun who is Israel, Eliyahu is Elia who is Yinon, Jesus is the same man, Haman is Hitler the wicked, meaning Amalek, Esau is the Roman Christian Empire, and Ishmael – the Arab tribes of the desert." Hezquel, meanwhile, removes his big white skullcap so as to observe it, and how drawn was he to the very prospect of this big yarmulke covering his head all day long and not just in shul. But then, he tells himself: "Once I have completed that many more mitzvahs, I shall don a skullcap and start wearing tassels. For now, I do still break the odd law."

Perhaps a nice cup of sugary mint tea would stop him feeling so sleepy; and maybe the sweetness of some rice in milk might lift his spirits. His thoughts drifted off again to the rabbi's beard. Maybe he, too, ought to cease his daily shaving ritual which only injures his skin and instead, grow a beard that elongates the face and endows it with Torah-like tranquility. And he smiles a heartwarming smile at his mentor that he, in turn, reciprocates in earnest, followed by words aimed directly at him.

A prayer is like a skewed wall, explains the rabbi. At times it is an antidote to grief and at others, it is grief epitomised. And Hezquel finds himself wondering whether this is the very meaning of prayer – drawing water from the well. He knows that when the great scholar Ovadia has grown old and weary, his disciples, who have now so lovingly dubbed him 'The Great Wise Abdullah – Servant of God', will no longer attend his sermons, and his hands shall have the strength to dress his hands and head in tefillin no more, and his lips will mutter all the prayers, and verses, and sermons in a voice so faint that only the Lord Himself could hear. However, he, Hezquel, would continue to call on him and give him a hand with his tefillin. And he would never deny his mentor the joys of teaching the Torah which the Hakham will carry on imparting unto him and no one else, to his dying day. He will continue to mentor him even when Hezquel's eyes are heavy and desperate to close from the toils of working nights, Friday nights included – Lord have mercy, for the coffers need their coppers, and the boss, the strength and stamina of his hands and back.

Hezquel spends three years under his mentor's tutelage. Five whole years his mind has been riddled with doubt and anguish over his father's death during which he had not set foot in a synagogue nor placed a single schoolbook in his rucksack; five years, until he finally turned 18.

In those five years he kept mostly silent and would often disappear on his mother, sneaking out of their narrow home to wander the streets of Jerusalem where he slept, utterly estranged from both school and shul. He couldn't quite recall either, whether his dream of becoming a women's hair stylist began in this five-year period or if it started even prior to his Bar Mitzvah, only to permeate long after. The only thing he knew was that he dreaded ending up in the same construction trade as all the other men in the family, working for Solel Boneh Contractors. His dreams had him go down a different career path. But then, his whole world caved in on him on the death of his mother, and his learned Torah mentor called on him at their home, instructing him to stay the course of the Shiva there, and to remove himself from street life. The rabbi stayed at his side and told him all about his younger days when, long before his beard had turned white, he had had the most devout of disciples – one Liyahu Nashawi, Hezquel's father, Lord rest his reverent soul, and recalled how he would channel all his earthly faculties into his spiritual ones and would give himself wholly to the sages' gospel. And after Hezquel had finished sitting Shiva, and after he had shaved off his 30-day-old mourning beard, he asked his mentor to teach him the Torah and to help him find a woman with whom he could make a home like all other men. And he would not serve in the army because how has this army ever served him? How has this life ever served him? He now wished to start afresh, living a life of faith – not fire. And in his first lesson, his mentor, the Hakham, began imparting Halachic law to Hezquel: He who sees Jerusalem in ruins must make a tear in his garment and then mend it so that he not have torn clothes. And Hezquel asked himself, which Jerusalem is this in reference to? The streets he grew up in, San Martin and Bar Yochai all the way to Pat Junction? After all, he sees them in ruins on a daily basis and would not have enough thread with which to even begin mending them. However, he approached his mentor's questions with prudence and was careful not to answer straight away, remembering his father's words about everything being two-faceted, and how every obverse had its hidden reverse. His father revealed to him that there were thousands of hidden ordinances that have remained heavily shrouded in mist ever since the Israelites were expelled from Mount Sinai. Not even the Great Rabbi Akivah was able to decipher the calligraphic ornaments and denotations the Lord himself had placed over the letters of the Torah so how could *he*, the least learned of the lot, even begin to tackle such profound Halachic questions? And all he could think was, what about a man ruined? What does one do? What does one do when one sees a man ruined?

Inside the shul, the Hakham started reciting hymns with added commentary explaining how, when discussing "The Binding of Isaac", one must remember that Isaac's brother Ishmael was bound, too; as was their father, Abraham, and their mothers, Hagar and Sarah, respectively.

Ishmael was bound when he collapsed under the merciless desert's blade and was virtually dying of thirst, whilst his mother distanced herself so as to avoid having to watch her son die; and he too was called upon by the Angel of Deliverance only after he had died on the inside and his heart was rendered blind.

And Sarah loathed Ishmael. And Hezquel listened as his mentor began waxing lyrical about how twice Abraham had got up early in the morning, saddled his donkey, filled his water canteen, then took his only son, whom he loved above all else, some place where no heavenly voices could reach them. And how Sarah laughed when Hagar was banished and how she wept the day Isaac was taken, and how she had no mercy for what lay ahead in the desert, but then could not bear the distance. It seemed to Hezquel that his mentor somehow knew of his half-brother by another woman, and of the pregnant belly his father had left behind in Beit Safafa[6]. How his love for her was not enough for him to have followed her or to have asked her to follow him, and how instead, he married a wife like Sarah who bore him two additional sons whom he loved that much less. That other woman carried on scrubbing and cleaning building stairwells when Hezquel was growing up, working on Hashomer Street and on Rabbi Zadok Street and at the school he attended, until her back finally gave way. His older half-brother he had only once laid eyes on at a distance as the boy was walking up to his mother, whilst Hezquel himself was out and about on the street with his parents. And his father was rendered speechless before them both, and his mother's jealousy of the other woman crept up on her at every corner. And he studied his older brother's face, looking for any signs of resemblance, but could find none. Only later, when the memory of his face came back to him whilst he was mourning their father whom they never got to share, did he find that resemblance. And he knew his mentor would say that this was akin to Sarah's hatred of Ishmael, son of the other woman. Seething jealousy had always ruled them both, yet Abraham had no hatred towards Ishmael. On the contrary. He loved and adored him, and was fond of him, and in his heart of hearts held him near and dear.

After 17 months of observing his progress, his tutor and mentor told Hezquel: "I am about to match you with a wife and you shall be like all others. She will be a vessel full of all things good, meek, and handsome, and you shall be ever so God-fearing, and you will be fruitful and multiply, and replenish the earth, and you both shall be two vessels emptied and refilled, and intertwined." And indeed, after eleven months when he did find Hezquel a bride, he guided him with gentle words, speaking softly and reverently:

"You are entering into matrimony, and I stand beside you at the chuppah to sanctify this union. And whilst the duty of intercourse is commanded by the Torah, it is untoward to engage in it on a daily basis. Rather, throughout the week, one ought to devote oneself to work, to prayer, and to educating oneself and one's family. Embrace this duty on the Sabbath when neither body nor soul are indisposed. This duty oughtn't to be performed at the start of a Friday night as the neighbours might hear one in the act, nor when one's stomach is also full, and his heart swollen with pride over the meal he has had and his home, so beautifully prepared for the holy Sabbath. One oughtn't to engage in this act in the morning, either, when your beloved is awash in light coming through the window, and one feels a rush of pride over her beauty, and the pangs of a growling stomach, and hunger, and the rush to get to shul. One should perform this duty in the middle of the night, rising for it after midnight like the disciples of scholars who go picking sparks in the fields, and you are to rouse her awake slowly, circling her and telling her, 'Out of all women, you are my wife, like a rose among the thorns.' You must approach her with playful words of praise and whimsy, and tender butterfly kisses. You mustn't swear at her or yourself, and do bear in mind that you are doing God's will and that where man and woman intertwine, the Divine spirit lieth."

Per the Halacha, Rachel's love for Jacob is not the same as Jacob's love for Rachel. Boaz's love of Ruth is not the same as Ruth's love of Boaz, whilst neither compares to Samson's love for his hair, or to Balaam's love for his jennet. And Hezquel recalled their first night, how he had put off approaching his bride, and how she sought him out with the sweetest words and began circling her betrothed and kissing him, whilst he could only manage a string of broken sentences, saying how he was "still full from the wedding feast . . . we'll leave it till after midnight like the scholars' disciples . . ." as he pulled away from her.

He realised that he was avoiding her body just as Amnon had after *that* act, only no such act had come to pass between his wife and him as of yet. Heaven forbid, he did not despise her, but rather was determined to keep his parts and orifices well away from hers, whispering: "In His wisdom and infinite wonder, the King of the Universe fashioned us these hollowed spaces, orifices and cavities – all designed for lust."

His whole form seemed to evoke his mentor's tips for reviving one's body and to summon the strength to go near her: every birth is the Creation told anew, and in its origins darkness was upon the face of the deep and the spirit of God moved upon the face of the waters. When heaven and earth were formless and empty; then came that which divided the waters, that reigned in all chaos, that swept up all mire and mud, that gave form to the formless, and that erected great columns out of intangible, elusive air, moulding them into a mound of sorts, arranging them as a type of wall, enclosing them like an awning, pouring water over them until they've turned to dirt. Birth and creation are constructed through speech and differentiation and name-giving, therefore that which the mouth cannot utter and the ear cannot hear, one body inside another cannot create. He told her that if he lacks the energy to talk about their act, then they won't have created new life. And so, he delayed their lovemaking night after night to the point that her body became panic-stricken. And she thought to herself, what kind of husband have I been matched with? He will not fulfill his husbandly duties. And after three weeks and four days, in the dead of one dark Sabbath night, he whispered in her ear: "The rabbi has told us we are to sire a male child and a female child. 'Be fruitful and multiply,' he said, 'all things in this life are cyclical; that which is made is later unmade, and tonight is the night for making.'" She woke up elated to feel his person and after he'd thrust his body into hers, he pulled away from her kisses, saying: "Not with hunger, not with gluttony, moderation is medicine."

His acts that night left him so mortified that for the next two months he dared not repeat them. His spirits eventually lifted and gradually, he began calling on her again every Sabbath eve, past midnight, in the latter part of the night, reciting a special prayer before and after the act which he had composed with his rabbi and mentor:

Protect me, oh Lord, like the apple of Your eye, and shield my gaze with Thine merciful wings that I need not witness a thing. Pierce the depth of mine ears with Thine gracious feathers that I need not hear any sound, nor be bound by any duty, nor speak Thine holy name in vain. Stop my heart feeling, and my thoughts distinguishing right from wrong, and my legs carrying me either near or far, and with Thine remaining feathers, with Thine everlasting grace, erect me a tent over my nether regions. That I be sexless, neither male or female; that I not rebirth myself in a new form stripped of all memory, donning a mother's womb or the proud mark of circumcision."

And she would hear his words and grow ever so sad. What kind of match has the great wise Hakham made for her, and why won't her husband seek out the love that burns within her? She wants to taste him, to see into him, yet to her he remains a closed book, or the most hidden, guarded of all fruit. She figured she would end up in sackcloth and ashes crying out: "I stand here before the Lord, I am bereft."

Moses imparted but the outer shell, whilst the fruity contents he left guarded for the sages' eyes and ears only. Hezquel found that his wandering mind left him wide awake and listening to the words of his mentor as he was saying them. And when he was reflecting both on himself and on the passage of time, he felt as if the rabbi's sermon had drawn out beyond his longest dreams, but also assumed it was bound to wrap up soon. Most likely, the Hakham would now say that there is double meaning in his words whereby the hidden fruit is only for the sages to retrieve on the one hand, or alternatively that it is only off limits to the sages, which leaves it to the unwise and unlearned for the picking. But instead, his mentor compared the bride to the hidden fruit, explaining that the act of matrimony is the revealing of that hidden fruit, which he then outlined in two parts: in the first, he explained that the virgin bride was the true Torah, available only to the sages who had to find her every orifice and cavity and become her husbands and proprietors; per the second meaning, the bride would only remain a virgin to the sages, waiting but neither saved nor privy to the truth, whereas he who is unwise and who has claimed his bride's virginity, it is as if he's unlocked the truth of the Torah, and has gained unfettered access and insight into every last secret.

He started muttering: "Who is like unto Thee, oh Lord, among the gods? Who is like Thee? Thou art holy and Thine Name is holy, and the holy praise Thee every day. Holy, holy, holy is the Lord, the whole land is filled with Thine glory."

Any minute now, the Hakham will conclude his sermon and Hezquel remains none the wiser as to whether it's a boy or a girl he'll be having in three months' time. Male and female He created them, and the bride He had given him now threatens to go to the rabbi, his mentor and declare that this arranged marriage, this husband he found for her may love the scriptures but he certainly does not love her. There is no true love in his heart for her. And she can't bear it, being unloved and lonesome with him in their home. Walking around with her belly heavy with child, undertaking the Torah's duty to be fruitful and multiply whilst wretched, not knowing how she could leave him with a baby in her belly. And Hezquel has tried to *dissuade* her from going to the Hakham. First with his silences, then with sweet nothings, describing his love like a light whose likeness cannot be captured on paper. Only if the page is heavy with darkness would one see the light contained within. Then, another time he tearfully pleaded: "What would the Hakham say if he found out? I'm practically a son to him, and I'm hardly the best catch out there as I'm sure he's told both you and himself. I am not wholesome. Please don't suggest to him any improprieties."

Hezquel decided to tread carefully with his mentor and to volunteer no information. He would exercise restraint, trust in the Lord, and hear what his mentor had to say. Who knows, perhaps he might not even think her words were such a big deal, or maybe he already knows everything; she quite possibly hasn't even been to see him yet because if she had, he would surely have felt it during the lesson, and he hadn't. But she may very well speak to him today or any day now, meaning he could yet stop her. He loved his mentor and his wise teachings. And now, his wife is suggesting she intends to leave him and he is lost in thought over how much he wanted a child yet at the same time did not want one at all. And seeing as how he couldn't just go ahead and have one on his own, he planted his body in hers. If the truth be known, he does have love in his heart, and he relishes how she moves in pregnancy. He was also quite fond of her morning sickness and all the ruckus with which she has disturbed the silence in his life. Perhaps he won't turn out as silent as his father, after all. He recalled how one night, a week or two ago when their separation seemed as imminent as one's next breath, he tried to explain to her that his childhood had stained every sheet and pillow in sight with tremendous sadness, then covered her body with adoring kisses.

The Hakham concluded his sermon and with his finger, beckoned Hezquel to approach. Hezquel, who already had one foot out the door, hoping he could slip out in time, could not pretend not to have seen his mentor's gesture and so approach he did. Hakham Ovadia indicated he should bow his head before him, and resting a heavy hand on his hair which he revealed under the skullcap, he began whispering, reciting with the utmost restraint: "Good riddance and thank the Lord I am unburdened of this one." And his mentor explained that from herein out "all curses and praises lie on your head; all rules and duties, and I shan't be made to interfere where the Divine spirit lieth between man and wife."

And in his heart, Hezquel echoed the words: "Good riddance and thank the Lord I am unburdened of this one. Thank the Lord he is unburdened of me. Thank the Lord."

Hezquel lumbered out of shul, taking slow, measured steps as he contemplated his mentor's double entendre. His mind conjured up the memory of his father's death and with his hand feeling ever so heavy, he wondered what place, in all his years, has love held in his heart? Whence does it enter, and whence does it exit?

He thought back affectionately to his nickname, saying it in his father's accent, "Hesquel, Hesquel", and started making his way back home and to his wife, wondering who should have created such opposites only to bring them together, whilst denying the likeminded their own kind.

He glanced at the narrow street that was right by the road he grew up on. There was no singing coming from any of the shuls along the street. The sun had either already set or was about to rise, making Hezquel feel as though he had just spent two whole days taking in sweet Halachic teachings as if he'd managed to go beyond the veil and back. Unsure of how steady his feet or the pavement were, he kept his mind sharp and awake with odes, hymns, and songs in prayer and hope of festive, better days. In his head, he was going back and forth: "The rabbi knows . . . the rabbi doesn't know." He then began fashioning letters into names until the names he'd thought up shone as bright as street lights which made Hezquel immeasurably excited. Indeed, daybreak was upon him and he found himself tripping on his words whilst reciting his morning prayers: "I offer thanks to Thee, for Thou hast compassionately restored my soul within me. Bless the Lord, oh my soul. Who coverest Thyself with light as with a garment. And I will betroth Thee unto me forever. Blessed art Thou who hath made me a bondman for Thy creator. Blessed art Thou who hath made me as He wishes, blessed He."

Chahla ve-Hezquel (Rachel and Ezekiel), is Almog Behar's debut novel, published by Keter Books, Jerusalem, 2010. 260 pages.

Notes:
[1] Eldest son of David, King of Israel
[2] Amnon's sister
[3] Hebrew for 'floor' and 'fiery ember'.
[4] Supposedly one of King Saul's mistresses.
[5] A shortening of Elijah the Prophet's name
[6] An Arab suburb in south Jerusalem.
[7] Chahla is a diminutive form of Rachel.

Shalom Darwish
(1913-1997)
Gender and Intersectionality

ORIT BASHKIN

Shalom Darwish was one of the most gifted writers of short prose in Iraq in the 1940s and 1950s. His prose captured many of the dilemmas characteristic of Iraqi and Iraqi-Jewish society, such as migration from the countryside to the big city, the status of women in Iraqi society, and family relations shaped under changing societal norms.

Born in the village of 'Ali al-Gharbi ('Amara district), Darwish moved to Baghdad as a child, where he studied at the Rachel Shahmon school. He obtained a law degree in 1938, and worked as a lawyer for many years. In addition, he served in Iraqi public life, assuming leadership roles in the Jewish community and in Iraqi politics, as a member of the social-democratic National Democratic Party (the NDP, al-Hizb al-Watani al-Dimuqrati). In 1947, he was elected as an NDP member of parliament. He was forced to leave Iraq in 1950, traumatized by the persecution that his community, and he himself, endured in the years 1949-1951. In Israel, he continued writing in Arabic, in the government-sponsored Arabic-language press, and working as a lawyer.

Darwish was a brilliant writer of short prose, and Arab critics at the time and later scholars of Iraqi and Arabic literature, such as Reuven Snir and Shmuel Moreh, hailed his pioneering work. Darwish, a man, wrote a great deal about women, and their struggles for emancipatory rights, as more Iraqi, and Iraqi-Jewish women, attained higher education, called for suffrage, and strove to choose the husbands they were to marry and shape a more equal vision of family life. Most Jewish intellectuals, such as Anwar Sha'ul, Mikha'il

Murad, Esterina Ibrahim, and Maryam al-Mulla, shared his worldview. His short story "In the year 2532" is constructed as a letter addressed to a female doctor in the year 2532, when women control the world. Switching the traditional roles of men and women, in Darwish's imagined future it is men whose freedom is curtailed under the presumption that equal citizenship rights might erode religiousness. The author forces his male readers to consider what might have happened to them, had they been barred from the labor force or considered simple machines of reproduction. Darwish channeled the radical voices of women that influenced the public debate in this period, and advanced the notion that oppression of women had more to do with sex, capital, and power than religious and family values.

SHALOM DARWISH

In the Year 2532

TRANSLATED FROM THE ARABIC BY URI HORESH

Madam Doctor,
   My parents have informed me that you have asked them for my hand in marriage. They have left me – and I do not think you will view this as odd – the liberty whether to accept or reject you.
   Madam Doctor, what I know about you is that you are a skilled physician, that hundreds of patients call on your clinic every day, and that you are beautiful and loved. People who know you describe you as compassionate and of good character; they say you are sublime and suave. All of this must encourage me to accept the engagement, except that I do not wish to put myself in a precarious position such as this without first adequately reflecting on it.
   Dear Madam, marriage is a social event of great significance, which – in my view – must not occur between two people who are unequal in their rights and obligations. As you know, we, as the weak gender, are slaves to our homes; we work tidying the house and raising children, as if we were unresponsive instruments, devoid of opinions and desires. We are destined to obey the women who control and supervise us.
   I was raised to think freely, and I therefore find in myself a strong tendency for frankness and boldness, in a manner that may be considered unsuitable for our weak gender. Except that I am free, as I have told you. I have a desire to break the shackles that have bound us for hundreds of years. And I have developed an aversion to marriage after the astonishment of witnessing my mother humiliating my father. You, too, may be painfully aware of the nature and degree of such humiliation. And you yourself might also be planning, at this very moment, how to subjugate and humiliate your new husband.
   I have been called 'effeminate' because I wish to leave the house and pursue the same jobs and professions that you all pursue. Answer me, in the name of God: how is it a threat to our morals and virtues that

a man should enter the market and work a respectable job, through which he can make a living and thus be free of having to beg his mother or sister or wife for his material needs? And why should this go against the notion of honor and violate the tenets of virtue? For is it honorable for a man to resort to begging for money from a woman? Is it virtuous that one gender should possess power, wealth and beauty, while the other remains deprived of all these?

If, Ma'am, you only knew how I yearn for the olden days of our venerable ancestors, about which we read in our history books; the days when men held power and hegemony, but today... We, Ma'am, back in the day, when we were in the proudest of our times, we did not humiliate and enslave you the way you do to us nowadays. We used to respect your weakness very much, we used to give you preference over us in every matter, we cherished your love and femininity. Where is all that in your control over and contempt for us?

You numb our nerves, each day to the tune of something else. I read something by a woman writer:

"What is it, men, that pushes you to rebel and revolt... and what are these imaginary shackles in which you claim to be bound? Here we are, toiling in order to spare you hard labor; we take responsibility for all of the hardships of life. And you do not do; you just want and want. Your requests are satisfied and your appetites taken care of. So, what do you all have to complain and whine about?"

And I ask you, in the name of God: what are we supposed to taste in that single bite that you all have given us as charity? What kind of bliss are we supposed to feel while in the bosoms of those who we know are our superiors and who only use us to pleasure their bodies? Those who can toss us away, whenever they wish, the way they toss out their old, worn-out shoes? You can justify this by claiming that we were sentenced to captivity by societal norms. And that the pleasure we find in your beauty and the gratification we derive from your companionship should preclude us from crying about our subordination. And that tidying our homes and taking care of our children should preoccupy us, sparing us the need to pursue careers, as you all do. And that the leisure we enjoy in the home is unparallel to your profound anguish in solving difficult problems. There may or may not be some truth in all of this, but, in any case, we shall continue our struggle to break down these antiquated restrictions and unhealthy traditions. We shall go out and live, and struggle for our lives, in a manner akin to your struggle for your lives, for the taste of labor and toil is much sweeter than that of humiliation and misery.

If, Ma'am, I ever find in myself an inclination to submit to that which I am unable to change and accept matrimony, giving in to these despotic societal norms, then, dear doctor, I shall not marry a doctor…

You may very well be astonished at this, but I do have justifiable reasons, which I shall explain to you, frankly and boldly, as follows…

How many hours do you work in a single day? This question may seem weird to you, but I believe it is of utmost importance. I would like to enjoy a good amount of joy with the woman who would be my spouse and life partner. I would like to spend with her – after laboring an entire day on tidying up my home – long, sweet, pleasurable hours. And you – how many minutes would you be able to spend at my side, after my prolonged hardship and extreme fatigue? A quarter of an hour? Do you believe that this is time enough for me to earn my share of joy and bliss? You, as a doctor, take a philosophical view of marriage, and your only goal in it is to fulfill your duty and propagate the human race. You maintain that fifteen minutes should suffice, or even exceed the time needed, for this goal. I, however, insist that my marriage should have another purpose beyond this one. I wish for it to sate my hunger for emotional bliss and quench my thirst for spiritual intimacy. I envision a marriage of the kind that existed hundreds of years ago, when a man aspired for his relationship with a woman to be about more than mere sexual pleasure and procreation.

And in these fifteen minutes, Madam Doctor, while I lie wrapped in your sturdy arms, you vigorously squeezing me to your bosom, me intoxicated by the bliss of this magnificent embrace and these gratifying kisses, immersed in the stupor of deep bliss – suddenly the bell rings and you are summoned to treat a patient. I know that your compassion and devotion to humanity surpass any affection in your heart, and I assure you that you would push me away from your bosom, forcefully and bitterly, and rush to your patient, indifferent to my sobbing and my melancholy.

No, Ma'am. I shall never consider marrying. For I am not impressed by this ludicrous role exemplified by my own father. I wish not to add to the shackles of prisoners yet a new shackle, which may be the cruelest of them all.

Jamil

IRAQI JEWISH WRITERS

MATI SHEMOELOF

Can't Prostrate myself at my Grandmother's Grave

TRANSLATED FROM THE HEBREW BY ERAN EDRY

*In loving memory of Granny Rachel Hazzaz,
22 March 2020, 2 Nissan 5780*

The poem's tomb opens, the poem's tomb is sealed,
You want to sing her a farewell poem in Aramaic
The heart's mind bursting with the ferocity of the memory of her laugh
The mind's heart shattered en route to her
And there is nowhere to return, and nowhere to advance in this poem
She stands underground waiting
for thousands of miles' worth of
your tears.

*

Granny Rachel Hazzaz
A brilliant exile who's rolled into the world sans script

And now you're the one playing around with this exile, but she's gone

*

Baghdad opens with a suitcase
Bedding she had sewn for her wedding day
are now in your wife's wardrobe in Germany,
the kibbeh that you have every Friday touched by the magic of your childhood
a plume of smoke in your adulthood,
Baghdad is sealed in a case of poetry
which you surrender to your little girl

*

After the rope had broken and the boat returned hollowed of words
to a beach bereft of seashells, molluscs, and starfish,
your daughter walks alongside you, asking 'Where's Gran?'
You tell her she's gone to heaven,
Your daughter repeats the question: 'Kannst wir Savta sehen ins Himmel?' (can we see Granny in heaven?")
on an empty boat's beach
letter by letter walk by, looking out for your poetry in the clouds

*

Gran,
We've been looking for you,
Unable to strip the house back to alien walls
Unable to carry on walking ahead, without looking back,
The longing stretches out after us like snails' saliva
The wormwood shrub orphaned of your hand
The pomegranate tree too shedding its fruit for naught
And the cats getting skinnier by the day, and already looking for another gran to care for

*

Every Friday, you come running out of school, trying not to slip on the barren soil
Turning right, Jaurès St., that's always looking out to the sea, a migrant neighbourhood that hasn't made the papers,
You step onto the path, surrounded by fruit trees, cacti, and herb plants, going past the common washing room
and stepping into your sanctum sanctorum. A small kitchen, a calendar, a photograph of the Maran*, a tight, well-worn tablecloth,
and then comes the question, what kind of kibbeh would you like? This rice-mounted creature appears riding on the back of a spherical spacecraft
You look at the small chair that's ready for Friday night candle lighting, and the cupboard in the storage room, which is where another piece of chocolate will come from at the end of the meal. It's nearly the Sabbath, and this is but a poem, because home is no more, and neither are you, only the words move about the present before hungry eyes.

*

Your roots don't grow into the land where she was born, Abraham
Your roots grow sideways, climbing upwards, heaven-bound
Shot out like clouds, into the very hearts of longing
Pining does not soothe
Yearning only numbs
The hankering hunkers down your poems entirely
You are more of a land in her heart, in her body, inside the place where she
lets you live in between the breaths of the memory of your Iraqi language,
angry that you have not returned to its embrace

---

* An honorific title for a leading, influential rabbi in the Jewish Sephardi community.

"Religion is for God,
the Fatherland is for Everyone":
Anwar Sha'ul and the Rise and Demise of Arabic Literature by Jews

BY REUVEN SNIR

In the pre-Islamic period, Jewish communities flourished throughout the Arabian Peninsula, and Jews were an integral part of Arab society and culture. One of the most notable of Arab-Jewish poets at the time was the female poet Sarra al-Qurayziyya, whose elegy for 350 noblemen of her tribe killed in a battle in 492 A.D. has been frequently cited in Arabic sources. In the next century, the personal integrity of another Arab-Jewish poet, al-Samaw'al ibn –'Adiya', became proverbial – he has since been commemorated by the saying *awfa min al-Samaw'al* (more loyal than al-Samaw'al). It refers to his refusal to hand over weapons that had been entrusted to him, even when a Bedouin chieftain laid siege to his castle in Tayma', north of al-Madina, and threatened to murder his son, which he eventually did when al-Samaw'al was steadfast in his refusal. Describing the moral superiority of his own tribe, al-Samaw'al composed a *qasida* about the noble qualities of the Arab man; the opening verse runs as follows:

When a man's honour is not defiled by baseness,
Then every cloak he cloaks himself in is comely.

Al-Samaw'al's poem, which has been highly regarded in the Arabic literary tradition, testifies to the existence of a past in which no one would consider being an Arab and a Jew at the same time to be paradoxical. From the mid-tenth to the mid-thirteenth century, Jewish culture in al-Andalus (Muslim Spain) had even more than elsewhere the

IRAQI JEWISH WRITERS

Anwar Sha'ul

closest of connections with Arab-Muslim culture through direct translation, imitation, adaptation, and borrowing. Such an atmosphere allowed for the inherited teachings of separate cultures to be actively exposed to one another and to fuse together.

As for modern times, Jews were nearly inactive in Arabic *belles-lettres* during the nineteenth century and the first two decades of the twentieth century. A new revival of Jewish involvement in Arabic literature occurred only during the 1920s, in fact, in modern times Jews have nowhere been as open to participating in wider Arab culture as during the first half of the twentieth century in Iraq. This involvement was an outcome of the process of modernization and secularization of the local Jewry – other Jewish communities in the Middle East and North Africa went through a similar process and started to interact in the political, social, economic, and cultural life of their countries, but, apart from Iraq, it is only in Egypt that can we find evidence of the intensive involvement of Jews in canonical Arab-Muslim culture.

Jewish writing in *fusha* (standard literary Arabic) during the twentieth century began in Iraq, predominantly in the field of journalism, and it developed as a result of the liberalization process that took place in the Ottoman Empire after the Revolution of July 1908 (also known as the Young Turk Revolution), and as a result of the arrival of modern education in the local community. From the beginning of the 1920s, Iraqi Jews started to produce Arabic belles lettres in *fusha,* and their works were brimming with Arab-Muslim themes and motifs as well as with enthusiastic Arab nationalism and Iraqi patriotism. These works quickly became part of mainstream Arabic literature and gained the recognition of Arab writers and scholars. Palestinian historian Abbas Shiblak (b. 1944) says of that period that the Jewish writers and artists of Iraq were part of the general cultural life of the Arab East, maintaining connections and sometimes forging relationships with writers and artists in other Arab countries. He writes: "It is significant that in Iraq (unlike Lebanon, Egypt, or Tunisia for instance) there were few if any Hebrew or Zionist newspapers. The works of the Iraqi-Jewish intelligentsia were Arabic in essence and expression."

An interesting, indirect testimony to that turning point was given in 1924 in *Nuzhat al-Mushtaq fi Ta'rikh Yahud al-'Iraq* (The Trip of the Man Filled with Longing into the History of the Jews of Iraq) by the Iraqi intellectual Yusuf Rizq Allah Ghunayma (1885-1950), who while describing the social classes of the Iraqi Jews remarked that the latter were involved with all kinds of occupations:

> But you cannot find among them writers and owners of periodicals and newspapers. The reason for this is that the Jew wants to work at what can benefit him while the market of composing and writing in our midst is selling badly. So in this matter they are following the Latin proverb which says: "Living comes first before philosophy."

However, on 10 April 1924, only a few months after Ghunayma's book was published, the first issue of *al-Misbah* (The Lamp) (1924-1929) was published: its owner, its editor, and most of its writers were Jews. The journal's aim was to contribute to Iraqi Arab-Muslim culture with no Jewish agenda whatsoever. In the first ten months during which the poet Anwar Sha'ul (1904-1984) led the editorial board, *al-Misbah* was a vehicle for the distribution of revolutionary ideas, a natural continuation of Sha'ul's dynamic activity in prior years. The Arabic literature written by Iraqi Jews at the time was a secular literature inspired by a cultural vision whose most eloquent dictum was *al-deen lil-laah walwatan lil-jami'* (religion is for God, the fatherland is for everyone). The Iraqi Jews who adopted this slogan were very much encouraged by Qur'anic verses that could be interpreted as fostering cultural pluralism such as *la ikraha fi al-deen* (There is no compulsion in religion) and *lakum dinukum wa-li dini* (You have your path and I have mine).

* * *

Born to an educated middle class family with European roots – his grandfather an immigrant Jew from Austria who arrived in Baghdad in the mid-nineteenth century – Anwar Sha'ul was a typical renaissance personality in the formative stage of the new Iraqi state. He was a writer of poetry and fiction, a journalist who published and edited periodicals, a translator and a man of theatre and cinema, a lexicographer and an educator, and in fact an encyclopedist and "a master of a thousand crafts" or jack-of-all-trades. In that he followed in the footsteps of the great Christian encyclopedists of the cultural revival (*Nahdha*) of Arab culture, such as Ahmad Faris al-Shidyaq (1804-1887), Jurji Zaydan (1861-1914), and Butrus al-Bustani (1819-1883). Above all, Sha'ul was a dominant figure among the Iraqi-Jewish secular intellectuals and created a movement inspiring many other young authors who were eager to implement the vision he started to push forward. Before he was twenty years old, he led a group of young Jews who started a library that included books on science and literature, in order to attract youth who would otherwise go visit "coffee houses, fun houses, and other places of recreation and money spending." At the grand opening of the library, as reported by the weekly *al-'Alam al-Isra'ili* (The Jewish World; French title: *l'Univers Israélite*) that came out in Beirut, enthusiastic speeches were given that encouraged youth to look at its books and to take on research projects. On this occasion, Sha'ul recited his poem "Nahdat al-Kiram" (The Renaissance of Noblemen), in which he called for the return of the glory of the past:

Gather courage and unite,
This is how you will fulfill your hope and ambition,
Hurry to fly high, but with judgment,
The leaper is not safe.
Reclaim the glory that was
Taken from you due to fate's turns.

There is no clue at all that it is a narrow Jewish renaissance – Sha'ul's activity during the next fifty years proves that he was actually calling for the revival of Arab culture and the Iraqi homeland. In the introduction to another poem, "al-Rabi'" (The Spring), Sha'ul published in the first issue of *al-Misbah*, he wrote:

Get up, get up – you writers and poets – Spring has come, the Lord of time, smiling, Nature has been smiling for human beings [...] And you – you writers and poets – why do I see you in deep silence, are you not the nightingales of literature?! So why don't you congratulate the Spring?

Here are some lines from the poem:

> Spring has come, surrounded by flowers,
> Birds are singing, welcoming it,
> Get up, my companion, let's visit a garden,
> Leave aside the troubles; let me not mention them,
> Please pass the wine in the gardens,
> Where the companions are birds and trees

Sha'ul's major early contributions however were in the field of the short story, and they came while he served as the editor of two journals, the aforementioned *al-Misbah* (1924-1929) and mainly with *al-Hasid* (1929-1938), the first issue of which was published on 14 February 1929. Sha'ul's desire to modernize Iraqi fiction came together with strong inspiration from traditional Arabic, canonical and folkloristic sources. No wonder that he sometimes wrote under the pen name of Ibn al-Samaw'al, an allusion to the aforementioned pre-Islamic Arab-Jewish poet, al-Samaw'al ibn 'Adiya'. Sha'ul's first story, "al-'Ashiq al-Ghadir" (The Unfaithful Lover), was published in 1924; it is about a young girl who, upon discovering that her lover was playing with her affections, decided to forget him. After publishing it, he gave up writing for three years, in order to free himself from the sentimental tendency from which most Iraqi writers of the time suffered. Sha'ul published his second story, "Fi Hisar al-Kut" (In the Siege of Kut), which deals with the suffering of the people in the province of Kut during the First World War – it was one of the first steps toward realism in the art of the emerging Iraqi short story.

Among his activities, Anwar Sha'ul was the most prominent Jewish intellectual at the time in Iraq struggling for women's rights. Inspired by such Iraqi defenders of women's rights as Jamil Sidqi al-Zahawi (1863-1936), whose commitment to that cause won him the title "The Woman's Liberator." His compatriot Ma'ruf al-Rusafi (1875-1945) in his poem "al-Mar'a fi al-Sharq" (The Woman in the East) saw an essential link between the status of women in society and the strength of Arab-Iraqi nation. As an editor, Sha'ul encouraged young female writers to undertake literary activity, among them Istirina Ibrahim (1914-1996), who later became Sha'ul's wife. In 1930, he published *al-Hassad al-Awwal* (The First Harvest), one of the first Iraqi collections of short stories. In the introduction to the collection, which includes thirty-one stories, he presents his conception that saw literature as a critical medium that must be used as a vehicle for social reformation. Literature cannot be based on "enthusiastic kisses exchanged by a couple of lovers"; rather, it must have its roots in the customs, traditions, and moral standards of a society along with all the shortcomings and confusions that accompany them.

Sha'ul's struggle for women's rights found its evident literary expression in the story "Banafsaja" (Violette), which is about the attractive and charming young woman who falls in love with a young man, but her family intends to betroth her to a wealthy man who is over forty years old. The girl decides to fight back – she is not "a piece of merchandise in the market place to be bought and sold according to their wishes". Locking herself in her room, she refuses to take part in the ceremony, and when her father threatens to break down the door, she responds with the following: "You may break down the door of the room, Father, but you cannot break down the door of my heart." In the anticipated happy ending the narrator receives an invitation to the wedding of Violette and her lover: "And so love won!"

* * *

On 14 December 1984, I was sitting in the news department of the *Voice of Israel*, Arabic section. One of our correspondents had just informed us that Anwar Sha'ul had passed away in Kiryat Ono near Tel Aviv. We broadcast this news along with a short biography. Over the internal telephone network, I called the news editor in the Hebrew section; it was important, I thought, to inform Israeli citizens that one of the last Arab-Jewish writers had passed away. "Anwar who?!" was her rather loud response. I briefly explained the situation to her, but she then replied, *ze lo me'anyen et ha-ma'zinim shelanu!* (it doesn't interest our listeners!). The Arab-Jewish encyclopedist, the master of a thousand crafts, with his wide literary reputation in Iraq of the first half of the twentieth century, was forgotten in Israel of the 1980s and plummeted into oblivion. But it was not a one-sided exclusion – the Arabic literature that twentieth-century Arabized Jews produced has also entirely been relegated to the margins of Arab culture and its scholarship. In a biographical dictionary of Iraqi personalities in the twentieth century published in the mid-1990s, the author Hamid al-Matba'i (1942-2018) omitted *all* the Iraqi-Jewish authors. The long and rich Jewish presence in the Arab world has been gradually erased and what has remained are only traces that are hardly mentioned.

* * *

We are currently witnessing the demise of Arab-Jewish culture – a tradition that started more than fifteen hundred years ago is vanishing before our very own eyes. The main factor in the Muslim-Christian-Jewish Arab symbiosis up to the twentieth century was that the great majority of the Jews under the rule of Islam adopted Arabic as their spoken language. This symbiosis does not exist in our time because Arabic is gradually disappearing as a language spoken on a daily basis by Jews. In the field of literature there is not even one Jewish author of record who was born in Israel after 1948 and who is still writing in Arabic. A Jew who today is fluent in Arabic must have either been born in an Arab country (and their numbers, of course, are rapidly decreasing), or have acquired the language as part of his training for service in the military or security services (and their numbers, needless to say, are always increasing). The Israeli-Jewish current canonical elite does not see Arabic language and Arab culture as intellectual assets – there is no better illustration of this point than the structure of the comparative literature departments at Israeli universities, where you can hardly find tenured scholars who have a knowledge of Arabic or who have taken the trouble to study its literature. In short, we all know that the chapter of Arab-Jewish symbiosis has reached its end, and that the hourglass will not be turned over anytime soon, if at all. Little did Sha'ul and his Jewish compatriots foresee during the 1920s that ideological and political developments in Palestine would crudely foreshorten what he considered as a new spring in Iraq, in fact in the Arab world as a whole. But, the great Arab poet Abu al-tayyib al-Mutanabbi (915-965), one of Sha'ul's favourite poets from the golden age of Arabic poetry, had already said:

> A man can never gain everything he hopes for,
> The winds blow contrary to what ships wish.

ANWAR SHA'UL

Me and the Unknown Other Half: Which of Us Sought the Other?

TRANSLATED FROM THE ARABIC BY ZEENA FAULK

In the early 1930s, I introduced my readers to my first book, my first collection of short stories, *al-Hassad al-Awwal: Ihda wa-Thalathin Qissa Iraqiyya* [The First Harvest: Thirty-One Iraqi Short Stories], in the beginning of which is the following dedication:

To my unknown other half!
To whom will share life with me tomorrow,
To the woman whom I have not set my eyes and heart upon yet!
Anwar

This dedication could be somewhat unique, it seems at first glance, perfectly clear, however, it does not take long before you would see it enigmatic it. Is it truly just an expression of innocent hope for a prospective soul mate? Is it an invitation to a female partner eager or fitting to be my "known other"? Is it perhaps a covered warning to a certain female human being? Or, is it a random, spontaneous whimsy? Or is it an inspired set of words I crafted at exactly the right place and time? Does that dedication mean something significant in my own life or nothing more than mere "prattle" about myself meant to stir up some idle gossip?

I myself had no clear answer at that time to any such questions that might have arisen in my readers' minds. It just so happened that such possibilities only began dancing in my head during a later period of my life, when I found myself reviewing this dedication in an attempt to fit all the puzzle pieces together.

ANWAR SHA'UL

During the 1930s – even before then, in fact – while penning this dedication and writing other works, I had a taste of love. At times, I was fed love straight, no chaser; I gulped it straight from wine glasses and other cups until I was drunk with passion. I was led through the groanings and ooh-aahs that only sensitive, open-minded, and visionary youths could feel. At that time (and in this very order), Sophia, Henriette, Marianne, and Bella, among many others, had come into my life.

Sophia would sit at her bedroom window, which afforded a view of the road outside her home. She sat at the window at a certain, precise time every day in the morning and evening as I passed by her home, my gaze ever turned skyward until our eyes would meet. I would see her smiling – or at least she seemed to be smiling – and wondered whether she was smiling at me. As soon as I perceived this smile, I became so petrified that I nearly stumbled. I wrote poems about her and published them at that time. But the question I was dying to have answered was whether she had ever read the poetry I wrote for her:

> I have made my route two routes
> To obtain a glimpse of your image.
> When my eyes met
> Your radiant shining face,
> I lowered my gaze , unaware of
> All that I have lost of my soul.
> Did my heart leap from my chest?
> Or did my brain take to the clouds?
> If only you knew
> What I hold in my heart,
> You would soften and
> Embrace Love happily.

Oh, how I thanked God later that my verses, mere words, would eventually become lost to time. The road I walked to glimpse her soon became shortened, altered, and truncated, until it finally disappeared altogether. Yet, I managed to keep my heart intact within my chest, and my brain firmly inside my head.

***

Henriette was a beauty and eloquent conversationalist. In one of my youthful, euphoric moments, as we drifted down the Tigris by boat, I extemporized the poem "A Boat under Moonlight" for her:

> Let me unveil the fervour of passion.
> Let me look at you and look more.
> Let me recite my affectionate canto,
> for I'm not a master of the chord.
> You have possessed [my] heart with your enchanting words
> with your magic eyes and thought
> Ask your tender heart about what my heart feels
> You will beget the answer with all lessons
> Come hither, let us bear witness
> To the sincerity of love against fate.
> Come hither, let us see these palm trees,
> The river, and the moon

But fate always held a sway over our lives that was stronger than the wild desire we felt for each other under the watchful eyes of the palm trees, river, and moon. Time eventually split us apart, and we never saw each other again.

***

Marianne was sophisticated and had a penchant for poetry. She was always keen to hear and revel in my sonnets. I found myself inebriated around her, utterly powerless and unable to awaken from my desperate, dream-like love for her. Nonetheless, I always warned her – and myself – that my heart might possibly recover at any time, especially in the following verse:

> Hear me, be fair to me,
> And comfort me with your love,
> Before my heart awakens.
> Deafen my ears with the tune of your words—
> A melody hidden in tones.
> Imbue my eyes with your glowing cheeks,
> And your eyes' radiant shine.

ANWAR SHA'UL

> Strew the dreams at night so I might feel
> The felicity and the pleasure of attainment.
> What's in love that makes you callous?
> Is your beauty mere fancy then
> To fill the eyes with a temporary shine
> Before dispersing among the creases of old age?

I recited this poem to the very last line to her. She listened attentively to my reading, as if these lines were melodies that the blustering wind would whisk away to the ends of the world, where they would never vanish nor settle.

***

One morning, out of nowhere, my heart awakened, and the lyrics ceased. I moved forward on my path, at times walking indolently, and at other times running and gasping for air. I felt that I had found my Unknown Other in the stunning, serene, and shy Bella. Her smile was the secret behind her allure. Her smile was her divine gift with which she mesmerized and smote the minds of her admirers. I fell head-over-heels with that smile, falling so hard for the woman that a mystical relationship, like that of a Sufi towards God, eventually grew. However, I fear this love might have been unrequited on her part. The first time that smile shone and caught my eyes was in a club, then in a park, and then a pathway. Finally, it dawned once again on a school stage, where she was called Bella, the one with the radiant smile. I wrote my poem "Smile to Me!" for her:

> Smile to me!
> Give me that smile for in it resides radiance
> Whose gleam drowns the darkness of despair.
> Smile to me for there is charm in it
> That always seeps deep to my soul.
> Smile to me like a bright star
> To cast out memories today and yesterday.
> Oh, daughter of light, with that radiant smile
> that gives forth like the rays of the sun.
> Your lips enflame the passions of the heart
> and inspirits the whims in each sense.

Almighty Allah refined these lips, then declared:
"Let thy glow be part of my godliness."

***

Some say that charm rests in the eyes
Where the muse wakens and slumbers,
Where the plumed arrows of love are charged
From the crest of the lids, darting from an arch.
Some proclaim that beauty lies in the hair,
With its beguiling ends, silky to the touch.
Some say secret charms rest in the cheeks
That beauty clads in the finest of clothes.
Still others find charm is in the form that
Fates have planted as the freshest seedling.
That's merely what others might see!
But my sentiment says intuitively
That in the lips alone and in nothing else,
Lies the whole secret in the ardent love of Qays.

***

Oh, daughter of light, your lips are a treasure
That God has not prior bestowed on a woman.
Did you grasp your radiance from the sun?
Or did you endow the sun with your light?
Or was it from dew-dripping morning flowers
That flaunt silks or a brocade?
I welcomed these smiles
With lips that inebriate from love without drinking.
Or was your light from a star in the darkness of nights
Crowning beautiful women with wedding wreaths?
Or from the light and force of electricity
That you seized its spark without even touching it?

***

Smile to me, for your beam boosts
My hope in life after anguish.
Your smile will make me pleased with life,
And after the grave takes me, continue to smile.
Your radiant smile avails me

> With that dazzling beam dissolves my agony.
> So smile to me for your lips are enough
> For a bosom forsaken by its lover.

It did not take long before Chronos, as always, forced us to drift apart. Her radiant smile and mouth had simply become a wisp from a time long past, a source of memories that sometimes sprang up from the depths of my soul. Strangely, any time her memory came rushing back to consciousness, it no longer cast the same spell over me, nor conjured the same image of that familiar enchantress. I no longer felt bound by her magical glamour:

> Myriad passionate desires burned in the heart.
> I thought their blaze would not ever snuff out.
> Fire uproariously flaming and erupting but in dry stalks
> Until they blew away and became barely scattered dust.

Days rolled past, and everything had changed. My feelings were transmuted, just as the lovebird changes his tune as he flies from one branch to another. This went on until I found a place to settle down with a life partner. My patient Other Unknown Half was soon to be – by the power of the Almighty, and without much contemplation – my Known Half.

It had not crossed my mind that she would become my life partner. Through my journal *al-Hasid* (The Reaper), I came to know Esterina Ibrahim, that promising young writer. Esterina became my companion in sickness and in health. She ambled with me, shoulder to shoulder, along the great path of life. She remained forever at my side as a wife, partner, lover, and a devoted mother to my boy, Dhia, and my girl, Wi'am, whom she raised patiently and tenderly.

Had this generous, open-armed person sought me out? Or was it I who searched for her?

We always asked each other this question; sometimes we settled on an answer, and other times we disagreed. We went on like this until we realized that neither of us was looking for the other. It had to be by the will of the most gracious and merciful God, Who simply said, "Let thee be each other's mate," and we obliged.

***

On a sunny winter morning in 1933, Saturday, December 26, 1933, to be more precise, I was strolling along Baghdad's alleyways toward the house of Ibrahim Haim Moalim Naseem, Baghdad's long-serving member of parliament. I strode along with resolute steps imbued with an unflappable conviction.

I gently knocked on the door, which opened wide before me, and the family received me in as a guest. Ibrahim thought that I had come to consult him over some matter, and thus welcomed my visit and asked his family to bring me coffee.

After a brief discussion about public health, weather, and sessions of the House of Representatives, I asked: "Sir, may I ask you a question? I would appreciate if you could reply candidly and without feeling uncomfortable." He stared at me, and it seemed that the "candidly and without feeling uncomfortable" part had piqued his interest.

"Go ahead," was his response.

"Do you consider me worthy enough to ask for the hand of your daughter, Esterina?" I asked without hesitancy. His firm answer came almost as quickly.

"Yes, I accept your request, provided that she herself agrees to marry you."

Esterina, in turn, consented to sail into the unknown with me.

Later that evening – in view of what I called the "holy torch", meaning the stove top in the house of Naima Soufir, my fiancé's oldest sister – we delved into the nitty-gritty of the engagement ceremony. We threw a modest yet lively party with the family, which was followed the next day by the religious rituals according to the rites of Moses and Aaron.

On March 14, 1934, we married in the Alliance School's synagogue in Baghdad, at the hands of the master, our uncle Shimon Effendi, who had the sweetest voice, with the chants of the choir's psalms and the melodies of the Iraqi Army Band, whose appearance was good surprise arranged by our pilot friend, Naji Ibrahim, as a wedding gift still remembered and cherished.

ISHAQ BAR-MOSHE

Iraqi Days

AN EXCERPT FROM THE NOVEL
IRAQI DAYS (AYYAM AL-IRAQ)
TRANSLATED BY JONATHAN WRIGHT

The only reason I can cite for failing to remember many details of my second year at Rusafa Middle School is that I was much less interested in my academic studies than in what was happening in the wider world around us. My academic routine definitely didn't suffer or change, except that I did my homework in a hurry so that I could start reading the newspapers to find out about countries where the situation was getting worse. The gloomy news from the outside world imposed itself on me. I think I was opening up physically and mentally but at the same time I was becoming more and more introverted. I was often hurt that the vast majority of people that I tried to draw into conversation on the subject showed less interest in it than I did. Some of them thought that what was happening was transitory and that the threat in Europe did not imply any threat in Iraq, and that the conflict between states would not do Iraq any harm, because it was not in conflict with any other state.

"This country works on the principle that if someone marries my mother I'll call him uncle."

"But the danger could come closer."

"The danger's to the big powers that are fighting. All of those states want to control as much territory as they can in the world."

"Don't you think there's a difference between Britain continuing to hold Iraq and Germany seizing control of it from Britain?"

"What's the difference? Iraq is a small, weak state. It's a dependent state, not a state that takes the lead. Small states follow big states like sheep."

"But it's different for us."

"That's true. Germany persecutes the Jews, while the English say they don't persecute anyone."

"I'm worried the Germans might get here."

"How? You think of some very silly and improbable things."

"I think about things that many people say could happen."

"Why bother? Cross that bridge when you come to it."

The answers I received were neither convincing, satisfying or adequate. People wanted to go about their business and were not interested in what was going on around them. In Iraq itself we had constant changes of government and we heard or read official statements speaking of the changes as being based on "the public interest" but the talk was of the chiefs of staff of the army who came and went and who were plotting against the cabinets, and of the colonels, brigadiers and generals who were setting up a "pressure centre" that they would aim at the king at the appropriate moment. We also heard about how the young new king was stupid and reckless, how he loved flying planes and driving fast cars, about his mistresses and his passion for the radio (he had set up a transmitter in the palace). My mind was busy with these things and I wasn't aware of anything in my immediate surroundings. I remember when I was in the second year of secondary school the classes were divided again. I was put with the brighter children in class 2A and we moved to a much bigger room than in the previous year. There was a strange story about this room. It looked out on the street and opposite it, or opposite the whole school, on the other side of the street there was a large coffee shop that could be seen in detail from the classroom windows. I remember that I sat next to the first window in the room and if I avoided the teacher's glances, I could see everything that happened in the coffee shop throughout the school day, especially during the classes that didn't require any special effort on my part.

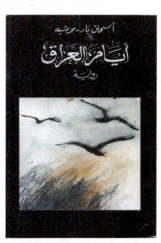

cover of Ayyam al-Iraq (Iraqi Days)

The coffee shop was empty for most of the day. A few customers would come from time to time to smoke shishas or drink cups of tea or coffee. Although the few customers meant the owner didn't have much work to do, he played a large His Master's Voice gramophone with a big trumpet for most of the day. When each record ended and the boy in charge of operating the machine was taking his time winding it up again, I could hear the boss shouting from across the street: "Hussein, where have you gone? Put the Zakiya George record on immediately." *

ISHAQ BAR-MOSHE

"Okay, boss."

Hussein put records on one after another, even if there were hardly any customers. The owner liked to create a good impression and he wanted everyone passing by to know that he had the latest records by both Iraqi and non-Iraqi singers. So in those days my mind wandered to the songs of Umm Kalthoum and I even got used to her long repetitions. I also listened to the songs of Mohammed Abdel Wahab, starting with "Sailing Along The Tigris", which he sang for King Faisal I, and ending with the songs from the film *The White Rose*. It wasn't the songs that attracted me, but rather the anguished, plaintive lyrics, which chased after delusions, the unknown, or nothing at all. I saw the songs as reflecting a state of collapse in society: women walking with veils over their faces, men singing of beauty that they couldn't see but could only surmise. The songs nonetheless reflected obscure yearnings, the delusions of love and suspicion of the unknown and the unseen. I too was chasing the unknown and it refused to let me approach it or see any of it. I realised at the time that the songs I heard were as sad as the things around me were sad, including the state of society, the state of the countries these songs came from and the state of the whole world. Besides these foreign songs that dominated the Iraqi music scene, the coffee shop had a set of Iraqi songs that, even if they differed in tone, reflected the same futile search for the unknown, finding solace in both sensual excess and mad impossible love. How my heart throbbed when I heard from across the street the voice of Salima Murad[†], Iraq's top female singer, denouncing the cruel behaviour of her lover. Her voice reached me over the noise of the cars that filled the street, clear and splendid despite its distinctive huskiness:

> *Your heart is like a boulder that showed me no mercy*
> *While you're so happy and full of joy, I'm in the state I'm in.*

Or, in matchless hyperbole:

> *If it wasn't for the flame of fire in my ribs, I would embrace you,*
> *I'd like you to become a rose, for me to smell all the time.*

These deep lamentations and mysterious sorrows were very similar to what I felt, though I wasn't in love and I didn't have a lover to weep over when we parted. But all the sorrows of the world came together in my life prospects and these songs reminded me of them.

After all that, I only remember a little of that school year. The painful thing was that some of the teachers had moved to other schools, and the others, for no good reason, were putting more and more pressure on the few Jewish children. I remember that Abdel Sattar, one of the teachers, came to us one day. He had been in a good mood all morning. He sometimes had to assemble the classes and read out the names of the children one by one, and they would reply 'Yes'. That day he stopped at the name of one Jewish boy called Shlomo Moallem who lived in our neighbourhood and was in my class. When Abdel Sattar called his name, he distorted it to make fun of it. "Shlimo Moallem," he said.

"Yes," the boy said, ignoring the distortion.

For no obvious reason, Abdel Sattar raised his voice and spoke in colloquial Iraqi. "God has afflicted us with you lot, Shlimo," he said. It made most of the class laugh but instantly made my heart bleed.

I think the boy smiled sarcastically and calmly, without saying anything. He was one of the simplest and most polite boys and I had never heard him speak in a loud voice. In the first break between lessons, I asked him: "Weren't you angry with Abel Sattar's impolite manner?"

"Of course, but what could I do?"

"Didn't you think of answering him back?"

"No. Answering him back in the same way wouldn't do any good and it might provoke him into harming me," he said.

"I wished you'd smashed his face in."

"There's no point in doing that to people of that kind."

"He's spreading Nazi propaganda," I said, "and he's trying to incite the other boys against the Jews."

"That's the hardest thing. Most of the boys take no notice of him. Those who do harass us don't do that because they've been influenced by Abdel Sattar's Nazism, but because they're growing up in an environment with many violent influences. They pick on us because we're Jews, not because they're Nazis."

"Aren't you frightened?"

"Frightened? Why?"

"Things could blow up against us, as Jews I mean."

"I don't think so, and I'm not afraid of anything."

Excerpted from *Ayyam al-Iraq* (Iraqi Days),
published by Dar al-Mashriq, Shafa Amr, 1988

* Ed: a recording of Zakiya George: https://www.youtube.com/watch?v=yBzABbZOJX4
† Ed: a recording of Salima Murad: https://www.youtube.com/watch?v=HhFA7ikD5Ig

Secularism, Spirituality and Reform – Ya'qub Balbul

BY ORIT BASHKIN

Ya'qub Balbul (1919-2003) was a Baghdadi-Jewish author and poet. He graduated from the Jewish Baghdadi *Alliance Israélite Universelle* school (established in 1864), which offered a French education to its Jewish and Muslim students. His knowledge of French and other Western languages later enabled him to find employment in the French Embassy as a translator. Concurrently, he published works of poetry and prose in the Iraqi and Egyptian press. In 1938, his collection of short stories, *al-Jamra al-ula* (The First Ember) appeared in Iraq. In 1936, a story in the Najafi cultural journal *al-Hatif* (edited by Ja'far al-Khalili) recognized his literary talents, noting, sadly, that he had to ask for his father's financial help in order to print his works.[1] Balbul's style and his thematic choices placed him at the forefront of Iraq's writers at the time. Youthful and angry, the undaunted Balbul tackled many taboos in Iraqi society: honor killings, the failed settlements of Bedouins in villages, and women's rights (or rather their absence). His poetry and short stories, moreover, reflected Balbul's patriotism and his mastery of the Arabic, and particularly Islamic, literary canon. Later in his life, Balbul edited the yearly journal of the Baghdadi Chamber of Commerce (*Majallat ghurfat tijarat Baghdad)*, of which he was a member.[2]

IN MY WONDROUS WORLD

In my wondrous world – do you know what amazes me?
Neither its stars nor its burning suns,
neither its galaxies nor its skies bewilder me,
its beauty is not created by burning matter.

I am unmoved by the achievements of human intelligence:
airplanes, ships, and electricity,
the turning of light into sound, and the factories
which produce perfumes. I am amazed by lights,

when they speak their secret language, the whisperings of furniture
when night comes, complaining silently
while silent forms reiterate their names.

I am amazed by passing, mysterious events,
uttering the secrets of this existence,
unveiling the mysteries of the grave.[3]

A Word on Balbul's World

In the interwar period, Iraqi poets and writers were interested in the sciences and in their potential to explain natural phenomena and improve the lives of mankind through technological inventions. Many Iraqis read articles about new approaches to science in Western philosophy in Egyptian and Lebanese journals, and reproduced these ideas in the Iraqi print market. Neoclassical poet Ma'ruf al-Rusafi wrote poems in honour of scientific innovations like the motor train.

In the 1930s, Rusafi wrote a book – deeply offensive to believers – entitled The Muhammadan Persona (*al-Shakhsiyya al-muhammadiyya*[4]), which interpreted the life of the Prophet from a scientific vantage point. Nonetheless, it reflected Rusafi's secularism, which was attested in many other public forms; in particular, in his staunch support of the 1908 Ottoman constitutional revolution, which he saw as the beginning of a new anti-sectarian dawn. Fellow neoclassical poet Jamil Sidqi al-Zahawi was a fervent Social Darwinist, and had popularized science in his poetry. In his long poem "Rebellion in Hell" ("Thawra fil Jahim"), scientists, free thinkers and philosophers attempt to conquer the heavens using scientific innovations. Some writers of prose were no less affirmative in their critique of religion. A group of young intellectuals called the *Sahifa* group, especially novelist Mahmoud Ahmad al-Sayyid and socialist writer Husain al-Rahhal, called intellectuals to reformulate a rational legal system and referenced Friedrich Nietzsche, Gustave Le Bon and Charles Darwin in their writings. Jews were impacted by these discourses and reproduced them, especially in articles in the press. They further demanded that certain Jewish practices relating, for example, to marriage or butchering be modernized and changed.

Balbul did not adopt the position that argued that science could explain each and every phenomenon in our universe, as his poem underscored the fact that not everything in our universe was measurable, or in accordance to a well-defined route of progress and decline. Balbul was greatly influenced by Henri Bergson (1859-1941), and this influence found its expression in his verse. He had been introduced to Bergson's thinking, in particular his book *L'evolution créatrice* (Creative Evolution), through his education at the Alliance school, as well as through Arabic newspapers and journals. Indeed, "My Wondrous World" speaks of the virtues of Bergsonian philosophy in placing the speaker at the centre while the universe is mediated through his questioning. Bergson critiqued the view that argued that nature was created to serve man. The poem itself shifts from nature and space, to man-made technology, to the most mundane. Yet it is not a paean to man's powers or nature's grand achievements; preference is given to the mysterious, the silent, and to nonhuman voices. What amazes the speaker is not the decipherable, but rather what is not perceptible by the speaker's senses and his spiritual awareness, which shapes his perceptions of time and space. At the same time, however, the divine is not represented in any way as the cause of the marvelous phenomena of the universe. The wonderment of the speaker does not lead him to admire, or even to search for the Creator, or the power behind the mysteries of the world, but rather to celebrate mystery in itself.

THE SPONGE

Motionlessly inert the sponge grew on his rock
as if the rock gave him life,
not knowing how he would live without it. His father,

as well as his uncle and grandfather
lived on the rock and found comfort.
When he saw the whale and the fish moving freely,
jumping high and falling back to the depths of the sea,
joyful, jubilant, without regretting what had been lost,
living mightily, between laughter and wonder,

his forehead was covered with shame, he shivered,
his cold blood gushed, and moved the rock beneath him;
he started asking for divine forgiveness and cursing the seas

because they had allowed a group of evildoers
to secretly and publicly mock the lives of rocks
by blithely swimming in merriment.[5]

On Balbul's Sponge

"The Sponge" caused much pain to Balbul. When he wanted to publish it, his editor in the newspaper al-Alim al-'Arabi was ordered not to print it. The director general of the ministry of propaganda summoned Balbul to his office to criticize the strange style of the poem. He wondered how Balbul dared apply the language of the unbelievers [kuffar] to the language of the Qur'an and advised him not to write such poetry any more. Balbul saw the affair as a manifestation of the lack of tolerance as far as freedom of expression was concerned, and the absence of democracy and freedom of publication even in the monarchical era.

What angered the readers of the poem?

Balbul's poem opposes two groups: those who object to motion (the rock, the sponge and his forefathers) and those who are constantly moving (the fish and the whale). The human sponge sanctifies immobility, which he identifies with loyalty to the traditions of his forefathers. Even when upset, he is unable to do anything more than pray and curse. The only factors capable of producing movement from the sponge are fear and hate; these are what make him move the rock under him and stir his cold blood. Those associated with movement are characterized as happy, willing to change positions (up / down), and interested in the present. The assumed motivations of the fish and the whale, however, are mediated through the sponge's perspective, who associates activity and joy with impiety, moral transgression, and shameful acts.

Images related to immobility and indifference occupied Arab intellectuals since the late 19th century. Many argued the idea that culture, religion, and civilization should not change in response to the circumstances of the modern world, and stifled the development of the East. In modern Arab intellectual discourses, the root causes for the stagnation [jumud] of the East were related to a host of practices and beliefs: the conduct of illogical ulama', the fact that contemporary Muslims turned their back on scientific inquiry, or, as argued in the mantra of some nationalists, the foreign influences (Turkish or Persian) that caused Arab culture to standstill. In Balbul's poem, stagnation is considered an extremely negative feature. It is associated with the sponge, a creature that clings to the familiar and the traditional, prizes inactivity, and is envious of those who lead a liberated life. It is worth noting that Iraqi political elites as well as religious authorities often rebuked the young effendia (the urban middle classes) for wasting their time in the pursuit of worldly pleasure and leisure. The sponge, then, could have signified any group of conservatives, religious and secular alike, who are hostile to free movement and mobility.

As opposed to the rigidity of the sponge, the poem celebrates movement. Social mobility, transformation, and movement were important themes in modern Iraq. Starting in the 1860s and continuing more vigorously in the interwar period, Iraq's communication and transportation services improved: construction of roads, bridges on the Tigris and the Euphrates, railways, and the pavement of streets within the cities linked quarters of the cities together, and made the movement from city to city safer and quicker. Iraqi intellectuals articulated the position that these acts were not only a mere improvement of one's living conditions, but rather symbolized modernity itself. The emergence of Baghdad as the cultural and political hub of interwar Iraq changed the movement of individuals within the city itself. As reading clubs and societies were opened and the number of schools increased, spatial practices transformed accordingly; individuals who walked the city's streets now included children moving between neighborhoods on their way to schools and students going to the colleges in the city; young men on their way to cafés, cinemas, literary salons, and nightclubs; as well as shoppers interested in merchandize in al-Rashid street or the newest Western commodities sold in Rozdi Beg Department

Store. The merry fish, and the emphasis on their constant leaping and jumping had to do with these new urban practices and the giddy effendia that roamed the streets of Baghdad. Mobility, however, was also the ability to change with the times, and the adoption and creation of new mores in literature, culture and science. Thus, when Balbul composed his poem about movement, when he hailed the ability to change, to transform from a state of rigidity to advancement, he was commenting on a society that was obsessed with the binaries of stagnation/progress, sleep/awakening, and rigidity/movement.

Despite the original difficulties to publish the poem, "The Sponge" was published a few years later in a collection of his poems. Balbul did not turn into an Iraqi 'Salman Rushdie' following its publication, but rather became a leading member in the Baghdad chamber of commerce. No doubt, Balbul was exceptionally bold. And yet, an intellectual in Iraq at the time was expected to be bold. Iraq definitely had its share of writers and journalists on the government payroll (or in the service of various political parties), court poets, and authors who shifted their political loyalties according to their personal interests. However, the most prominent intellectuals at the time, be it the Christian Rafa'il Butti or the Shi'i 'Ali al-Wardi, were courageous in critiquing their own religious communities and the communities around them. Audacious poets like Muhammad Mahdi al-Jawahiri and Muhammad Bahr Salih al-'Ulum found themselves in jail because they were confident enough to criticize the state. Self-assured and fearless, the young Balbul likewise defied certain conventions, just as Jews like writers Shalom Darwish confronted certain Iraqi and Jewish norms. This was what an intellectual had to do: take on dangerous themes, and endure the consequences.

Notes:
[1] Al-Hatif, 4:161, 31/March/1939, 1
[2] Shmuel Moreh, "Introduction" in Selections from "The First Ember" and "A Mind's Plight"/Ya'cov [Balboul] Lev – Mukhtarat min "al-Jamra al-ula" wa "Mihnat al-'aql"/Ya'qub Balbul Lev, Jerusalem: Agudat ha-akadema'im yoze'y 'iraq, 2006, 9-16; 75-79; Reuven Snir, 'Arviyut, yahdut, zionut: Ma'vak zehuyot bi-yetziratam shel yehudei 'iraq, Jerusalem: Yad ben tzvi, 2005, 74-76; 112-118; 166-168
[3] and [5] Balbul, Mihnat al-'aql, 90-91 and 12.
[4] It was published in Arabic by Dar al-Jamal, Köln, Germany, 2002, and was banned in a number of Arab countries.

HAVIVA PEDAYA

Baghdad

A POEM

TRANSLATED FROM THE HEBREW BY HOWARD COHEN

1
In Berlin at its heart a former wall of separation we met
passing through the divisions of time and space
from Baghdad and Beer Sheba to Berlin we travelled
to speak one with another
and from Sweden and from Dubai and from Tel Aviv and from
　Ramat Gan we came
to say to one to another I love you I need you
without you I am betrayed.

And before the Arab poets the envy grows.
With you the present continues, with you my childhood appears.
You are the ventriloquist through which my effaced parents and my
　dead grandfather speak again
more animated than ever.

2
Going out from Baghdad, time moved on.
There it was slow, even eternal, and then all at once it sped up,
a past time now lacerated within
whilst every moment not an essence of that past is hidden.

Now Baghdad is behind you
and what have you to say, Father.

In fleeing Baghdad
time has been plundered and betrayed
time of dreams, time of rice sacks in braided stems,
time of simple basic words capturing the whole of existence
because our great mother is our *Nana*.[1]

Her face hidden behind an *abaya* without a reply
and with that first moment of silence I will emerge a Hebrew mute
for Arabic was my language of strength –
there I spoke, there I was a poet
while here I gained my strength from within the regime.
I stood before that dispossessed man and my heart wept
for that which was taken from me so abruptly and which still
   remained in his hands
and upon his lips
and before him I stood as one robbed and in love.

3
Going out from Baghdad what have you to say, Grandfather.
The spaces between those kabbalist letters I taught were full of
   Arabic
and so to explain the contraction[2]
I said: *Maalum*[3]
It will take time to dismantle these crowded words.
We came from the rivers of Babylon and the markets of Baghdad
separated from each other only by force as our baggage fused with
   our bodies.
We danced upon the white sand in Dizengoff balls and searched for
   the cafés open on the Sabbath
but always we remained devout to our God
for we were enshrined with the Tel Aviv of Yehezkiel's vision on the
   Baghdad beach.

4
Going out from Baghdad what have you to say, Mother.
Still you gather the sacred words, the sacred water, the amulets
and go forth daily to work for the social security services.
What have you to say when every day you set out your vision.

HAVIVA PEDAYA

I promise you all the future lost from a butchered past
because revered grandfather would cast out spirits.
In Mahane Yehuda neighbourhood he pictured those red knights
   coming to slaughter
and in '42 he rolled in the dust beside Rachel's Tomb
onto the charred remains of his brothers
striking the arks so that the swallowed souls should go forth.

5
Going out from Beersheba to Berlin whilst in my head
steps reverberate from Jerusalem to Beersheba,
words of Jewish Arabic exploding in my head –
a celebration of *hosa,* arabesque sounds masquerading as a Berlin
   cabaret.[4]
I wish to clarify:
that I deliver to others does not mean that I am delivered into the
   tradition of my heritage
that I break into crises does not mean that I myself am breaking
for even if I have that courage to be broken I also can break.
I do not always go on
because the sobs gush forth in waves
but that is not to say that I do not laugh out loud,
I laugh and do so to the fullest, for depression will never take its
   pull.
Yet a Baghdadian melancholia constrains the laughter
and you who came from Baghdad to Berlin reveal to me
that weeping is typical for the Jews and Arabs of Baghdad,
weeping also at university without discern without discipline
teaching Jewish Thought whilst I am that history weeping alone;
rivers of Baghdad continued to flow from me
between the cubes of grey concrete and the desert
and I took upon myself the right to cry out, and I was banished for
   no reason.

6
Going out from Baghdad
assessing robbed time
betrayed measured gauged,
long ago you left that eternity

like a dried and fragile flower ripped out from between the pages,
pages of days when Baghdad was the Heavenly Jerusalem
and Jerusalem the Heavenly Baghdad.
Meeting now people who whilst in Iraq
sought out talismans to keep away the demons
and in Israel wept at night as they longed for them once more.
Meeting people who there sought out a sage to excise the spirit
    from within
and in Israel themselves became spirits lost in limbo.
You ask to meet again that crazy demon in the market or the street
whom Naqqash witnessed drowning on the beaches of Tel Aviv.
Your disjointed dispersed body
with no understanding of the unconscious within it
with an arrogant certainty only of the present.
Your organs scattered through time and space like the objects
    abandoned in Baghdad,
like the demon that was excised or the spirit which was worn down
for, yes, we must always be precise about what those remains are.
What it is that remains behind, while it is you who yearn for us
telling us photographing us giving us the gift of these fragments,
opening our eyes to what will become of us in Israel.

Our discarded bodies here, our derelict houses there.

Empty bookcases
houses made from delicate wooden frames for watching and not for
    being watched,
preserved archives, floating corpses
ornamentation over the doorposts
locks in rusty doors
windows blocked up with bricks
an isolated blue house between the highest of trees.
There 'Bait al-Yahudi' ("the Jew's house")
drying for you whilst it remains
spilling Baghdadian tears.
And you are that broken body that opens out into scratches and
    blockages
the life that was there cannot go on, you know that.
Its time was cut off, their time flowed out

and without realizing it, we reached this place saturated in madness
    at a time of purity
descending upon us, all those hunted and wounded souls from
    Europe;
greetings to you, Berlin, but not our thanks.

7
So how do we separate the yearning from the yearning, the
    upheaval from the upheaval.
It's not just the physical Baghdad,
it's the lack of that uniqueness of Baghdad that forced your father to
    adapt himself
until he became no more than air in the streets of Jerusalem.
Your father was robbed of himself as you were of your father, and
    therein lies the pain.
There was no mix of channels.
All of Baghdad's time flowed into another channel and we were the
    distortion, we were the disturbance
You busy yourself with the weight of the sacred, clogged with
    muted sand,[5]
that sand that flowed into the heart and its clock is called the
    Qur'an.
AbdelWahab and the *al-Kuwaitis* and *Filfel al-Gourgi* and the market
    and the cafés.[6]
That's the problem: you all thinking we are mourning something
    that was born to be broken
as you take upon yourselves the mastery even of our unconscious,
the blocked time inside the hourglass that gave rise to a lost land in
    Israel.

What say you, my parents, what does our holy grandfather whisper?
How you disagreed: father with his nostalgia and mother with her
    utopia.
Where are we left to grow up, where is that fine line of a present
    that does not collapse?
You reply: what we see in those photos from Baghdad
no longer reflects in the mirror for us
that same mirror in the old cupboard in the old house under the
    road

and we were as worms and not men
that is the breaking;
we know how voluminous we were, how much vision we had
whilst here we have become gaunt
others see us as they see a picture
and we are negated by the reflection.

8
What do you say, children, what do I say now.
What are we and what of us and what of Berlin, that pushed us out into that Israel?
And what of the land that we are in and what of the land between us that stifles Arabic and Hebrew?
Do we have a chance to weave out a new story of creation?
So much light and darkness in that pit within us
even the earth and the waters of Genesis that the sacred letters
    ZMRKD wanted to merge together as one[7]
even they have difficulty thinking of a new beginning
escaping from the abyss of great forgetfulness.
Into which Tiamat that cruel Babylonian was booted to ensure creation?[8]
But who will boot now inside this packed chaos cluttered up with occupation with weakness with sand and with dust?
So much sanctity lacking a correct language lacking a tonality.
Shall we make believe that German and English did not impregnate our Arabic and our Hebrew,
that it is all just an analytical language.

9
Through the strength of the secret we move between the being and the absence inside us
and *Akoo* and *Makoo* remember us even from the beginning of days as we keep our language intact.[9]
We Babylonian Jews we Babylonians from Baghdad who register our being and our absence in all that we do
in our theology and in our coffee and in our milk from the corner store.

10

Akoo and *Makoo* these two clowns pulling at our strings
walking behind us mocking us and the *eyib* captured in our
   reflections
for we are shame within shame the shame of being Jews from
   Baghdad who sing and cry in Arabic
the shame in our weakness at being neutered at becoming officers
   of power against new weaklings
the shame of the blocked hourglass turning us into a language
   robbed of its sanctity
the shame of the occupied land which lost us our right to our
   Jewishness and imbued us with weakness and shame
the shame of our reception turning into a grasping[10]
the shame of the clear and narrow spiritual letters and light
the shame that only in our prayers we are still permitted to weep
because our great weakness has been routed now towards the will
   to power.
The tears of the master have no rights
and there is no solace now in forgetting

Notes:
1 *Nana* is a fond nickname in Arabic given to the mother.
2 The grandfather with his limited Hebrew taught Lurianic Kabbala, a gnostic theosophy in Judaism containing the key notion of the contraction of the Godhead to make way for the creation of the world.
3 *Maalum* in Arabic means 'of course'.
4 *Hosa* in Jewish Arabic means 'noise'. Jewish Arabic was a dialect spoken by Iraqi Jews.
5 in Hebrew means both 'sand' and 'secular'. The play on words could not be preserved in English, but the idea that the sand that no longer flows refers also to the loss of sanctity experienced by Iraqi Jews in their displaced lives.
6 Abdel Wahab, al-Kuwatis, Filfel al-Gourgi were all well-known Arabic singers among Iraqi Jews.
7 ZMRKD is a transliteration of the Hebrew letters, and here refers to an amulet made up from the last letters in the first five Hebrew verses of Genesis: Earth, Water, Light, Darkness, One
8 Tiamat is the god of the abyss: according to the Jewish Midrash, God kicked Tiamat into the abyss in order to create the world.
9 These are Arabic words exclusive to the Mesopotamian region for denoting 'being' (*akoo*) and 'absence' (*makoo*).
10 There is a play of words in the Hebrew word which means both 'reception' and 'kabbala'.

On the Poetry of Haviva Pedaya

ALMOG BEHAR

Haviva Pedaya was born in Jerusalem in 1957. She grew up in the local neighbourhood of Mekor Baruch, after her family had emigrated from Baghdad, Iraq. She is the great granddaughter of acclaimed Kabbalist and author Rabbi Yehuda Fatiyah (1859-1942), who, in 1933, left Baghdad and arrived in Jerusalem, where he then settled. In his lifetime Rabbi Yehuda Fatiyah penned and published volumes of Kabbalah books, as well as four liturgical poems – all of which appeared in his book, *Prisoners of Hope*, with each poem dedicated to one of the Four Matriarchs. He also wrote an additional liturgical poem, in memory of his late son[1]. Haviva Pedaya is the granddaughter of Rabbi Shaul Fatiyah (1908-1982), son of Rabbi Yehuda Fatiyah who, himself, was also a Kabbalist, and who had passed down the musical tradition of Jewish-Iraqi liturgical poetry to his grandchildren, including the poet Rabbi Yehuda Ovadia Fatiyah, Haviva Pedaya's brother. Haviva Pedaya began her studies at Jerusalem's Hebrew University at the age of twenty. There she studied Kabbalah and Jewish Thought. She is a Jewish Mysticism scholar and has written, amongst other things, about the origins of Jewish occult, Kabbalah in Spain and in Provence, Nachmanides, the beginnings of Hasidic Judaism, the role of sight and sound in mysticism, and the place that myth and ritual occupy in Jewish time. Pedaya moved to the city of Beersheba in the south of Israel where she is a full-time professor at Ben Gurion University's Department of Jewish History.

Her earliest poems appeared in 1994 in the magazine *Rooms* (Chadarim). Her debut poetry collection, *From a Sealed Ark*, was published in 1996. Her follow-up book, *Birthing of the Anima*, appeared in 2002. Both poetry books are heavily reliant on the Kabbalah world of iconography and ideas, as well as on Hebrew scriptures, Midrash (biblical exegesis,) prayer, and poetry, and are profoundly influenced by ancient Hebrew. What is more, at the heart of many of her poems is the mystical experience, or one's longing for some kind of mystical connection, alongside movements between one's own inner spaces and the metaphysical planes, in addition to notable appearances by God, angels, mythological scenes, and dreams. Her third book, *Blood's Ink*, was published in 2009 and marked, as hailed on its cover, "a reversal of the covert-overt dynamics in the layers of her poetry". The book also contains explicit references to her move from Jerusalem to Beersheba and features the first instances of her protest and Mizrahi (Jewish Middle Eastern) poetry. Her debut prose fiction novel, *The Eye of the Cat,* was published in 2008. She has since published an additional two poetry books, and two novels. In 1988, Pedaya received the Hebrew University of Jerusalem's Harry Hershon Award. In 1997, she won the Bernstein Prize for her debut book of poetry, the President's Literature Award for her second poetry book (2004), and the Yehuda Amichai Literary Award for her third book of poems (2012).

The title of her first collection, *From a Sealed Ark*, contains the range of meanings associated with the word 'ark', and its so-called sealed nature. The ark is the written word; in Hebrew, it is also used to refer to a musical bar; it is also the Ark of the Temple (as the Ark of the Covenant was previously known, and the name that was later given to the table on which the Torah scroll is laid). An 'ark' is also the sealed box, as well as an echoing of Noah's Ark that had spent many a day sealed. Its description as 'sealed' also references the division between the scriptures' closed sections that begin midline, versus the open sections that begin at the start of a line. This title is also evocative of a line from the poem, *Rachel's Virtue*, written for Rabbi Yehuda Fatiyah, Haviva Pedaya's grandfather: *And I shall open those sealed arks / containing the souls of the subsumed*[2], in which the Lord informs Rachel that He has decided to show mercy and that salvation is nigh, including the resurrection of the dead ('the subsumed'). With this name, Pedaya remarks on her hailing from a word that either defies interpretation or is not easily interpreted. Alternatively, it is a word that lends itself to a multitude of meanings and interpretations. She is fiercely protective of the prospect of remaining sealed off and uninterpretable on the one hand, and of the desire to move away and break out of the confinements of the word, on the other.

Prior to the 1996 publication of her first collection, in 1994 Haviva Pedaya published a series of poems in the magazine, *Rooms*, which included the poem, *A Man Walks* that was written in Delphi, Greece in 1992, but which was only published in her third collection that came out in 2009. For me, this poem holds the key to unlocking both her early and late works – in poetry, prose, and philosophy:

Notes:
1 See Ben-Yaakov, 1970, pp.382-386
2 Ibid, p.385

Read more online

The Mani Brothers
Poems for the Incarcerated
with introduction by Almog Behar

Studio Ronny
A Poem by Ronny Someck

The Light's Chrysalis
A poem by Haviva Pedaya

The Liberation of a Slave
A Short Story by Shalom Darwish
Translation from the Arabic by Uri Horesh

The Revolt of Ignorance
A Short Story by Ya'qub Balbul
Translated from the Arabic by Uri Horesh
Introduction by Orit Bashkin

www.banipal.co.uk/selections/

BOOK REVIEWS

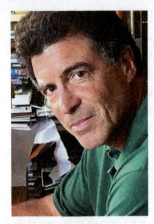

Trino Cruz reviews
**Poems of Alexandria and New York
by Ahmed Morsi**
Translated from the Arabic
by Raphael Cohen
Banipal Books, London, September 2021.
126 pages. Pbk: ISBN: 978-1-913043-15-5,
£9.99 / USD16.95.
Ebook: ISBN: 978-1-913043-16-2, £6.99

Ahmed Morsi: The Poet of Two Cities

The publication of Ahmed Morsi's *Poems of Alexandria and New York* provides us with a welcome doorway into a fascinating and unifying creative universe. Born in Alexandria (Egypt) in 1930 and residing in New York since 1974, Morsi's work thrives on the rare breadth of his independent and eclectic spirit.

"*My world, exists and has existed since time immemorial. It is a world where everything is seen, perceived and understood differently. Your world is bound by conditioning, preconceived habits. In mine, the senses are free.*"*

The poet dares and reveals what he discovers. For millennia poetry and images have endlessly enriched one another, providing us with invaluable clues and insight about ourselves and others.

A few words are due about Ahmed Morsi's personal periplus. Departing from Alexandria in 1955, via Baghdad, then Cairo and eventually settling in New York in 1974. However, there are firm rumours that a part of Morsi never left Alexandria at all. Breaking away and yet never wanting to do so fully, or in Cavafy's own words:

"*You won't find a new country. Won't find another shore.
This city will pursue you.*"

Wherever an artist moves, he carries his dreams and demons with

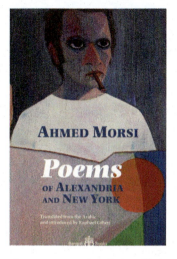

him, totally unaware of how he may have equipped himself for his journey. Morsi's entourage of loved ones and members of his fraternity, Cavafy, al Niffari and al Farahidi, Edwar al-Kharrat, Alfred Faraj, Abd al-Wahhab al-Bayati and so many others, have accompanied him wherever he has gone.

Morsi has been a dedicated and original artist for the whole of his creative life, from the late 1940's onwards. Images and words have always been the substrate from which he has drawn to express himself. A mystic tension pervades all his work.

"Art for me – whether my poetry or paintings – is an expression of my personal experiences; unbounded by time and place. I prefer not to make of art a utility and rather to allow it the utmost freedom to just be."*

Morsi's lifepath has resulted in two clearly defined poetic periods, the first from 1949 to 1968, when he was based between his native Alexandria, Baghdad and Cairo, and the second, which starts in 1996, when the poet had already lived for over 20 years in New York. The poems in this book are those which inaugurate this second period.

Morsi's poetry and painting were closer during the first period. The prolonged silence in his poetic writing resulted in a point of inflection in which there was a divergence from his painting and artistic expression for which there was to be greater continuity. In his poetry, the 30-year silence resulted in a changed poetic voice.

This book, in the excellent translation of Raphael Cohen, beautifully juxtaposes two inspired and contrasting gazes, which are closely interwined and ultimately fuse into one. *Pictures from the New York Album* and *Elegies to the Mediterranean*, two of Morsi's best-known collections of poetry, marked his return to poetry after his prolonged silence.

We realise that in Morsi's creative universe, Alexandria and New York are two faces of the same city. Multiple side-doors, lanes and corridors connect them, through them an inexhaustible creative energy freely flows. These two cities have come together in Morsi for a purpose. They have coalesced in the life of the artist, in his tireless memory which tells us of the world differently.

In the opening lines of the book, Alexandria's Eastern Harbour already surfaces, and becomes an important anchor-point and reference throughout:

> *The sky over the Eastern Harbour*
> *I remember was a deaf mirror,*
> *dripping the bodies of the dead.*
> *Were they the bodies of the living?*
> (Details from a Mural)

The poet, so sensitive to the lives of others around him, senses in his midst, through the lives and deaths of his ageing neighbours, Larry, Rachel, Victoria, in that strange and dynamic vertical community of residents of a city building, those who fear the pursuit of Death, and the futile defying of its snares.

> *. . . I was curious to know*
> *where the old Rachel*
> *had disappeared to, and how silently she had gone?*
> (The Lady in Appartment 12 E)

His own hospitalisation experience is recounted and reflected upon in the poem "5 days in Cornell Hospital", in which he explores the unfathomable relationship between the living and the dead which so intrigues the poet.

> *Which of us knows whether we are alive*
> *or dead?*

> *The corridors echoed with the groans of the elderly*
> *awaiting the appearance of Death*

The surrealist and metaphysical influences sharpened Morsi's language early on, giving rise to an original and powerful idiom which has drawn wisely from the deep memory of human existence and culture. A language where East and West, North and South have en-

Ahmed Morsi in his home in Manhattan, December 2018, photo by Samuel Shimon

riched their meanings beyond recognition, new bearings are exposed which anchor this space in a sense of being which goes far beyond the merely superficial and the narrow paths of our individual histories. A wonderful example of this is his memorable poem "The Road to Manhattan" in which the surreal atmosphere and powerful imagery engulf us:

> Manhattan loomed in the distance
> like tall Giacometti figurines
> plucking the fins from fish
> submerged in the clouds.
> . . .
> Manhattan slithers forward
> stretching dragon hands, smashing drawers
> out of which the secrets of poets fall
> . . .
> Was I too
> searching for something lost?

The down-to-earth familiarity with which Morsi converses with al Niffari, Cavafy or Al-Farahidi, shows us the artist and intelectual projecting himself through the refracting lens of his own life and experience. He quietly and lucidly shows us how alive they still are, how relevant they are to this day. The present demands to be the open meeting place for these gifted beings who have shed so much light on us. These poems in turn serve to connect us with their voices. Morsi combs the streets of Soho for the great 10th century sufi mystic, al-Niffari:

> . . . *seeking for a lover*
> *one thousand years old.*

As he continues his search on West Broadway, he stumbles over a body:

> *I avoided checking the truth,*
> *averted my face*
> *and continued walking aimlessly,*
> *a question ringing in my ears,*
> *a deep echo:*
>
> *Did I stumble over my body*
> *or did I stumble over yours?*
>   (Adventures in Search of al-Niffari)

Al-Niffari followed our poet from Alexandria to New York, an unexpected stowaway who has remained silent all these years, and is now in open dialogue with him:

> *It's enough to wrap yourself*
> *whether you come evening or morning*
> *in your* Mawaqif

As Al Niffari is brought to life, walking the streets of lower Manhattan, he reminds us of the power and relevance of his *Al Mawaqif*. This is a precious cultural gesture, years after the Mahjar writer, Ameen Rihani, had brought the great Al Ma'arri to New York when he translated his *Luzumiyyat*.

Without the burden of blurring nostalgias or backward-looking distortions, how portable is one's homeland, does it not fit untidyly into one's heart, one's memory and imagination? Is not each day, wherever we may be, our only homeland after all!

On Canal Street I rummaged
through boxes of things
nobody wished to reclaim

looking for my own homeland
               (Lament to the Sea I)

The recurring theme surfaces in the book's second section:

to search in the corners
of your forgotten suitcases
for a homeland
that you speak of
  as though something lost.
             (Impression 23)

A homeland that is so deeply rooted in oneself:

now back in Manhattan
having returned from the dolorous journey,
seeking a homeland forgotten
but in the features of your face.
             (Impression 24)

In the poem "Café Reggio", he pays tribute to poet, friend and fellow-exile Joseph Brodsky:

in the colony of cursed poets,
trying to kill the birds of poetry.

Throughout the book there is a blurring of boundaries between life and death. The book's first section closes with the poem "Greeting Card" in which:
the sea trenches fill with the bodies of sailors and fish
to erect a tomb for the living.

As we enter the book's second section, *Elegies to the Mediterranean*, we turn our gaze inwards towards Alexandria as its Eastern Harbour resurfaces.

The poet *drags the nets of exile* across the twenty-six "Impressions of Anfoushi". The Alexandrian neighbourhood of Anfoushi imposes itself, and becomes another important anchor-point for the poet's memory and imagination.

Does it matter that the traces of
your childhood are dead and buried
In the ruins of your sunken city . . . ?
     (Impression 1)

In *Impression 5*, the poet traces back to his seven-year-old self, that spark which has driven his search and creativity to this very day:
You weren't afraid to soar in search of secrets
on the surface or underwater.
You weren't afraid of secrets.

The uncovering of that richness which must be retrieved and shared:
Things and places
that have left no trace
visible to the eye
     (Impression 7)

The shadowless beings which so often inhabit Morsi's paintings also move freely through his poems.
When he left Alexandria
did he know
his body would no longer cast
a shadow, long or short,
on the cobbles of its streets
like an alien being
rejected by the Earth and rendered shadowless.
     (Impression 8)

We are swept on by the torrent of things grown so familiar that they cast no shadow. We float, we float . . . These beautiful words from Virginia

Woolf's *The Waves* also echo within me.

What is the nature of these failing shadows?
In "Impression 18" the poet asks:
Have you poured over all the maps of the invisible cities?
Perhaps you concealed your shadow one day
in the interstices of nowhere.

Alexandria is a symbol, a city of myth and flesh, invented by its inhabitants who are in turn the expression of it. Alexandria, the timeless city of the Delta, great source of images and memory which endlessly flow into our world. The inexhaustible crossroads of trade and myths, linking imaginations across continents, the city which surfaces again and again, is all too real. But what will all this mean to those who follow. To his daughters the poet says:
You did not really intend
to give them
a fake legacy
when you gave them a rusty key
to unlock the city of Alexandria.

You never knew
that what you had to pass on
was never the key
but illusion on illusion.
           (Impression10)

In "Impression 17", we are suddenly walking the streets of Manhattan, having returned unexpectedly through an Anfoushi alley, you realise how inextricably they are both connected in the poet, one and the same being breathing both cities to its lees.

The "*country of the others*" where he has lived for so long is now his own, is there anything at all that has remained unchanged?
What he left behind no longer exists:

all cities of imagination and desire disappear.
           (Impression 14)

Why are we nostalgic for places that don't exist
and never have existed
in either the land of the living
or the land of the dead?
             (Impression 18)

Expressions of exile, anonymity, dislocation, and estrangement, which have often been remarked in Morsi's painting, also find expression in his poetry:
a strange sense of estrangement
after a quarter century of diaspora
in the wastelands of this enchanted city.

And what is the past?
A being or a thing?
             (Impression 19)

With the sea drying, and the canals and Delta of the past now silted, the restless cities, which inhabit us endlessly, change their faces, while that which remains unchanged appears merely lifeless!

In "Impression 19", the poet refers to his poetic silence. What could have held back the poetry for over thirty years, what prolonged this gestation? The breaking of this silence, opened up new territory for the poet.
the phoenix of poetry rises
from its stupor in a dead space
after thirty years' slumber
in hibernation.
             (Impression 19)

Cavafy is never far, he has been shadowing Morsi for a lifetime!
Now and again I saw Cavafy
In the shadows of Perfumers Street
             (Impression 20)

In a beautiful and significant poem, in the closing section of the book, *Five Poems*, the poet traces back to winter 1945 in Alexandria, a day he still remembers, of how Al-Farahidi, the great eighth-century philologist from Basra, uncovered in him a sense and ignited a

passion which have not abandoned him ever since:
awed by the naked bodies of words.

. . .

*worlds of sound opened up to me
and the desert beasts' rhythmic beat.
(Surgery on Al-Khalil..)*

Morsi, the great Mediterranean artist and poet, knows himself to be a part of that powerful river that flows from the East, constantly renewing itself. Like so many other artists who crossed the Atlantic before him, he pays tribute to Picasso, Matisse, Braque, Beckmann and Morandi in his poem *The Eighth International Fine Art Print Fair*. His words also remind me of the Mahjar movement, with Gibran, Rihani and Naimy, arriving in New York from the Mediterranean Levant at the beginning of the twentieth century.

He knows he is one of those:
*who came to Manhattan
from another world, guided by the force of their visions.*

The sharing and communication of human experience and knowledge via our creative work, is the backbone of our civilization. Its immense value lies in that it captures the essence of our existence, fleshes out the heartland of our memory, something which would otherwise just fizzle out traceless.

This deceivingly slim volume is a precious threshold into an exceptionally rich universe. When we close this book there is a sense of having lived further, of having shared and delved deep into the creative life of a generous and gifted human being. The reader can only be infinitely grateful for such a timely and reassuring gesture of such deep significance.

Sources:
*The Flying Poet, Aicon Gallery New York, December 2018-January 2019:
http://www.artbreath.org/interviews/ahmed-morsi
http://officemagazine.net/flying-poet

BOOK REVIEWS

Susannah Tarbush reviews
**The Madness of Despair
by Ghalya F T Al Said**
Translated by Raphael Cohen
Banipal Books, UK, 2021. 256 pages
ISBN Hbk: 978-1-913043-21-6
ISBN Pbk: 978-1-913043-12
ISBN eBook: 978-1-913043-13-1
Hbk £22.00, Pbk £11.99, Ebook £6.99

The love triangle that becomes a vicious circle

In this novel the Omani fiction writer, poet and museum founder Ghalya FT Al Said explores the love triangle between three Arab émigrés living in London: Maliha, her husband Nafie and their friend Nadim, an urbane and successful doctor. Nadim is secretly Maliha's lover although he is married to an Englishwoman by whom he has several children.

The picture on the cover of *The Madness of Despair* hints at the psychological state of Maliha. It is a 2019 painting by Iraqi artist Afifa Aleiby entitled *Silence of the Dwellings* and portrays a young woman, an expression of anxiety and desperation on her face, standing in a darkened interior, an open window behind her. When Maliha first meets Nadim she tells him: "Since coming to this country, Doctor, I've lived a totally isolated and lonely life, skulking behind these walls. I don't know a soul. Again and again, I've resolved to break out of my isolation. I suffer so much."

Maliha had never wanted to marry Nafie. Back in her home country her brutal older brother had forced her into wedlock with this old friend who had been working in London. In revenge, Maliha decided that "her wedding night would be turned into her husband's curse". When she awoke at dawn the next day she "screamed for all to hear in the alleyways that her husband was impotent". To escape this public humiliation Nafie fled back to London with his new bride.

Maliha is from a poor family and Al Said gives us poignant glimpses

BOOK REVIEWS

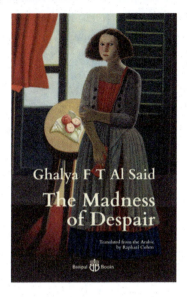

of her deprived childhood. She had some success as a pedlar of small items as a girl, but her brother snatched away the meagre earnings she had hidden in a box. She still cherishes dreams of becoming a businesswoman and from time to time in London she tries her luck as a street trader.

At the time of her marriage Maliha was deceived by Nafie into believing that he had prospered and lived a life of luxury in London. She is devastated to find herself living with him in a wretched run-down hostel and then in a cramped council flat in a block on cosmopolitan Goldhawk Road in Shepherds Bush, West London.

She spends much time gazing out of the window at the busy shopkeepers across the road: the Indian jeweller, the Sudanese draper, the Lebanese furniture seller, the Moroccan purveyor of shoes and bags, the British butcher, the Italian restaurateur. She wishes Nafie was an enterprising shopkeeper rather than having his "crap job in a shoe factory, whose smells of rotten leather, burnt plastic, and chemical dyes he brings home with him. Even his fingers and nails are dyed".

Ghalya Al Said was educated in the UK and has a PhD in international relations from Warwick University. She is the author of six novels, but *The Madness of Despair* is the first to appear in English translation. Al Said uses her intimate knowledge of the UK and its Middle Eastern diaspora to good effect in her writing. Four of her six novels are set in the UK. They include her 2005 debut *Ayam fil Jena* (Days in Heaven) an excerpt from which was published in *Banipal 51*, in translation by Charis Olszok.

The Madness of Despair was first published in 2011 by Beirut-based Riad El-Rayyes Books under the title *Junoun al-Ya's*. Katia al-Tawil's review of the Arabic original appeared in *Banipal 71* together with the first chapter of Raphael Cohen's translation. Cohen is a professional translator and lexicographer who studied Arabic and Hebrew at the universities of Oxford and Chicago. He has translated many literary works from Arabic and his translation of *The Madness of Despair*, much of which is in dialogue, has a commendable naturalness and sensitive choices of colloquialisms.

In *The Madness of Despair* Al Said takes us into the world of marginalised Middle Eastern immigrants in London, surviving on poorly paid jobs and welfare payments. The couple's neighbours in the council block are mostly Arab and Muslim, from traditional and conservative societies. They are simultaneously intrigued and outraged by the strange relationship between Maliha, Nafie and the Doctor. Nadim is the couple's constant visitor, bringing them endless supplies of food and consumer goods and seeming to control the household. The neighbours speculate about his nationality and origins and come up with various outlandish theories in the face of his refusal to answer any of their questions. At one point they subject him to violence.

Al Said shows herself to be a gifted and inventive storyteller as she depicts the descent of Maliha from discontent into hysteria, depression and a loss of grip on reality. Maliha is no mere passive victim however and has a streak of obstinacy and rebelliousness. On his side, Dr Nadim resorts to ever more extravagant and manipulative behaviour to indulge his passion for Malia and to exert and maintain control over her and Nafie, partly through becoming their benefactor.

Although Maliha shares a bed with Nafie she refuses to have sex with him, employing various ruses and excuses. She meets Doctor Nadim for the first time when he arrives for dinner at her and Nafie's flat before Nafie has returned home from work. For both, this encounter is a shattering *coup de foudre*. Before long they embark on a steamy affair, conducted in his surgery out of hours. Their physical union is described in rapturous, at times somewhat overblown, terms: "The planets stopped in their orbits, humanity froze, wind, rain and clouds stopped."

Maliha and Nadim, swept along by powerful emotions, initially find their affair fulfilling. Nadim has reached a stage in his life where he longs to reunite with his culture – "He had a hankering for anything Arab and oriental: people, food, customs, climate, clothing, even the streets and alleyways." He collects Middle Eastern artefacts and the walls of his waiting room are crammed with oriental prayer beads, and other mementos. "Maliha's beauty evoked the beauty of his distant country" and she fits the bill as an idealised Arab woman. On her side, Maliha was "dazzled by his smart appearance, clean clothes, deep voice, easy smile and kind eyes." She envisaged that her life would go from strength to strength with "the dear cultured man who encouraged her to move forward".

But although Nadim's marriage has grown cold and distant he refuses to consider divorce because it would break up his family and bring him financial ruin. As time passes Maliha realises nothing will change and the triangle becomes claustrophobic.

The trio spend many evenings eating, sitting and talking together in the Goldhawk Road flat, Nafie seemingly oblivious to the sexual relationship between Nadim and Maliha. She regularly berates Nafie for what she sees as his defects and failures as a husband. "As much as he could he avoided her gaze in fear of her hurtful words and blazing looks." He retreats at one stage to a corner of the room in which he has placed a wooden trunk containing his personal treasures: dried food, photos, complete poems of Antara, tapes of old songs, and so on.

The Doctor is at his most devious when Nafie puts Maliha under increasing pressure to have a child. Nadim hatches a secret plan whereby Maliha will become pregnant without having sex with her husband. But motherhood brings Maliha no joy: she fails to bond with her baby son and his rearing is left to Nadim and Nafie.

Al Said has a well-developed sense of tragedy and comedy and she portrays the love triangle with many touches of humour, such as when Nadim tries to turn Maliha into his vision of the ideal woman. "I love you as an Arab woman, not anything else. Look how vivid and beautiful Middle Eastern clothes are and how funny modern Western blouses and dresses look. Just seeing you in them gives me a terrible headache, especially when you wear those damned blue jeans. Blue jinns more like!" In one episode, in an effort to please Maliha, Nadim buys a whole lamb's carcass. When he is carrying it on the underground, wrapped in a cloth, blood starts to drip onto the floor and the police are called as the passengers suspect Nadim is transporting a human corpse.

Towards its end *The Madness of Despair* grows increasingly dark. "The three friends, Nafie, Maliha, and the Doctor continued living this bizarre vicious circle of despairing monotony for so long it verged on madness," Al Said writes, as the novel builds towards to its dramatic and shocking denouement.

BOOK REVIEWS

Hannah Somerville reviews
**Sarajevo Firewood
by Saïd Khatibi**
Translated from the Arabic
by Paul Starkey
Banipal Books, London, September 2021
ISBN: 978-1-913043-23-0. Pbk, 320pp,
£11.99 / USD19.95.
EBook 978-1-913043-24-7 £6.99

A singular tale of survival and self-realization

This excellent third novel by Algerian writer and journalist Saïd Khatibi is a masterful rumination on war and genocide, place-memory, independent inquiry and self-actualization. More than that, it's completely unique. First published in Arabic in 2018 and newly translated by Paul Starkey, the intricate plot of *Sarajevo Firewood,* which was shortlisted for the 2020 International Prize for Arabic Fiction, charts the respective, ultimately intertwined trajectories of Salim, a harassed former reporter from Algiers, and Ivana, a waitress and aspiring playwright from a broken home in Sarajevo. Both are compelled to leave their civil war-ravaged countries of birth for Ljubljana, Slovenia. In the frigid non-embrace of this third city, both are shellshocked to learn the truth about their family origins and crimes committed by those closest to them, under cover of armed conflict. With refreshing honesty and peculiar grace, the book invites us to consider the true meaning of fealty – and freedom – for those whose fates appear circumscribed by those that came before them.

In his Ibn Battuta Award-winning account of travel in the Balkans, *The Inflamed Gardens of the East* (2015), an excerpt of which was published by Banipal in autumn 2019, Khatibi recounted his first visit to Sarajevo: a city where football matches are screened beside mass graveyards, still sunk in poverty and the nightmare of its recent past behind the glossy, tourist-friendly façade. The Bosnian War and ensuing ethnic cleansing of 1992-95 saw 100,000 people killed, 80,000

BOOK REVIEWS

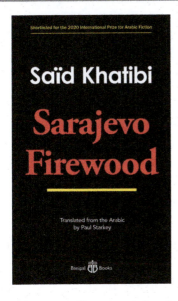

of them Bosniaks; fatalities in the conflict between the Algerian government and Islamist insurgents from 1991 to 2002 were of a similar magnitude. "Today I feel that I left a part of my heart in Sarajevo," Khatibi writes. "A city which resembles me as I resemble it, to a point almost of identity: lazy like me, elegant, poor and proud of itself."

This tribute to a trauma-twinned city emerged fully formed three years later in the character of Ivana. Downtrodden and mortally dissatisfied, this young woman's myriad internal complexes are presented as the outcomes of her parents' violent marriage, child abuse by a now-dead father accused of collaborating with the Chetniks, having a sister who lost her mind overnight, and walking day after day through still-tense city streets built over the corpses of the dead.

In Ivana's plaintive first-person narrations, the city is also obliquely encountered: like Sarajevo, her mother, mired in depression and languor, can offer neither the answers nor the emotional nourishment she seeks. Likewise Khatibi does a brilliant job of presenting a nuanced approach to trauma, both individual and collective: when describing instances of male brutality or cold, transactional sex, Khatibi has this normally loquacious, quick-to-anger protagonist subtly disengage. The language becomes more detached, cursory and to the point. Rather than cruelty and injustice being repressed or revolted against, there is a great sense of both being lived with pragmatically: "If I had been imprisoned in Sarajevo," Ivana reflects, "I would not have been afraid, for our freedom there is a vast prison, where we play tricks with our vocabulary in order not to call it by its real name."

More than 900 miles away in the Algerian capital, we are introduced to Salim: a newly out-of-work journalist, born in Bou Saada as a child of the now-supine War of Independence generation. Salim's daily errands are punctuated by beige meals eaten on the hoof, the eternal pursuit of forged visas and documentation, and the fleeting but always horrific spectre of Islamist atrocities. Every element of lived existence in Algiers is presented as fragile, transient, and perpetually under siege: from a young graduate smashed to smithereens in a traffic accident to Salim's strained relationship with an older teacher, Malika, which appears strangulated by the welter of things unsaid.

Khatibi has not lived in Algeria for 10 years. But his recollections of day-to-day turmoil in his country of birth emerge clear as a bell, and always in fresh, creative forms. So too the state of mind: "We sat in the kitchen," Salim reports at one stage, "and she gave me a cup of coffee with the strongly flavoured thyme that grows on Djebel Kerdada, which overlooks the town like a customs officer lying in wait for secrets, and teems with poisonous snakes and scorpions". Bou Saada, through how its people cross the road, is "like a man who had been emasculated".

In turn, Khatibi illustrates Ljubljana through the eyes of the two new arrivals. Installed with his uncle Si Ahmad, who owns a café in the "city of bridges and pretty women", Salim's early observations on the behaviour of the Slovenes are thrilling; later, though, he notes that the residents of that city, "wrapped in its silk blanket of security", would be unable to comprehend "the monsters that had sprung up in the East and ripped apart the wombs of Sarajevo". Ivana is disillusioned from the start, encountering the city chiefly through its vicious and lascivious men while trying to hold down a new job, coincidentally at Si Ahmad's cafe. She takes refuge in the theatre, and in writing a play modelled on the 1959 French romantic drama *Hiroshima Mon Amour*: a vocation that crystallizes after the pair finally meet. "In the theatre," Ivana writes, "I can manoeuvre destiny, speak harshly to it, knead it and conquer it. On the stage, I grow muscles, my face wears a smile."

DIGITAL BANIPAL

An annual subscription gives access to the complete archive

Subscribe to
Digital Banipal
with Exact Editions:

https://shop.exacteditions.com/banipal

After a chain of shocking events in Slovenia wrenches the pair apart, their true, shared purpose becomes clear: a type of resurrection. Horrified into near-stasis by a murder in Ljubljana and revelations about his family's past, Salim finally embarks on a fact-finding journey on Ivana's advice: "Look for the whole truth and do not be satisfied with the testimony of one person." As the details unfurl, Ivana immortalises their stories onstage: discovering along the way, with al-

Saïd Khatibi

most painful poignancy, that there exist after all individuals willing to help her succeed in good faith. By interrogating the untold secrets of the "wars that had no name", each finds a way to resolve, or at least render bearable, their own internal war.

With *Sarajevo Firewood*, Khatibi offers a singular tale of survival and self-realization. It's also a tale of two cities, worlds apart but bonded by appalling violence and individual forbearance. In his interview for IPAF last April, Khatibi noted "a deeply entrenched literary tradition which seems to be dying out in modern times: that the majority of writers were once journalists." *Sarajevo Firewood* is a case study in how one craft can inform the other for the better: Khatibi writes fiction with the empathy and attention to detail of a seasoned reporter, but also with a constant half-an-eye on ensuring the reader comprehends the subjects at hand. Translated beautifully by Paul Starkey, the prose is spare, uncomplicated and precise, with not a word wasted. But the observations that spill from each page are brand new, and perfectly crafted to be enlightening beyond their base content. This is a compelling and edifying read, worthy of every praise.

BOOK REVIEWS

Fayez Ghazi reviews
Al-Hamaqa kama lam Yarwiha ahad (Foolishness as No One Told It)
by **Samir Kacimi**
Published by Editions Difaf, Beirut, 2020 and Editions El-Ikhtilef, Algiers, 2020
ISBN: 978-614-02-1851-2

The naked truth of silver-tongued corruption

Trilogies in Arab and international literature, in which writers build a progressive narrative and the successive development of characters, are something of a fashion. For a writer to destroy everything he built in his first novel and reconfigure the characters, keeping their names but taking on new roles that have nothing to do with what they were before, and then to destroy this second structure to complete the events of the first novel, is truly rare to find, and I think a first in Arabic literature.

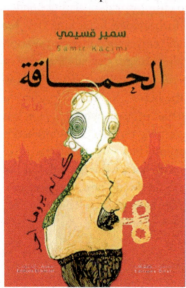

Cover of the Arabic edition

Such is the case with *Foolishness as No One Told It*, the seventh novel of Algerian journalist and writer Samir Kacimi. It takes up afresh the themes and characters of *The Stairs of Trolard* (2020) that was longlisted for the 2020 International Prize for Arabic Fiction, and was described as "a daring and prophetic novel which re-imagines the political history of Algeria – and through it Arab history as a whole – in a satirical style, using fantastical elements to simulate reality".

In two parts, the first, entitled "Fools of the Don di Carr", begins with a letter from a publisher to a writer inviting him to write about food and dogs because readers hope to forget reality, not confront it. The writer replies: "The master is an illusion that only slaves believe in."

The protagonist, Jamal Humaidi, the son of a clairvoyant (Awyush), runs a brothel. One day, he has a dream and soon finds it is the dream of the country's

Samir Kacimi

President, and that it was imprinted on his subconscious because he watched an analysis of it on television. The general background is that the President tells his mistress, Aisha La Rolex, about his dream and assigns his security services to search for its characters in the real world. Aisha carries the dream to "the man with the medals", another of her lovers. And here begin plans and counter-plans to oust the President from his position.

"The man sitting there knows that he is accused of something. He has been accused from the moment he was born in this country."

Besides Jamal Humaidi, there is Ibrahim Bafalolo, a diligent public servant for thirty years in a petty job, and Essam Kashkasy, a handsome young man, the lover of Bakhta an unlucky gambler, and the electronic publisher going by the name Dalilah Ghandrich, who looks like Trotsky. Other secondary characters include Moha Bou Khanouna and Olga, a lonely ex-prostitute, Ahmed al-Selouqi, Saeed al-Deeb, Chief of Protocol, and Officer Salem al-Jamal.

Society is divided into two categories: "pre-threshold beings"– who are the great majority (the people, the marginalized, and commanded slaves . . .),; and "post-threshold beings" – who are the ruling minority (presidents, ministers and senior officers). Kacimi deconstructs reality, starting with the figure of cultural corruption represented by Issam Kashkasi, and the Historian, followed by that of flagrant political prostitution in the character of Aisha La Rolex (a brothel madam who became Minister of Tourism); to the sharp criticism of writers, critics and the directed press (p. 51-52). Kacimi satirizes French speakers in higher circles, the military and their limited brains (p. 181 to 184), the ignorance rampant in public administration (p. 101), immorality in official positions, and the lies of history and its repeated reformulations.

This part ends with Jamal Humaidi lying unconscious in a junk yard, where in a dream he meets friends who have moved "beyond the threshold", and with the silver-tongued Aysha comparing her previous work in prostitution with her later work in politics.

"You have to believe me if I tell you that what you consider to be whoredom, will remain – even if I spend all my life in it – more honourable than politics."

The second half of the novel is entitled "The Fool Always Reads", in which it appears that the first part was in fact a dream which Jamal Hamidi wakes up from to find he is President of the Republic. This dream narrative as a convention resembles the end of Milan Kundera's novel *Identity*, however, Kacimi places it at his novel's centre. At this point, Kacimi reconnects this novel to his preceding one *The Stairs of Trolard*, laying out possible paths for events, a fictional re-

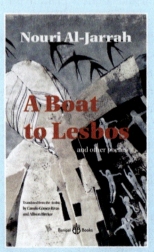

A Boat to Lesbos
and other poems
by Nouri Al-Jarrah

This powerful epic poem by Syrian poet Nouri Al-Jarrah, in the form of a Greek tragedy, bears passionate and dramatic witness to the horrors and ravages suffered by Syrian families forced to flee across the Mediterranean.

"The delicate, heart-breaking poems in A Boat to Lesbos *find in Sappho's exile a common bond between the island's most famous poet and Syrians escaping civil war."* Ruth Padel

Translated from the Arabic
by Camilo Gómez-Rivas and Allison Blecker
Cover & inside paintings by Reem Yassouf

The poet's first collection in English translation
ISBN: 978-0-9956369-4-1 • 120pp • £9.99 • €13 • US$15

reading of history, or a reformulation of what might have been, showing his supreme ability to destroy what he had already created and rebuild again instantly! If *The Stairs of Trolard* was based on the idea of disappearing doors and what they symbolize, then this second half of "Foolishness as No One Told It" begins from the idea of people losing their ability to read and its symbolism of illiteracy and ignorance.

It is a brave move – Samir Kacimi kills off his protagonist, the President, and re-weaves the events of *The Stairs of Trolard,* choosing and appointing a new president – through intertextuality – suggesting that life is a closed circle where history repeats itself as a new farce that differs in name only.

After the president's death and everyone's ability to read is lost, a former officer is summoned by a group of retirees who have an idea of finding a solution through the ways of deep state. Ironically, Colonel Saeed al-Deeb can only read *No One Writes to the Colonel* by Gabriel Márquez. After ten years, he finds a solution, which leads to the appointment as President of Salim Ghashi, known also as Salem al-Jamal [the Camel] after the two humps on his back.

Kacimi continues his harsh criticism in this second half: how the people are being fooled and used, how leaders are made, the rule of the military disguised with a civilian *façade*, the decision-maker who lives overseas, and the general ignorance of the people, their backwardness and rampant illiteracy.

"In an illiterate country, you do not need to read until you become their master. All you need is to realize that they are ignorant, and to make them imagine that they are not. In such a country, nothing is better than a stupid people pretending intelligence who carry you on their back, thinking that you are the one carrying them."

Foolishness as No One Told It is the truth as no one told it: the lowest is a slave of the highest and the highest is a slave to another abroad. Kacimi deftly exposes fraud, deception, falsification and the distortion of the past, the present and perhaps the future. Ignorance and lies compromise everyone – from the doorman to the ruler. He delivers this naked and clear truth in a more compelling language than in *The Stairs of Trolard,* with a breadth that reflects social reality, and a depth that probes political reality, making this one of the best modern Arab novels.

BOOKS IN BRIEF

Beirut 2020: The Collapse of a Civilization, a Journal
by Charif Majdalani

Translated from the French by Ruth Diver
Mountain Leopard Press (UK) Other Press (USA) July 2021. ISBN 978-1914495038.
Hbk, 174 pages £14.99 / $14.99

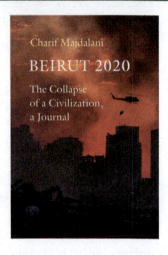

This journal is more than a cry from the heart and it lays bare far more than the feelings and emotions that came violently to the surface in Beirut during 2020, and especially July and August 2020. Spread over 75 short chapters, it ends with an anguished note: "Our lives, like that drink can, and that cigar, thrown to the winds …"

Charif Majdalani, who was born in Lebanon in 1960 and teaches French literature at the Université Saint-Joseph in Beirut, has written a special Preface for the English-language edition, to explain to Anglophone readers the special centuries-old "religious mosaic and cultural diversity" that make up Lebanon and that explain why the country "avoided dictatorship and the so-called socialist models" of the rest of the Arab world.

He recounts living the day by day modern horror story of Lebanon's disintegrating economy while explaining its 100-year history as a modern state, and in particular its leaders' transformation over years from enthusiastic young men, to career soldiers, to warlords, to politicians and finally to corrupt oligarchs – often the same families and actual persona.

The breakdown of the infrastructure builds to the crescendo of corruption that resulted in the port explosion on 4 August 2020 and its horrendous destruction, loss of life, and gruesome injuries.

"As if that entire collapse I was describing was not happening fast enough, as if this degeneration was not swift enough, some unknown malignant force decided to precipitate them and in a matter of seconds hurled everything that was still standing to the ground."

Rather than give figures for the destruction, Majdalani gives personal and individual descriptions of the awful effects inflicted on friend after friend – Reina, Jad, Karim, Omar, Paula, Monique, Marwan, Nada, Hatem, Michel – the people of Beirut. A spontaneous movement of volunteers begins the process of clearing, cleaning up, sweeping, sorting, and giving out food and drink. But the survival instinct of the oligarchy in power means citizens were left to do as best they can, with banks shut and virtually no electricity. The country is under siege from the inside – "The government is trying to overthrow the people", Majdalani concludes.

As they clean and clear up, the young, however, are resisting – red and white banners proclaim: "We will never leave, we will rebuild."

BOOKS IN BRIEF

No One May Remain: Agatha Christie, Come, I'll Tell You How I Live
by Haitham Hussein
Translated from the Arabic by Nicole Fares
Dar Arab, UK, August 2021
ISBN: 9781788710817. Pbk, 208pp, £7.00

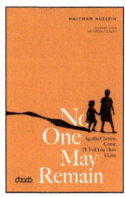

The book begins with a note from Agatha Christie saying that her memoir, Come, Tell Me How You Live, which details her life in Syria in the 1930s, was "small beer – a very small book full of everyday doings and happenings". Novelist and journalist Haitham Hussein hoped to create the same, and he has done – magnificently – recounting his experiences in story after story after arriving at UK passport control and claiming asylum. But he also lends to each episode an extraordinary depth and dimension by inquiring into the countless crucial existential questions of memory, identity, place, family, space, culture and traditions (all needing to be answered) that face asylum seekers, refugees and all the displaced and uprooted who need to "escape the inferno of death in its many form".

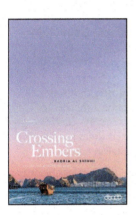

Crossing Embers
by Badria Al Shihhi
Translated from the Arabic by Sawad Hussain
Dar Arab, UK, August 2021
ISBN: 9781788710824. Pbk, 284pp, £10.00

Zahra's husband has left her and their mountain village in Oman, wanting to travel – maybe to East Africa to marry a black African slave, say the rumours. The village regards him as dead, and Zahra faces marriage to her cousin Abdallah to avoid disgrace. She has no power to refuse these demands of her family, and society, so takes the only way out. An African family slave helps her plan difficult sea journeys from Sur to Malindi, to Mombasa and Zanzibar – she has a new life, until a slave uprising, burning farms, gunshots and war, confront her with a final desperate decision. This historical novel is the author's debut novel, first published in Arabic in 1999.

Without
by Younis al-Akhzami
Translated from the Arabic by Michelle Hartman and Caline Nasrallah
Dar Arab, UK, July 2021
ISBN: 9781788710800 Pbk 256pp, £10.00

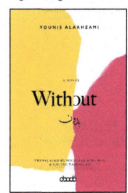

Omani author Al Akhzami is a short story writer and novelist. This, his fifth novel, follows the difficult life of a transgender young person in the Middle East. At the start he riffs on a quote from Jack Kerouac to warn: "This is a novel of pain, love and danger". But it is very much a novel of love, friendship, survival and acceptance, as Alia and her family deal with a complex challenge. Alia is a Yemeni girl living in Khobar, Saudi Arabia, and Sana'a in Yemen. When her periods don't start her mother arranges various unsuccessful treatments, but growing signs of a moustache prove to Alia she is not actually a girl. With the support of her father she moves to study in Swansea, UK, and makes the decision to transition and change her name to Ali. Ali undergoes many operations with several delays and more tests, and more delays until one day he is without hope..

A Dove in Free Flight by Faraj Bayrakdar
Upset Press, USA, October 2021
ISBN 978-1-937357-00-9. Pbk, 128 pp, USD22.95

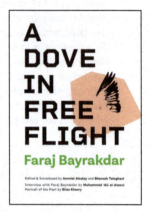

Poems by Faraj Bayrakdar, Interview by Muhammad 'Ali al-Atassi with the poet after his release from incarceration, and 'Portrait of the Poet' by Elias Khoury. Edited & introduced by Ammiel Alcalay and Shareah Taleghani and translated by the New York Translation Collective comprising Ammiel Alcalay, Sinan Antoon, Rebecca Johnson, Elias Khoury, Tsolin Nalbantian, Jeffrey Sacks, and Shareah Taleghani. The poems making up this fourth collection for Bayrakdar were written while he was incarcerated in Syria's Tadmor, Palestine Division and Saydnaya prisons. Smuggled out, they were published in Beirut without Bayrakdar's knowledge and became a means "to mobilize international, intellectual opinion, particularly in France, in order to set the poet free". Moroccan poet Abdellatif Laabi translated them for the French edition, *Ni vivant, ni mort* (1998) and there is also an Italian edition.

Packaged Lives by Haifa Zangana
Translated from the Arabic by Wen-chin Ouyang
Syracuse University Press, December 2021.
176 pages. Pbk: 9780815611370. £12.50 / USD14.95.
eBook: 9780815655411

Ten short stories and a novella by Iraqi-Kurdish author and activist Haifa Zangana. Iraqis living in exile come to life as men and women caught between two worlds, portrayed keenly, sensitively and lovingly, but without compromise. They cannot return to Iraq and are forced to wait for news from afar while at the same time being unable to fully adjust to life in Britain and make new homes. The question "What is home?" is at the heart of each story as the protagonists, stuck in ready-made or "packaged lives", struggle to set themselves free from relationships they have been caught up in, and rely on art, poetry, and nature to provide escape.

BOOKS IN BRIEF

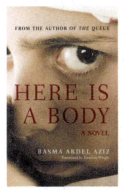

Here Is a Body by Basma Abdel Aziz
Translated from the Arabic by Jonathan Wright
Hoopoe Fiction, September 2021
Pbk. 340pp. ISBN: 9781649030818. £12.99 / USD18.95

The author debut's novel *The Queue* is followed by this passionate and fluid work that takes to task, like a dog to the proverbial bone, the inhuman savagery of state oppression – through the eyes of a street kid. The story of its dirty deceit, its deliberate dehumanization of citizens it doesn't like, its blackmail and threats to life that can only arouse fear and terror in a normal person's soul makes for stressful reading. The struggle for life is the struggle for humanity itself. Survival against the odds. How to remain an individual? How to escape? How to resist? Or is the only chance of life to succumb to the oppression? Dynamic and powerful writing, brilliantly translated by Jonathan Wright.

Like We Still Speak by Danielle Badra
University of Arkansas Press, October 2021
ISBN 978-1-68226-176-7. Pbk, 84pp, USD16.95.
Winner of the 2021 Etel Adnan Poetry Prize

Conversation and memory are at the heart of this award-winning poetry collection by Danielle Badra, an Arab American poet and poetry editor of the literary and arts journal *So To Speak*. Fady Joudah and Hayan Charara write in their preface to the book: "This is a deeply spiritual book, all the more so because of its clarity and humility. Yet, we cannot walk away from the addictive command that so many of these poems ask us to follow: to read them along plural paths whose order changes while their immeasurable spirit remains unbound. Each poem is a singular vessel—of narratives, embodiments that correspond with memories, memories that recollect passion . . . *Like We Still Speak* is a sanctum. Inside it, we are enthralled by beauty, consoled by light, sustained by making."

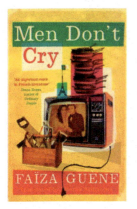

Men Don't Cry by Faiza Guene
Translated from the French by Sarah Ardizzone
Cassava Republic Press, UK, August 2021.
ISBN: 978-1911115694. Pbk, & Ebook: 216pp, £11.99.

A touching and humorous coming-of-age story by the acclaimed author of *Kiffe Kiffe Tomorrow* and *Just Like Tomorrow*. Protagonist Mourad Chennoun is born and grows up in the south of France in an Algerian family – his father spends his days fixing things in the backyard while his mother bemoans the loss of her natal village in

Algeria, and all mention of Mourad's rebellious feminist sister Dounia, who escaped to Paris and became a lawyer, far from the traditions and control of her family, is taboo. Mourad's nightmare would be to end up stuck at home, so he also leaves and starts a teaching career in the Paris suburbs. This is a fast-moving tale of a young man's struggle to juggle loyalties in life, with familiar tropes of tensions between first and second-generation immigrants, which under the pens of Faiza Guene (and her brilliant translator) never feel clichéd.

Zabor, or the Psalms by Kamel Daoud
Translated from the French by Emma Ramadan
Other Press, USA, March 2021.
ISBN 9781635420142. Pbk, 384pp, PB. £13 / $17.99

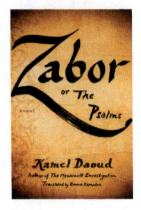

Second novel by the author of *The Meursault Investigation*. Having lost his mother and been shunned by his father, Zabor grows up in the company of books, which teach him a new language. Ever since he can remember, he has been convinced that he has a gift – if he writes, he will stave off death, and those captured in the sentences of his notebooks will live longer. He becomes committed to writing, but will this set him free from a pre-ordained destiny? That is the question.

Between Beirut and the Moon by Naji Bakhti
Influx Press, UK, August 2020
Paperback 288 pages ISBN 978-1910312551

In this debut novel by an author born and raised in Beirut, Adam comes of age in the post-civil-war city, with gunfire, turmoil and comedy liable to erupt at any moment. He wanted to become an astronaut but "who ever heard of an Arab on the moon?" his father, a secular, book-loving journalist, told him. It's an affectionate family saga with vivid vignettes of day-to-day scenarios and a host of Beiruti characters including his teacher Mr Malik, his best friend Basil, who is Druze and wants to go and fight in Syria, and above all his father, who was nearly killed by militiamen wielding AK47s when trying to get supplies of toilet rolls.

The Funambulists: Women Poets of the Arab Diaspora by Lisa Marchi
Syracuse University Press, USA, November 2021
Pbk ISBN 9780815637523 £25 / $29.95
eBook 9780815655473 £17.22

An exploration of contemporary Arab diasporic poetry from a transnational, gendered, and multilingual perspective, illuminating the distinct artistic voice of each poet and highlighting the aesthetic and political relevance that unites their works. The six women poets are Naomi Shihab Nye, Iman Mersal, Nadine Ltaif, Suheir Hammad and Mina Boulhanna. Despite their varying geographical, linguistic and political backgrounds, Marchi finds common ground in themes of injustice, spirituality, gender, race, and class.

Writing Palestine: Palestine Book Awards
Edited by Victoria Brittain and Haifa Zangana
MEMO Publishers, UK, June 2021
ISBN 978-1-907433-47-4. Pbk, 136pp. £15.00

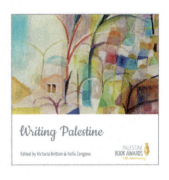

The book, with Arabic and English texts, brings together texts by Rima Khalaf, Salman Abu Sitta, Ramzy Baroud, Ilan Pappé, Richard Falk, Karen Abu Zayd, Salim Vally and Eugene Rogan, who were either keynote speakers at the annual Palestine Book Awards or recipients of awards.

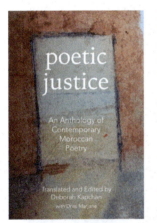

Poetic Justice: An Anthology of Contemporary Moroccan Poetry, edited and translated by Deborah Kapchan, with Driss Marjane.
Center for Middle Eastern Studies, University of Texas at Austin, July 2019. Series: CMES Modern Middle East Literatures in Translation
ISBN: 978-1-4773-1849-2. Pbk, 434 pages. £16.34 / USD21.95

This anthology is "a superb achievement" of scholarship and poetic endeavour by Deborah Kapchan, professor of performance studies at New York University. The book brings into English eighty-four Moroccan poets writing in Arabic, French and Tamazight. Opening with a fascinating essay entitled "On Translation and Ethnography" in which Kapchan describes how "translation takes place in the register of parole, not langue – that is, speech and the sentence and not the abstraction of grammatical language", the book primarily includes poets who began writing after Moroccan independence in 1956 and includes works originally written in Moroccan Arabic (darija), classical Arabic, French, and Tamazight. Why *Poetic Justice*? Moroccan poetry (and especially zajal, oral poetry now written in Moroccan Arabic) is often published in newspapers and journals and is thus a vibrant form of social commentary; what's more, there is a law, a justice, in the aesthetic act that speaks back to the law of the land. *Poetic Justice* because literature has the power to shape the cultural and moral imagination in profound and just ways.

internationales literaturfestival berlin 2021

Director of the Berlin International Festival of Literature, Ulrich Schreiber, is a keen follower of Arabic literature and always invites a number of Arab writers to participate, along with writers from many other countries around the world. In the twenty-first session of the festival, which took place from 8 to 19 September 2021, four writers from the Arab world participated. One, the French-Moroccan writer Leïla Slimani, was invited to give the opening speech of the festival.

On the second day of the festival, *Banipal* magazine editor Samuel Shimon participated in a symposium with German writer and translator Stefan Weidner entitled "The Future of Arabic Literature in Europe". Samuel Shimon spoke about the beginnings of *Banipal* magazine and the role it has played translating Arabic literature into English over its 24 years of publishing to date. He also spoke about the Spanish edition of the magazine, and announced that there was an idea to publish the magazine in German.

Among the Arab writers participating was Algerian author

Leïla Slimani

Samuel Shimon and Stefan Weidner

Abdelouahab Aissaoui, whose novel *The Spartan Court* won the 2020 International Prize for Arabic Fiction. Set at the beginning of the 19th century, with the country under Ottoman rule and at the start of the French occupation, it looks at this period from the perspectives of five characters – a French journalist, a former Napoleonic soldier, an Algerian businessman, a revolutionary, and a prostitute.

On the last evening, 18 September, a seminar was devoted to Jordanian writer Jalal Barjas, who spoke about his writing experience as well as his novel *Notebooks of the Bookseller* which won the 2021 International Prize for Arabic Fiction earlier this year. This novel depicts a world of poverty and uprooting: a bookseller, who finds himself homeless after losing his bookshop, loses himself in the identities of characters from novels and commits several crimes until he meets a woman who changes his life. Despite this, there is no call for him to despair; rather, reaching the depths of such pain is necessary in order to realise new dreams and stand on firmer ground, this time with hope.

Jalal Barjas   *Abdelouahab Aissaoui*

CONTRIBUTORS

Ammiel Alcalay is a poet, novelist, translator, critic and scholar. His books include *After Jews and Arabs*, *Memories of Our Future*, *Keys to the Garden*, *from the warring factions*, and *a little history*. Published in 2021 are *A Dove in Free Flight*, poems by Faraj Bayrakdar, with Shareah Taleghani and the New York Translation Collective, *Ghost Talk*, and *A Bibliography for After Jews & Arabs*. He received a 2017 American Book Award from the Before Columbus Foundation for his work as founder and General Editor of Lost & Found: The CUNY Poetics Document Initiative (lostandfoundbooks.org).

Ishaq Bar-Moshe (1927–2003) Ishaq Bar-Moshe was born and. raised in Baghdad. He was educated at the Rachel Shimon elementary school, Rusafa middle school and completed high school at the Ahliya Jewish school. From 1945–48 he studied at the Law College. He worked as an editor at a number of newspapers including *Al-Shaab* and *al-Ahali*. After being forced to emigrate in 1950, he left Iraq for Israel, where he founded the Jerusalem-based newspaper *al-Anba'a*. Ishaq died of heart disease in Manchester on December 9, 2003. His first collection of short stories was *Wara al-Sur* (Behind the Walls), followed in 1974 by *al-Dibb al-Qutbi wa-Qisas Ukhra* (The Polar Bear and Other Stories) and *Raqsat al-Matar wa-Qisas Ukhra* (Rain Dance and Other Stories). The first part of his memoir, *al-Khuruj min 'Iraq* (Exodus from Iraq) appeared in 1975, followed in 1988 by the novels *Ayyam al-Iraq* (Iraqi Days) and *Bayt fi Baghdad* (A House in Baghdad).

Orit Bashkin is a professor of Middle Eastern history at the University of Chicago, working on the intellectual, social and cultural history of the Arab world. She received her PhD from Princeton University (2005) with a thesis on Iraqi intellectual history. She has written over forty book chapters and articles on Iraqi history, the history of Iraqi Jews, the Arab cultural revival movement (the nahda) in the late 19th century, and the connections between modern Arab history and Arabic literature. Her books include *Impossible Exodus: Iraqi Jews in Israel*, Stanford University Press, 2017; *New Babylonians: A History of Jews in Modern Iraq*. Stanford University Press, 2012 and *The Other Iraq – Pluralism and Culture in Hashemite Iraq*, Stanford University Press, 2009

Almog Behar is a poet, novelist, translator, editor and critic. Behar was born in 1978, and now lives in Jerusalem. He has published six books, the latest being *Kdey She-Hamelach Yitpazer al Ha-Ahava* (Rub Salt into Love, 2021). His novel *Chahla ve-Hezkel* (Rachel and Ezekiel, 2010) was translated into Arabic and published in Cairo in 2016.

CONTRIBUTORS

Behar is one of the founders of the Judeo-Arabic cultural studies program at Tel Aviv University, and teaches in the Literature Department at Tel Aviv University. His other books: *Zim'on Be'erot* (The Thirst of the Wells, 2008), *Ana Min Al-Yahoud* (I am one of the Jews (in Arabic in the original), 2009), *Chut Moshekh Min Ha-Lashon* (A Thread Drawing from the Tongue, 2009), *Shirim Le-Asirei Batei-HaSohar* (Poems for the Prisoners, 2016).

Dan Cern is an English teacher and a graduate of Bar Ilan University with an MA in information science, and later, an MA in English literature.

Trino Cruz, born in Gibraltar in 1960, is a bilingual writer and translator. He grew up in the Straits region, between Gibraltar, Morocco and Spain, an upbringing which has deeply influenced his personal vision of the Mediterranean. He is currently involved in a number of regional cultural initiatives, and is on the editorial board of *SureS*, a literary journal in Tangier, Morocco, and revista *Banipal*, the Spanish Banipal. His published works include several poetry collections, notably *Lecturas del espacio profanado* (1992) and *Rihla* (2003). *Memoria del Polizón*, his writings to date in Spanish, is forthcoming. He has collaborated in numerous translations of Arabic and French poetry to Spanish, and read his poetry in venues and poetry festivals in Spain, Morocco and in South America.

Eran Edry is a Tel Aviv-born screen and stage translator, and children's screenwriter. Highlights of his recent translation credits include award-winning playwright, Maya Arad-Yasur's critically acclaimed *Amsterdam*, Nili Lamdan's political family drama, *Land of Onions and Honey*, director Eran Riklis's thriller, *Spider in the Web*, and lots more. Eran lives in north London with his partner and their dog, and is currently working on his debut children's book, and latest stage translation.

Yuval Evri is Assistant Professor of Near Eastern and Judaic Studies on the Marash and Ocuin Chair in Ottoman, Mizrahi and Sephardic Jewish Studies at Brandeis University. His research focuses on the cultural and political history of Palestine/Land of Israel focusing on Sephardi and Arab-Jewish culture. His recent book entitled: *The Return to Al-Andalus: Disputes Over Sephardic Culture and Identity Between Arabic and Hebrew* was published by Magnes press in 2020.

Fayez Ghazi is a Lebanese writer whose first novel *Munay* (My Wish) was published by Dar Abbad in 2013, and his second *Azhar al-Mawt* (Flowers of Death) in 2020 by Dar al-Farabi, Beirut. He writes for several Arab newspapers and websites.

Oded Halahmy (born in Baghdad, 1938) is a Babylonian Jew whose family fled Iraq in 1950, settling in Jaffa, Israel. He studied at Saint Martin's School of Art in London, UK, from 1966-1968 alongside artists such as Gilbert and George. He taught at Ontario College of Art and has lived in New York since 1970, the home of his own Pomegranate Gallery. His dynamic mainly bronze and metal sculptures are held in many major collections.

Uri Horesh is Senior Lecturer in the Department of Arabic Language and Literature Instruction at Achva Academic College, having previously taught at academic institutions in the US and the UK. Their research in variationist sociolinguistics has appeared, inter alia, in *Journal of Sociolinguistics*, *Zeitschrift für arabische Linguistik*, *Language in Society* and *Encyclopedia of Arabic Language and Linguistics*. They are a co-editor of *The Routledge Handbook of Arabic Sociolinguistics* (2019) and a co-author of the textbook *Arabic Sociolinguistics*, to be published in 2022 by Cambridge University Press.

Tami Israeli (PhD) is the head of the department of literature and Children's Literature at the Levinsky College of Education, Tel Aviv. She is a literary editor and her research focuses on modern Hebrew poetry. She is the author of *Hedva Harechavi: A Monograph* (2019).

CONTRIBUTORS

Hana Morgenstern is a scholar, writer and translator of Middle Eastern literatures. She is an Associate Professor in Postcolonial and Middle Eastern Literature at Cambridge University and a Fellow at Newnham College and currently co-convenor of the Revolutionary Papers and the Archives of the Disappeared Research Projects.

Hadas Shabat Nadir is Head of the literature department at the Kibbutzim College of Education, Technology and the Arts, Tel Aviv. She is the founder and manager of the Jewish-Arab Program at Ben-Gurion University of the Negev.

Mati Shemoelof is an Arab-Jewish poet, author and editor, born in 1972. His writing is diverse and includes six poetry books, plays, articles and one collection of stories. His works have won significant recognition and prizes. A German edition of his poems was published by AphorismA Verlag, Berlin, in 2019.

Yehouda Shenhav-Shahrabani is an Arab Jew. He is a professor of sociology at Tel Aviv University, and chief editor of Maktoob, a book series for the translation of Arabic literature, at the Jerusalem Van Leer Institute. He is also Membre du Conseil Scientifique de l'Institut d'Études Avancées de Nantes. Among his books: *The Arab Jews* (2006, Stanford University Press) and *Beyond the Two State Solution* (2014, Polity Press). He has translated 15 novels from Arabic to Hebrew, among them works by Elias Khoury, Mahmoud Shukair, Ali al-Muqri, and Salman Natour.

Reuven Snir is professor of Arabic language and literature at the University of Haifa. He teaches courses on Arabic poetry, Palestinian theatre, Sufism, and Arab–Jewish culture. Prof. Snir has published in Arabic, Hebrew, and English and has translated poetry between the three languages. His last books in English: *Baghdad: The City in Verse* (Harvard University Press, 2013); *Who Needs Arab–Jewish Identity? Interpellation, Exclusion, and Inessential Solidarities* (Brill, 2015); *Modern Arabic Literature: A Theoretical Framework* (Edinburgh University Press, 2017); and *Arab–Jewish Literature: The Birth & Demise of the Arab–Jewish Short Story* (Brill, 2019).

Hannah Somerville is a London-based investigative journalist and former health reporter. She has a BA in Arabic and Spanish from the University of Leeds and an MA in Arabic Literature from SOAS, University of London. Her dissertation focused on body politics in new Egyptian 'dystopian' fiction.

Susannah Tarbush is a freelance journalist specialising in cultural affairs in the Middle East. She writes the Tanjara blog, and is a consulting editor of *Banipal* and regular reviewer, and a trustee of the Banipal Trust for Arab Literature.

Nael el-Toukhy is an author, translator and journalist from Egypt. He was born in 1978 in Kuwait, and moved to Egypt in 1981. He published his first collection of stories (Technical Changes) in 2003, and has since published 2 novellas and 3 novels. He has also translated three books from Hebrew, including *Chahla and Hezquel* discussed above. In 2009, he started a blog to translate texts from modern Israeli literature.

Jonathan Wright studied Arabic, Turkish and Islamic History at St. John's College, Oxford University. He is an award-winning translator of fiction by Arab authors, including Mazen Maarouf, Amjad Nasser, Ahmed Saadawi, Hassan Blasim, Saud Alsanousi, Youssef Ziedan, Hamour Ziada, Khaled el-Khamissi and others. His latest work is *God 99* by Hassan Blasim (Comma Press, 2020).

Ryan Zohar is the Librarian at the Middle East Institute, New York University. He writes about Middle Eastern Jewish intellectual history, the politics of Mizrahiyut in Israel/Palestine, and Iraqi-Jewish cultural production.

For more information on all the authors in *Banipal* 72 and all the translators, writers and reviewers, please go to: www.banipal.co.uk/contributors/